A Guide to Teaching
with
The Norton Field Guide to Writing

A Guide to Teaching

with

The Norton
Field Guide
to Writing

Richard Bullock

WRIGHT STATE UNIVERSITY

W. W. NORTON & COMPANY

New York • London

W. W. Norton & Company has been independent since its founding in 1923, when William Warder Norton and Mary D. Herter Norton first published lectures delivered at the People's Institute, the adult education division of New York City's Cooper Union. The Nortons soon expanded their program beyond the Institute, publishing books by celebrated academics from America and abroad. By mid-century, the two major pillars of Norton's publishing program—trade books and college texts—were firmly established. In the 1950s, the Norton family transferred control of the company to its employees, and today—with a staff of four hundred and a comparable number of trade, college, and professional titles published each year—W. W. Norton & Company stands as the largest and oldest publishing house owned wholly by its employees.

Composition: Matrix Publishing and Carole Desnoes
Production Manager: Diane O'Connor

ISBN 0-393-92661-3

W. W. Norton & Company, Inc., 500 Fifth Avenue, New York, NY 10110
www.wwnorton.com

W. W. Norton & Company Ltd., Castle House, 75/76 Wells Street, London W1T 3QT

1 2 3 4 5 6 7 8 9 0

Preface

> First-year writing is the best course
> in the university to teach.
> —*Toby Fulwiler*

Toby is right: First-year writing courses may be hard work, requiring of instructors more time and energy than some other courses, but they're immensely rewarding. We get to work with small classes, coming to know our students in ways lecturers in large halls seldom do. We get to help students learn their way around the new academic environment of college, sharing in their excitement and anxiety. And we get to help them explore ways of writing and reading that are often utterly new to them, from embedding significance in a narrative to dissecting a nonfiction text, from immersing themselves in research to considering how best to persuade an audience. When we teach first-year English or other writing courses, we combine complex, challenging content and strong interactions with individual writers as they go about creating unique texts. This is a book of resources for teachers using *The Norton Field Guide to Writing*.

Like the *Field Guide* itself, this book doesn't try to tell you everything there is to know about teaching writing. Instead, it tries to tell you what you're most likely to need to know as you teach first-year writing courses. If you want to know more, you can find additional information at the end of each chapter, in lists of useful readings. These lists are not intended to be comprehensive. Instead, they present one, two, or more essays or Web sites that offer useful information and helpful advice for teachers—and, usually, a good bibliography of additional sources on that topic. You're busy and may not want to wade through a lengthy bibliography; therefore, these readings are good starting places for learning more about basic issues in teaching writing.

This book has two parts. Part I consists of nineteen chapters with advice on teaching writing, from designing a writing course to meeting the needs of students and adapting to a new role as a teacher. Each chapter offers specific guidance on developing and teaching a first-year writing course and aims to be as practical as possible. Although knowing rhetorical and composition theory is important—you need to know why you teach as you do, and theory provides that understanding—this book isn't the place to provide theory. My assumption, and the assumption of my co-authors, is that you need first of all to be ready to walk into your own writing course on the first day of class and both be prepared and seem prepared to your students:

to have a plan for your course, a syllabus to share with students, activities to do in class, and the ability to respond to and grade students' writing. These chapters will help you do that.

Part II gives advice on teaching with the *Norton Field Guide*. The *Field Guide* is designed to be flexible: you can create any number of course plans and sequences of writing and reading assignments by combining its chapters in various ways. If you're new to teaching or comfortable with a traditional guide to writing, you might start by using Chapters 6–9: WRITING A LITERACY NARRATIVE, ANALYZING A TEXT, REPORTING INFORMATION, and ARGUING A POSITION. These four chapters present sequences of readings and assignments that lead students from understanding of the key features of the genre to the completion of a finished essay in that genre, and you can structure your class activities and assignments to follow the chapter's advice. Whichever path you choose—or if you decide to mix writing guides and assignments you yourself create—you should find useful advice in Chapter 20, "Developing Course Plans Using *The Norton Field Guide*." The other ten chapters offer advice, tips, and ideas for using each of the chapters in the *Field Guide*.

Of course, this book reflects my own experience as a teacher of writing teachers. Knowing my own limits, however, I asked some of the best writing teachers I know—some of them former students, others colleagues and collaborators—to contribute chapters to the book. I think you'll find that they succeeded admirably, presenting good advice on teaching narrative, teaching ways

to use readings, being an effective teacher and graduate student, and dealing with special populations of students, including those whose first language isn't English and those with various disabilities. I want to thank these teachers publicly for making this guide for teaching better than it would otherwise be: Brady Allen, Adrienne Cassell, Jimmy Chesire, Carol Cornett, Deborah Crusan, Melissa Faulkner, Scott Geisel, Maureen Daly Goggin, and Melissa Toomey.

There are others I need to thank, too. Jane Blakelock, Assistant Director of Writing Programs for Computing in Wright State's English Department and also the department's and our college's Webmaster, taught me most of what I know about designing electronic texts and how best to teach them. Catherine Crowley sensitively edited several chapters, and other instructors, lecturers, and professors in Wright State's English Department contributed many ideas that found their way into the book: Debbie Bertsch (now at Columbus State Community College), Vicki Burke, Byron Crews, Sally DeThomas, Stephanie Dickey, Jeannette Horwitz, Beth Klaisner, Peggy Lindsey, Nancy Mack, Cynthia Marshall, Sarah McGinley, Michelle Metzner, Kristie Rowe, Bobby Rubin, Cathy Sayer, David Seitz, Tracy Smith, and Rick Strader. Thank you all.

I owe a special debt to Paige Huskey and Mike Boblitt, whose work in revising and editing this manual has greatly improved it.

Special thanks are also in order for the people who have supported me as I've worked on these two field guides. Henry

Limouze, the chair of Wright State's Department of English, has been unfailingly supportive. Marilyn Moller is the finest editor in the textbook business and has helped me in ways too numerous to mention. Nicole Netherton, associate editor, has been helpful and cheerful in equal measure. Thanks also to Donna Reiss, who copyedited this manuscript, Anna Palchik, who designed the book, and the other fine people at W. W. Norton who helped make this book happen; all deserve their share of the credit for this book. And finally, thanks to Barb Bullock, my wife and best teacher, who each day by precept and example teaches me to open up to life.

Richard Bullock

part 1

Teaching Writing

Designing a Writing Course   **1**

Whenever we teach, designing the course we're about to teach presents challenges. As a new teaching assistant, you've been given a general outline of the writing course you're to teach, along with some intensive training. Organizing the weeks that stretch ahead when you've never taught before, though, is daunting, even with the help you've been given. If you're a newly hired adjunct instructor, you may already have experience in the classroom, but you need to adapt what you've done before to the requirements of a new writing program. If you're a seasoned faculty member, you've taught many writing courses, but perhaps not recently, and not with this text or this course outline. No matter where you fit in these scenarios, you can use some help in designing your course. This chapter offers advice on planning a writing course that suits your preferences and your students' needs.

Thinking about Course Design

A writing course is akin to a set of boxes within boxes: the largest, outermost box is the complete course from start to finish. Within that box are instructional units that typically begin with the introduction of a writing assignment and end with its com-

pletion. Each unit is made up of sequences of assignments that move the class and the assigned writing along. And each class period includes various activities that move students through the sequence of assignments. When you've considered your course on each of these levels, you can plan every period of every week of the term so that every class period's work builds on what went before and prepares for what comes next. Of course, having a plan gives you something to diverge from and improve on without losing your way or being reduced to wondering, "What do I do on Monday?" Here's how to devise such a plan.

The course as a whole. Determine the writing program's goals for the course: What does the program or department or university want students to achieve by completing this course? Sometimes these goals are clearly spelled out; in other situations, you may need to ask the writing program administrators, the department chair, or faculty who regularly teach the course what the institution's expectations are. If the goals of the course are left to you, consult the WPA *Outcomes Statement* at the end of this chapter for help. That statement defines outcomes that soundly designed first-year writing courses should include, according to the Council of Writing Program Administrators, a national organization of writing program directors and specialists in composition and rhetoric.

The goals for your course will guide your planning. For example, if a goal is to "develop flexible strategies for generating, revising, editing, and proofreading," then you need to include those activities in your course plan. If a goal is to "respond appropriately to different kinds of rhetorical situations," then your plan should include opportunities for students to write in various genres for various reasons. If a goal is to "control such surface features as syntax, grammar, punctuation, and spelling," then including instruction in those surface features should be part of your overall plan. Once you've established your goals for the course itself, you can meet those goals by dividing the course into units.

Units. Designing a writing course is akin to other complex tasks best broken down into smaller parts that can be dealt with more easily, rather than trying to think of the whole at once. A writing course usually consists of a number of units within which students create a certain sort of writing, such as a personal narrative, an argument, an analysis, or a researched report. As you teach each unit, you lead students through a sequence of assignments that help students through writing processes from finding a topic, thinking about and researching it, drafting and revising, to polishing a final draft and assessing their work. The number of units you create depends on how many pieces of writing you want students to finish and how much time you want to

spend on each of those pieces. For example, a typical first-term, first-year writing course might consist of three or four 3-week units, each of them focusing on a single genre.

14-Week Semester:
Weeks 1–3 Personal Literacy Narrative
Weeks 4–7 Text Analysis
Weeks 8–10 Film Evaluation
Weeks 11–13 Argument
Week 14 Portfolio Preparation, Assessment

10-Week Quarter:
Weeks 1–2 Personal Literacy Narrative
Weeks 3–6 Text Analysis
Weeks 7–9 Film Evaluation
Week 10 Portfolio Preparation, Assessment

The length of a unit is highly flexible, of course. Some instructors may teach five- or six-week units to allow students to delve deeply into a subject and write lengthy, extensively researched essays; others may design two-week-long units to give students a flavor for certain genres and to make time for others. The length of each unit is finally like the length of a good essay: as long as it has to be to get the job done.

Assignment sequences. Within a unit, the sequence of specific assignments creates the momentum that gets students writing and keeps them progressing from beginning to end. This sequencing involves several variables: how many days your class meets each week, which days you meet, how long your class sessions are, and what you can expect students to do in class and between classes. Let's deal with each one separately:

How many days each week does your course meet, and which days? Your course schedule—Mondays, Wednesdays, and Fridays for fifty minutes each day; Tuesdays and Thursdays for 75 minutes; Monday nights for three hours—determines the rhythm of your assignments: what you ask students to do, how much you ask them to do, how much work you do in class, and how much work you ask students to do independently. For example, if your course meets on Tuesdays and Thursdays, you will probably ask students to do much more work outside class over the long period between

Tuesday–Thursday Schedule

Day	In-Class Activities	Assignment for the Next Class
Tu	Introduce literacy narrative assignment, begin generating activities	Read essays in ch. 6; write 1-page responses to each
Th	Share responses and discuss essays; go over Key Features; start developing possible topics through freewriting, looping; introduce the rhetorical situation	Read "Choosing a topic," pp. 30–31; choose a topic; answer questions in "Considering the Rhetorical Situation," p. 31
Tu	Topic conferences: Be prepared to describe your topic and the rhetorical situation as you see it.	Do "Generating Ideas and Text" activities, pp. 31–33
Th	Workshop on choosing pertinent details;minilesson on organizing a narrative	Read "Ways of Organizing a Literacy Narrative," pp. 33–34, and "Beginning and Ending,"ch. 28. Write a complete draft, 3–5 pp. long

Monday–Wednesday–Friday Schedule

Day	In-Class Activities	Assignment for the Next Class
M	Introduce assignment, begin generating activities	Read Bragg and Bullock essays in ch. 6; write 1-page responses to each
W	Share responses and discuss essays; go over Key Features	Read Nichols essay in ch. 6; write 1-page response
F	Discuss Nichols essay; minilesson on topic selection; introduce the rhetorical situation	Do activities in "Choosing a topic" and "Considering the rhetorical situation," pp. 30–31
M	Topic conferences: Be prepared to describe your topic and your rhetorical situation as you see it	Read "Ways of Organizing a Literacy Narrative," pp. 33–34 and "Beginning and Ending," ch. 28. Write an outline and first paragraph

Thursday and Tuesday than between Tuesday and Thursday; if your course meets Mondays, Wednesdays, and Fridays, you'll probably assign more balanced amounts of independent work. On page 5 are a couple of examples, one from a Tuesday-Thursday course and one from a Monday-Wednesday-Friday course. In each, students are beginning to write a personal literacy narrative. The left-hand column shows the day of the week; the middle column describes the activities to be completed during class, and the right-hand column shows the students' assignments for the following class.

Charting your assignment sequences can help you see how each class relates to those preceding and following it and how each assignment helps students make progress, using what they learned in class to do something that prepares them for the activities of the next class.

How long are your class periods? Within the term, unit, and weekly schedule, you need to develop a rhythm for your class periods, too. A fifty-minute period has a very different feel to it than a seventy-five or ninety-minute period. Chapter 4, "Managing Class Activities" in this book provides more detailed advice on structuring your class meetings, but in general, in an effective class period you will accomplish the following:

- Review what the class has done so far
- Clarify the relationship of students' previous work and current tasks
- Introduce activities or help students with upcoming tasks
- Prepare students to do the next assignment

Putting the parts together. Here is a set of guidelines for planning a course by considering the course as a whole, the units that make it up, the assignment sequences that students will follow, and the class activities that will help them progress.

1. Determine the goals of your course and what you must do to achieve them.
2. Decide on the number of units and what each will achieve.
3. Estimate how many weeks—or how many class days—the class will need to achieve each unit's goal; make sure your units don't exceed the number of class periods in the term. Note that some tasks take more time and instruction than others.
4. Consider how much preparation students will need in order to write a draft. For example, students might draft a personal narrative after a day or two of generating ideas and material, but they might need several weeks to write a report. Consider also what they will need to do—what assignments you will give them—before they write a draft, during drafting, and afterward. Consider too how many drafts you want them to write and what sort of response you can give them along the way. (See Chapter 9, "Responding to Student Writing" in this book.)

5. Plot out the unit on a calendar or chart, playing with the placement of the due dates for each student assignment. Think about how much time each assignment will take and how that fits into the time students have between class meetings.

6. Now start filling in the details. What, exactly, will you expect students to have done before each class meeting? What will you do during each class meeting? Chapter 4, "Managing Class Activities," offers detailed advice on using your time with your students effectively. What will the assignment for the next class meeting be? Chapter 3, "Designing Writing Assignments," Chapter 7, "Using Writing Activities in Class," and Chapter 8, "Using Readings to Teach Writing," can help you create appropriate tasks for students to complete on their own. For each unit, consider creating a plan in the form of a table that provides you and your students with that information.

Being Prepared and Flexible

Creating a plan for your course can relieve much of the stress of teaching, especially the first time you teach a course. A danger, though, is that if you follow your plan too closely, it can become a straitjacket that confines, rather than enables. Students may need more or less time on a task than you've scheduled; you may find that providing students with the instruction they need takes more or less time than you had thought; and events beyond your control, such as the weather or electrical power interruptions, may force you to change your plans. Maintaining flexibility to meet students' needs and to anticipate the unforeseeable is just as important as knowing what you'll do each day. You can incorporate flexibility into your plan in several ways. You can build a couple of open class periods into your schedule at the end of a unit, so if you need more time you can use those periods without squeezing the next unit's schedule. Or you can create detailed unit plans one at a time, giving students the overall unit topic and main deadlines but waiting until you've gone through much of one unit before filling in the details of the next. As you gain confidence in your teaching abilities and get to know your students, you'll find balancing planning with flexibility will become easier.

Unit			
Class Day	Goal of Day's Work	Class Activities	Assignment

WPA Outcomes Statement for First-Year Composition

This statement was adopted by the Council of Writing Program Administrators (WPA) in April, 2000. A version of this statement was published in WPA: *Writing Program Administration* 23.1/2 (fall/winter 1999): 59–66. It offers a clear description of the student performance goals most university writing programs seek to provide by the end of first-year writing courses (or sequences of courses). A good way to assess your own writing course plan is to see how well it helps your students achieve these outcomes.

Introduction

This statement describes the common knowledge, skills, and attitudes sought by first-year composition programs in American postsecondary education. To some extent, we seek to regularize what can be expected to be taught in first-year composition; to this end the document is not merely a compilation or summary of what currently takes place. Rather, the following statement articulates what composition teachers nationwide have learned from practice, research, and theory. This document intentionally defines only "outcomes," or types of results, and not "standards," or precise levels of achievement. The setting of standards should be left to specific institutions or specific groups of institutions.

Learning to write is a complex process, both individual and social, that takes place over time with continued practice and informed guidance. Therefore, it is important that teachers, administrators, and a concerned public do not imagine that these outcomes can be taught in reduced or simple ways. Helping students demonstrate these outcomes requires expert understanding of how students actually learn to write. For this reason we expect the primary audience for this document to be well-prepared college writing teachers and college writing program administrators. In some places, we have chosen to write in their professional language. Among such readers, terms such as "rhetorical" and "genre" convey a rich meaning that is not easily simplified. While we have also aimed at writing a document that the general public can understand, in limited cases we have aimed first at communicating effectively with expert writing teachers and writing program administrators.

These statements describe only what we expect to find at the end of first-year composition, at most schools a required general education course or sequence of courses. As writers move beyond first-year composition, their writing abilities do not merely improve. Rather, students' abilities not only diversify along disciplinary and professional lines but also move into whole new levels where expected outcomes expand, multiply, and diverge. For this reason, each statement of outcomes for first-year composition is followed by suggestions for further work that builds on these outcomes.

Rhetorical Knowledge

By the end of first year composition, students should

- Focus on a purpose
- Respond to the needs of different audiences
- Respond appropriately to different kinds of rhetorical situations
- Use conventions of format and structure appropriate to the rhetorical situation
- Adopt appropriate voice, tone, and level of formality
- Understand how genres shape reading and writing
- Write in several genres

Faculty in all programs and departments can build on this preparation by helping students learn

- The main features of writing in their fields
- The main uses of writing in their fields
- The expectations of readers in their fields

Critical Thinking, Reading, and Writing

By the end of first-year composition, students should

- Use writing and reading for inquiry, learning, thinking, and communicating
- Understand a writing assignment as a series of tasks, including finding, evaluating, analyzing, and synthesizing appropriate primary and secondary sources

- Integrate their own ideas with those of others
- Understand the relationships among language, knowledge, and power

Faculty in all programs and departments can build on this preparation by helping students learn

- The uses of writing as a critical thinking method
- The interactions among critical thinking, critical reading, and writing
- The relationships among language, knowledge, and power in their fields

Processes

By the end of first-year composition, students should

- Be aware that it usually takes multiple drafts to create and complete a successful text
- Develop flexible strategies for generating, revising, editing, and proofreading
- Understand writing as an open process that permits writers to use later invention and re-thinking to revise their work
- Understand the collaborative and social aspects of writing processes
- Learn to critique their own and others' works
- Learn to balance the advantages of relying on others with the responsibility of doing their part
- Use a variety of technologies to address a range of audiences

Faculty in all programs and departments can build on this preparation by helping students learn

- To build final results in stages
- To review work-in-progress in collaborative peer groups for purposes other than editing
- To save extensive editing for later parts of the writing process
- To apply the technologies commonly used to research and communicate within their fields

Knowledge of Conventions

By the end of first-year composition, students should

- Learn common formats for different kinds of texts
- Develop knowledge of genre conventions ranging from structure and paragraphing to tone and mechanics
- Practice appropriate means of documenting their work

- Control such surface features as syntax, grammar, punctuation, and spelling

Faculty in all programs and departments can build on this preparation by helping students learn

- The conventions of usage, specialized vocabulary, format, and documentation in their fields
- Strategies through which better control of conventions can be achieved

Useful Readings

Murray, Donald M. A *Writer Teaches Writing*, Revised 2nd ed. Boston: Heinle, 2003 (especially chapters 5 and 9).

Deen, Rosemary. "Notes to Stella." *College English* 54 (1992): 573–585.

Elbow, Peter. "Embracing Contraries in the Teaching Process." *College English* 45 (1983): 327–339.

Creating a Syllabus 2

In every class you took in college, the instructor gave you a syllabus that provided an outline of the course. If you transferred credit from one college to another, you may have shown the syllabuses for some of those courses to advisors at the other to make sure the courses were equivalent. As an instructor, you may be required to provide a copy of the syllabus for your own course to your department office to be kept on file. A course syllabus is more than simply information for students; it is a promise to those students that the course will be conducted in a certain way and a record of how the course was conducted. The audience for your syllabus includes students, faculty, and administrators, so taking care to create a complete, clear syllabus is well worth your time. This chapter offers advice on how to construct a good syllabus for a writing course.

Contents of a Good Syllabus

A good syllabus anticipates and answers students' questions:

- How does this course fit into the curriculum? Why must I or should I take it?

- What is the content or subject matter of the course?

- What teaching style or methods of instruction will be used? Will the course be primarily a workshop course? Lectures? Discussion? Online? A combination?

- What are the prerequisites? What knowledge or ability does the instructor assume I already have?

- What are the requirements? How much work is there?

- How will my work be evaluated? Will there be a portfolio, tests, quizzes, written assignments, projects, presentations? How many?

- When are assignments due? How will I need to use my time to get the work done?

- What books and materials must I have? What must I purchase? What will be available through the library, online, in class, or as handouts?

- What are the rules for the course, for attendance, submitting work, and participating in class?

- How can I contact the instructor, and when can I do so?

Building a Course Syllabus

A typical syllabus for a writing course contains much of the following information but is unlikely to include all of it. Even if you don't want to put an item in your syllabus, you may find that thinking about your policy on that issue can help you anticipate students' questions or behavior.

Basic Course Information

- Course title, section number, call number, number of credits
- Room and time(s) where the class meets
- Semester or quarter and year
- Prerequisites: other courses, placement scores, or test scores

Your Personal Information

- Your name and title
- Your office location, with directions if it's hard to find
- Your office hours, email address, office phone number, and Web page address, if you have one
- Your home phone number and times when students may call, if you wish
- How you'd like students to address you (as Mr. or Ms. _____, as Professor or Dr. _____, with your first name)

Textbooks and Other Materials

- Each textbook's title, edition, author, publisher, and date of publication; ISBN number; clear identification of required and recommended texts; URL of textbook Web page
- Additional materials to be assigned and where they may be found (in the library's reserve room or on your Web site, for example)
- Where students may get help with accessing electronic materials (online reserve materials or materials on your Web site, for example)
- Other required materials or fees (such as a lab or printing fee, photocopying fees, floppy disks, two-pocket folders)

Course Description

- Can repeat your school's catalogue description, or you may write one (or both)
- Typically includes the major themes, topics, knowledge, and skills to be addressed in the course

Course Objectives

- Cognitive: what students should understand
- Affective: what students should appreciate
- Behavioral: what students should be able to do

Course Requirements

- Summary of assignments and due dates
- Reading assignments
- Number and type of papers and other

assignments such as oral presentations or group projects

- Attendance requirements
- Class participation requirements (in-class or electronic, on bulletin boards, email)
- Your expectations of the amount of time and work students should anticipate

Course Calendar

- Reading assignments with due dates
- Deadlines for drafts and other projects
- Dates of tests, special events, final exam, and course evaluations
- Deadlines for dropping or withdrawing from the course

Grading Policies and Procedures

- The course grading system (A-F, plusses and minuses, points, percentages, etc.)
- Percentage or amount each course requirement counts toward final grade (make sure percentages add up to 100%)
- Rubrics for evaluating papers
- Use of quizzes, surprise or scheduled, and whether or not they can be made up
- Penalties for late work (for example, "All assignments must be submitted at the beginning of the class on their due date in order to receive credit.")
- Extra credit policy, if any
- Policy on incomplete grades (for example, "No Incomplete grades will be given except in extreme circumstances.")
- Policy on incomplete portfolios (for example, "Incomplete portfolios will receive an F.")
- Policy on making up work (for example, "No work may be made up unless you have talked with me. It is your responsibility to initiate this meeting. Penalties for turning in work late may still apply.")

Academic Honesty Policy

- Your academic honesty policy (must correspond with your department's or university's policy)

Other Useful Information

- Campus resources such as a writing center, study skills center, technology help desk, or counseling center
- Space for two-three classmates' names, telephone numbers, and e-mail addresses

Some Tips to Help Students Do Well

- Most learning takes place out of class. The time students are expected to work outside class is usually 2 hours for every class hour.
- Read each reading assignment several times. Once is seldom enough.
- Come to class; sit in the front of the room.
- Ask questions and participate.
- Go to the writing center.
- Study with peers.

Course Rules

- Recording class discussions
- Eating food in classrooms
- Behaving appropriately (class decorum issues)
- Other issues

As you can see, a course syllabus may be quite elaborate—or it may be fairly brief. Look at syllabuses for other courses like the one you're teaching to see what instructors at your school customarily include in their syllabuses (or syllabi, or course plan— that's another term that varies from school to school).

A Sample Syllabus

Here is a sample syllabus for a ten-week-long writing course, annotated with commentary.

ENG 101: Processes of Writing[1]
Call no: XXXXX
Section XX, Fall 200X, 0XX Millett Hall, 11–12:15 Tuesdays and Thursdays
Instructor: Richard Bullock
Office: 541 Millett
phone & voice mail 770-0000; email rbinstructor33@wrightstate.edu
Office hours: Tuesdays and Thursdays, 2:00–3:00 and by appointment

This course aims to help you become a better reader and writer of academic and other nonfiction writing. You'll write several drafts of three essays: a memoir focused on your own literacy, a critical analysis of a text, and an evaluation of a film. You'll also write several evaluations of your own work, which you will compile in a writing portfolio. Along the way, I hope you'll come to understand yourself as a writer and reader better than you do now and be able to assess your own writing's strengths and weaknesses.[2]

In some courses, you must read and learn a certain amount of material that is fairly well-defined. In a writing course, however, you can interpret writing activities as requiring a lot of time and effort, or a little. Consistently interpreting assignments as something to dash off quickly, rather than as something to think about, consider, and spend time on, is likely to affect your performance and final grade. Note, too, that in college, you're expected to spend about two hours studying and working independently for every hour you spend in class.

Note: Everything you turn in should be as error-free as you can make it. Get into the habit of editing and proofreading, because your instructors will expect clean, correct prose, in informal as well as formal writing.[3]

---

[1]Provide basic information at the top.
[2]Give a general description of the goals and desired outcomes of the course.
[3]This note is intended to counteract the effects of students' Instant Messaging and email habits while continuing to establish expectations.

ATTENDANCE AND PARTICIPATION: You'll be doing a lot of group work in this class, and failing to attend hurts both you and your group members. So don't miss, and don't schedule other activities during class time. As an incentive, remember that *something will be due every class period*—something either written for the class or written during the class; I won't accept it from anyone but you, and I won't accept it after I've collected it in class.[4]

Much of the work of the class comes during class time, so you must be present, doing the work along the way; *I won't accept at quarter's end a portfolio of work I haven't seen beforehand in draft form, during class.* If I haven't seen it while you've worked on it, how can I know that you wrote it?[5]

I also reserve the right to let your preparedness and participation affect your grade. In other words, if you don't come prepared, or if you choose not to participate in class activities, your grade may[6] suffer.

EMERGENCIES: Sometimes—very seldom, but sometimes—things come up that may force you to miss class or be unable to submit an assignment. If they do, **CALL** or **EMAIL ME** *ahead of time.* I'm more inclined to be flexible if you talk with me than if you stop coming to class or simply disappear.[7]

TEXTS AND MATERIALS: Richard Bullock, *The Norton Field Guide to Writing*
   A writer's handbook—see departmental approved list
   At least $5 worth of copy card credit—you'll be making copies
   Your campus username, password, and email address

GRADES:
- **10% Test** on reading selections to be announced
- **10% Daily work.** 5 points per day, 100 in the quarter; lose more than 20 points or 4 days' worth and you lose all. Showing up matters.
- **20% Midterm Portfolio.** Must include *literacy narrative* and *self-evaluation*, your weekly letters, and your daily work.
- **60% Course Portfolio.** Must include two of these three: *literacy narrative, critical analysis, and evaluation; self-evaluation of portfolio contents*; and all drafts of all 3 essays listed above.[8]

[4]Some instructors prefer a simple policy, e.g., 3 absences and the student's grade drops a letter, and drops another letter for each additional absence. If you prefer such a policy, combine it with an attendance sheet students sign on arriving each day, to eliminate arguments over whether or not a student was present; if the student doesn't sign the sheet, the student is counted absent.

[5]This rule, along with deadlines for committing to topics of essays, can greatly reduce students' opportunities to submit plagiarized work and establishes your expectation that they must write multiple drafts and participate in the course activities.

[6]Soft language here gives you flexibility to take individual students' situations into account.

[7]Advice on how to behave responsibly in a new environment. Some students believe that if they're absent when something is due, instructors have to let them turn it in late.

[8]Make sure your points or percentages add up to 100%!

INTERIM EVALUATION: Anytime you want to know what your grade would be before the course portfolio is due, make an appointment with me. Bring your working folder, with everything you've written for the course labeled and in order, and I'll gladly go over it with you, to let you know your grade *if I had to give you one at that time.*[9]

COURSE PORTFOLIOS: Rather than being graded on every piece of writing you do, you're better off if you're evaluated on a body of work you've compiled over an extended period. Here's why:[10]

- You've got more chances of doing a good job. If you buy 10 raffle tickets instead of one, your chances of winning improve.
- You'll present a more realistic view of your writing abilities and achievements than you can with any single piece of writing. An album of photos better shows what you look like than your driver's license photo does.
- You'll have the opportunity to rewrite, revise, edit, and polish, to visit the Writing Center—to show me your best work—right up until finals week, so you can do a better job than you might otherwise do.

For all those reasons, the midterm and course portfolios represent your evidence to me that you deserve a certain grade. An incomplete or missing midterm or course portfolio will earn a final course grade of **F.**[11]

Your course portfolio grades are based on your achievements—on the *quality of the writing*—not on effort (how hard you worked) or intention (what you meant to do).[12]

WEEKLY LETTERS: Each Tuesday, plan on writing a letter from you to me. Make it at least a page (250+ words) long. Address it "Dear Rich." Each Thursday, I'll write a "Dear Class" letter via email.

FORMAT: Final drafts in the portfolios should be printed out double-spaced, using a 12-point font, 1" margins; include your name in upper right-hand corner, along with description of assignment and date due. Assignments marked "informal" may be handwritten, but must be legible and not written on paper ripped out of a spiral-bound notebook. Other work should be done in Turnitin.com or WebCT. Submit weekly letters and essay drafts as Word documents in the appropriate assignment in Turnitin.[13]

---

[9]Knowing that students can take this option relieves many of their fears, even though very, very few students will do it!

[10]Many students are used to receiving grades on every piece of writing they submit. Explaining the rationale for portfolios can start the process of relieving their worries; their experience in the class will help them see the advantages of earning a grade on a portfolio of work they've revised extensively.

[11]Lack of evidence for a grade makes grading impossible. This policy shows that you're serious about them doing the work—all of the work.

[12]Again, you establish your expectations—that they submit the best work of which they're capable—and forestall arguments of this sort: "I came to class every day and worked really hard, so I deserve a better grade."

[13]Explain how students should submit assignments: on paper, as email attachments, on a Web discussion board, or in an assignment posted on courseware.

Keep everything you write for this course in some organized fashion: an accordion folder, a three-ring notebook, a stiff plastic or cardboard envelope, a separate folder in your computer files. Save your work in at least 2 places!!! Keep everything in order—you'll need it to compile your portfolio and write your self-assessment essays.[14]

UNIVERSITY WRITING CENTER:[15] The University Writing Center, in 104 Wilson Hall, can help you improve your writing through one-on-one conferences. Please go early, go often—it's free and will be useful to you. (I may require some of you to go there, if your writing shows that you need additional help.)

DISCLAIMER: This syllabus may well change to reflect my sense of your needs. I won't make changes that are potentially harmful to you, however, without negotiating.[16]

CONTACTS: Write down the names, phone numbers, and email addresses of three class-mates. Call or write them if you need help with something to do with this class and you can't contact me.[17]

_____

_____

_____

Advice from students who've taken ENG 101 in the past:[18]
"If you are taking English 101, then you are probably a new student. College isn't what you thought it would be, is it? . . . if you don't like taking advice, get over it. Next off, go to class and finish all of your assignments. (You will find that this tip is useful in any class.) Grades can easily fall without you even noticing."

"My first word of advice is—make sure you have your papers before you leave the house! When you have a draft or a revision due, always do it—write something. Even if you're having trouble, and it's not your best work, it will most likely help you work towards your final draft."

"Do not take the little assignments lightly. Those little assignments, in the long run, make or break your papers. He gives you things like that to better prepare yourself for the big assignments, and trust me when I say, you need those little ones."

---

[14]Again, advice to help students be successful in a course in which they'll generate a lot of material.

[15]It's always good to tout support services available to students.

[16]The class you teach depends in part on your students' abilities and needs as well as your developing sense of how to teach them. Language like this lets you adjust your course to meet the students' needs.

[17]If your school doesn't place students in learning communities—and even if it does—helping your students create support networks with their peers can help them succeed.

[18]As in many things, students often take the advice of other students more seriously than they take ours. Asking them at the end of the course to give advice to future students can give you a wealth of good ideas to share—and give you insights into your course as students see it.

"I can tell you now that I am not, nor ever will be an English major. So here are a couple of suggestions to help you get through this class smoothly. First of all, procrastination has got to go. Until this year I was the crowned queen of procrastination. I'll let you know now that it is considerably **<u>less stressful</u>** to do things in bits and pieces and not to wait until the last minute to start things. It will also improve your grades greatly."

"You can <u>never</u> have too many drafts! We all hate revising and changing our papers, I understand. However, sitting down at midnight to start your paper that is due at 11 a.m. is not going to cut it in college! Trust me."

"English is <u>not</u> like most of your other classes. There are few people per class, so the prof knows if you're there and attentive or not."

"My advice to you is to take risks and enjoy what you are writing."

"You don't have to write a perfect paper the first time. Take your time; you will have <u>many</u> chances to revise papers. I'm sure this will annoy you, because I know it did me, but it really does benefit you a lot."

A Useful Reading

Baecker, Diann L. "Uncovering the Rhetoric of the Syllabus." *College Teaching* 46:2 (Spring 1998): 58–63.

Designing Writing Assignments   **3**

When you hear faculty complain that the writing their students submit to them is horrible, the fault often lies not so much with the ability of the students but with the quality of the assignment. Vague, incomplete, poorly constructed assignments elicit—guess what?—vague, incomplete, poorly constructed student writing. On the other hand, carefully constructed assignments can aid students as they write, guiding them to well-written texts. That's why it's important to craft your writing assignments carefully: You get what you ask for.

Developing Assignment Sequences

When you plan assignments, think in terms of sequences that move students through a series of activities toward the goal of a finished piece of writing. Reading, working in groups, generating ideas and text, drafting, getting response, revising, editing and proofreading, evaluating—each of these activities helps students write better texts. You may well think initially of a course as made up of a few assignments— a literacy narrative, a text analysis, a report, an argument—but each of these

products results from a carefully plotted sequence of in-class and out-of-class assignments, each of which contributes to the quality of that final product.

Using *The Norton Field Guide to Writing*

The *Norton Field Guide* is designed to help you develop good assignments. You may use one of the longer genre chapters (Chapter 6, WRITING A LITERACY NARRATIVE; Chapter 7, ANALYZING A TEXT; Chapter 8, REPORTING INFORMATION; and Chapter 9, ARGUING A POSITION), each of which presents a sequence that leads students from initial exploration of a genre through editing and proofreading and self-assessment of their work. If you're new to teaching, you may find those chapters useful models of successful assignment sequences. If you'd like to design your own sequences, the activities in those chapters can provide a framework for creating assignments using various parts of the *Field Guide*.

1. Introduce the genre (Chapters 6–20), using readings
2. Define Key Features of the genre (as defined in the Genre chapters)

3. Provide help in choosing a topic (presented in each Genre chapter and in Chapter 22, GENERATING IDEAS AND TEXT)

4. Have students consider the Rhetorical Situation (Chapters 1–5, with advice in each Genre chapter as well)

5. Ask students to generate ideas and text (with activities in each Genre chapter or in Chapter 22) and do appropriate research (Chapters 39–45)

6. Have students organize their material, plan their text, and use appropriate writing strategies (from Chapters 28–38) as they draft (Chapter 23)

7. Ask students to assess their drafts (Chapter 24), get response and revise (Chapter 25), edit and proofread (Chapter 26)

8. Have students assess their written product, either by itself or as part of a portfolio of their work (as described in Chapter 27)

Of course, each of these steps may be expanded or contracted to suit the assignment and the needs of your students. For example, you may give students only a few days to generate ideas and text and organize a memoir, on the assumption that they are familiar with narratives and have the necessary information in their memories. By contrast, students writing a researched essay arguing a position may need several weeks to generate ideas and find sources before they attempt a draft. For more assignment sequence possibilities, see Chapter 20, "Developing Course Plans Using *The Norton Field Guide*."

Making Your Expectations Clear

A good writing assignment gives students all the information they need to complete it. As Erika Lindemann notes, providing clear information about the rhetorical situation of the text you expect them to produce will help students understand both what you want and what they should do. The elements of the rhetorical situation that you should address include the following (adapted from Lindemann 212):

- Students' interest in the topic and what they understand about it

- Purpose of the text—what it should try to accomplish

- Intended audience for the text

- Genre in which students should write

- Stance students should adopt

- Criteria—including the Key Features as well as format and deadlines—for a successful text

All of the Genre chapters in the *Norton Field Guide* provide questions for each element in the rhetorical situation as well as a list of each genre's Key Features. You can ask students to explore what they know about their topic using several of the activities in Chapter 22 of the *Field Guide*. Here's an example of a good writing assignment:

Arguing a Position. Take a stand on an issue that affects your life as a student, a worker, or a citizen. Your argument should include: a thesis declaring your position, evidence supporting your position, an explanation of your reasoning, and acknowledgement or refutation of other positions. Your purpose is to convince your readers that your position is reasonable—though you may attempt to persuade them to consider a certain position or to do something. You are writing to an informed, intelligent audience, perhaps readers of the *New York Times* or the *Atlantic Monthly*, so your stance should be thoughtful, balanced, and reasonable. Your essay should be 4–6 pages long and should include at least four scholarly sources in your Works-Cited list, documented using MLA guidelines. You must submit a topic proposal on February 1, present a research portfolio on February 10, and submit a complete draft on February 15. You may revise until the course portfolio is due during finals week.

This assignment provides students with considerable freedom to choose a topic of interest to them while giving them a clear indication of the rhetorical situation in which they must write, including important due dates and procedural information.

Assigning Topics or Giving Choices

Whether you assign specific topics or let students choose their own depends on numerous factors. If you want students to work together as a class on a project, you may assign a topic or a cluster of related topics on which individual students or groups of students might work. When asking students to evaluate a film, for example, you might provide a list of suitable movies and ask groups of students to choose one. If you're using the assignment to teach specific skills, you might assign everyone the same task so they can discuss its intricacies and compare their attempts, a useful tactic for teaching summarizing and paraphrasing, for example. Some instructors ask students to work from a limited set of source materials to write a researched essay on a controversial topic chosen by the instructor in order to teach them how to use sources appropriately. When you assign a topic, you gain control over significant aspects of your course. However, you run the risk that your students may not find the topic as engaging or as interesting as you do. Even if your writing program offers courses identified by their theme, students more often sign up for courses by time of day and availability than by course topic. Also you lose variety in your student drafts, something to consider when it comes time to read and respond to twenty or twenty-five drafts.

If you allow students to choose their own topics, you must help each of those two dozen students solve unique writing problems; however, you gain the opportunity to read and discuss many subjects you might never have otherwise encountered. More important, you offer students the opportunity to explore topics in which they have an interest, resulting in more engagement in the work of your class and better writing. In general, don't leave assignments completely open. Stipulate a genre within which students must write, help students narrow or broaden topics to fit the constraints of their abilities and the course, and veto topics that are unmanageable or difficult to write well on. Consider an assignment to be like a game: Establish the rules and set the boundaries of the playing field, and then let your students be as creative as they can within those rules and boundaries.

Helping Students Interpret Your Assignments

No matter how elaborately instructors define assignments, students need to interpret them in order to begin. Part of that interpretation involves making a judgment about the ease or difficulty of accomplishing the tasks. One student may understand an assignment as requiring several hours of library research, the creation of a detailed outline, and a schedule that will permit the writing of several drafts. On the other hand, another student in the same class, interpreting the same assignment, will assume that it can be knocked off with an hour's research on the Web and a single, quickly written draft. One, if not both, of these students may be misinterpreting your expectations, so it's important to clarify them. Breaking a large assignment into a sequence of activities, each with a due date and a product to be submitted, is helpful; so is a suggested timetable. Consider, too, showing good examples of the amount and quality of work you expect. You don't want your conscientious students spending hours on an assignment you consider a brief learning tool, and you want to prod your less conscientious students to adopt suitable work habits.

Doing the Assignment Yourself

Whenever possible, do assignments yourself before you give them to your students. You will accomplish two important things: one, you can find out whether the assignment works—if it's doable or leads to unanticipated difficulties—before students are led into a swamp; and two, you develop an example that you can show them and discuss, not necessarily as an expert, but as a fellow writer who sometimes struggles with an assignment. Students rarely see the writing of their teachers and even more rarely see that writing with its dead ends, revisions, and rough edges, and they find the process fascinating. Show students your own writing, and you'll not only show them how they might approach assignments, you'll gain credibility in their eyes as someone who does what you ask your students to do, as writing teacher Jimmy Chesire points out in Chapter 17 of this book.

Useful Readings

Lindemann, Erika. A *Rhetoric for Writing Teachers,* 3rd Ed. NY: Oxford, 1995.

Rankin, Elizabeth. "From Simple to Complex: Ideas of Order in Assignment Sequences." *Journal of Advanced Composition* 10.1 (1990).

Sommers, Nancy. "Revision Strategies of Student Writers and Experienced Adult Writers." *College Composition and Communication* 31.4 (December 1980): 378–388.

Managing Class Activities   **4**

You may remember most vividly your upper-division courses, which were probably a mix of lecture and discussion. As a new teacher of writing, however, you're faced with a different situation, a course in which the subject is writing, and the goal is primarily the improvement of students' writing—not the learning of a body of content. How can you fill 150–200 minutes of class time a week on writing? This chapter offers some advice on structuring your class time in ways that will engage students and help them improve their writing.

Structuring Classes

The primary model of college teaching is the lecture that fills the entire class period, no matter how long. Various observers have noted, though, that students' attention begins wandering after about twenty minutes, suggesting that varying class activities will maintain students' interest and improve their learning better than doing any one activity for the whole class period. Your class will likely run more smoothly and be more interesting to you and your students if you follow a predictable overall pattern during class but vary the activities within the pattern. One pattern that works well includes these tasks:

- Review what the class has done so far.
- Clarify the relationship of students' previous work and current tasks.
- Introduce activities or offer information to help students with current and upcoming tasks.
- Prepare students to do the next assignment in the unit.

Each of these tasks may require one or more activities and take up more or less time, depending on your purposes and your students' needs. For advice on coordinating your class activities with your assignment sequences and overall course goals, see Chapter 1, "Designing a Writing Course."

Planning Class Activities

Here are some activities that successful writing teachers use to achieve their purposes in class.

Workshops and conferences. Writing workshops and student conferences are the primary activities in most writing courses, often being the predominant use of class time. For detailed advice on setting up and running workshops in class, see Chapter 5, "Conducting Class Workshops." As preparation for workshops, you can ask students to read about collaborating in Chapter 21 in the *Field Guide*, and to do several of the activities together in workshops. Many activities in the Genre chapters lend themselves to collaboration. For example, several of the activities in chapter 7, ANALYZING A TEXT, are best done in class by groups of students working together.

Although students working together can accomplish much, sometimes you need to discuss each student's writing individually. Chapter 6 in this book offers detailed advice on scheduling and holding conferences.

Minilessons, presentations, and lectures. Minilessons are brief, five-to-ten-minute lessons on a specific topic. They may include information students need to know, such as the importance of the rhetorical situation; procedures for class activities, such as how to respond to others' drafts or how to collaborate successfully; lessons in specific writing strategies or processes, such as options for generating ideas and text, editing, or narrating; lessons on topics that may give students trouble, such as citing Web sites; or lessons on specific aspects of writing, such as using semicolons. Minilessons are successful because they are clearly focused and brief. Many instructors start class periods with minilessons that focus students' attention on the day's work or answer a question that came up in a previous class. You might end some days with a minilesson that explains an aspect of the students' assignment or intersperse minilessons throughout a class period as you move from activity to activity.

Presentations using PowerPoint, overhead projector transparencies, audio, or video often accompany minilessons or may comprise longer segments of a class period. For example, you may show a brief video clip to introduce a writing or research assignment. As always, though, such a presentation should have a clear pedagogical purpose. Although students like to be entertained, they understand that what goes on in class should relate to their purpose for being there. So make the connection between a presentation and their writing explicit, both orally and through followup activities that ask students to analyze or use the presentation in some way. For advice on creating effective media presentations, see Chapter 48 in the *Field Guide*.

Lectures may be useful for transmitting content, but they are usually inappropriate for writing classes, where information is presented to be applied in students' own writing. You may find an occasional lecture useful, but if you do, treat it as a carefully crafted, focused explanation of a specific topic. To aid students' understanding, accompany your lecture with visual presentations of the material; again, see Chapter 48 in the *Field Guide* for advice.

Discussions. Discussions can be useful for helping students think about and articulate their thinking on issues related to their writing and reading. After asking students to read several literacy narratives, for example, you might ask them to discuss the way each writer expresses the significance of the events portrayed in the narratives and which ways are most effective. Or, you might ask students to describe a situation in their lives where they evaluated a movie or a song and then compare that evaluation to a formal, written evaluation of a movie or a song. Having a good discussion involves getting students to participate, moving the discussion forward toward your goals, and dealing with emotional or interpersonal issues as they arise. Here are some tips for conducting whole-class discussions.

Getting students to participate. Students are often hesitant to participate in discussions. They may be unsure of the reaction their comments will elicit from you or from their classmates. They may feel unprepared. They may not know where to begin. When you start a discussion, consider these tactics to help students become comfortable and more likely to respond:

- *Consider the seating arrangement.* It may sound touchy-feely, but people's physical relationships to one another influence the quality of their interactions. Having students face one another, in a circle or some other arrangement, creates a better dynamic for discussion than sitting in rows. It's also harder for students to hide.

- *Begin with writing.* Ask students to write for five minutes on the topic you wish them to discuss. Then ask some or all students to share what they've written. This simple technique gives students a chance to think about the topic and rehearse what to say; it relieves pressure and permits thought.

- *Start with a common experience.* If students can relate the topic to something in their own lives, they're likely to have something to say; for example, a life event that everyone has likely gone through or knows about such as the loss of a pet or a family member. A shared event or presentation might take place in class: a brief video, a common reading, even a staged skit.

- *Pose a problem.* You might present a scenario or point out a contradiction between two ideas or positions and ask students to explore ways of dealing with it. Your challenge here is to keep the possible options for dealing with the situation open as long as possible so students don't latch onto the first solution and settle for it, effectively ending the discussion.

- *Start with a group activity.* Some students, indeed some classes, find discussing topics in small groups easier than talking as a class. If so, begin discussions by asking students to write briefly; to share their writing with three to five classmates in a group; and then to solve a problem, reach a consensus, or otherwise carry the discussion forward. Have the groups report to the class, using their reports to start the whole-class discussion. This activity can be done quickly: for example, in workshops on writing across the curriculum, Toby Fulwiler asks participants to write for five minutes, share in groups for five minutes, and then report. The discipline of a brief time limit keeps everyone on task.

- *Conduct discussions online.* Holding a discussion in a computer classroom through the computers may seem odd, especially as you hear students engaged in discussion only by the clicking of fingers on the keyboard. However, some students who would never contribute to a spoken discussion will reveal strong voices in online discussions. And some classes that simply won't talk to one another will write to one another.

Moving the discussion forward. Once you have a discussion going, here are some tips for keeping it going:

- Plan for possibilities, but don't assume you can predict the shape of the discussion. To prepare, know the subject as well as you can and identify your goal in having the discussion. Then, as students talk, you can interject responses and questions to nudge the discussion in the direction you want it to head. Avoid creating a script or flow chart for the discussion, however; your plan is likely to be useless within five minutes.

- Use silence as a tool. Too often, when teachers ask a question, they don't wait long enough: The silence makes them uneasy, and they either call on someone or answer the question themselves. Don't. The silence following a question may make you uneasy, but it makes students uneasy, too, and sooner or later one of them will say something to break the tension. Allowing a period of silence following a

question also shows respect for students' need to think before speaking.

- Use writing and groups to refocus students' attention or jumpstart a dying discussion. If a discussion heads in a direction you don't want—it peters out, dissolves into irrelevancies, or becomes argumentative, emotional, or personal— reset it by having students do a brief writing, share it in groups, and then come together again as a class.

- Make sure everyone participates or has the opportunity. You may have a couple of students who monopolize the discussion. If that happens, you may need to deal with the problem. For example, you might take the monopolizers aside, thank them for their strong contributions, and ask if they would allow others to participate more, to help their classmates gain the skills they already have. Chronic nonparticipants should be drawn out, again privately. Tell them you value their opinions and contributions and want them to share with the class. Asking students to write, and then asking all students to read what they've written, allows everyone to participate, too. Consider, too, offering students a couple of "free pass" opportunities; if called on, they can cash in one of their free passes if they aren't ready to respond.

Dealing with emotional or interpersonal issues. Sometimes students become agitated, angry, or upset during a discussion. This display of emotion can be a positive sign that students are engaged in the topic, but it can also make you (and them) feel uncomfortable or threatened. If you feel that you are losing control of a discussion or that students are becoming too argumentative, you can ask the class to stop and write briefly on the contended topic, giving everyone a chance to gather their thoughts. Then ask the class to articulate the arguments on both sides, perhaps listing them on the board and asking the class to look for areas of common ground. Refer to authoritative sources to resolve disputes that have a basis in fact or turn the dispute into a writing assignment, which can lead to a followup discussion during the next class period or be posted on an online discussion board. In a particularly contentious situation, you may need to spell out rules—perhaps creating them with the class—for acceptable behavior during discussions, for example, "no personal attacks," or "before you attack someone's position, you must restate it in your own words." Your goal should be to create a class atmosphere in which students feel safe in expressing their opinions.

Using Class Time Effectively

Taking attendance. Most instructors maintain an attendance policy, stated in their syllabus. You may take attendance orally, checking off each student as you read his or her name. This method is useful at the beginning of the term, when you're trying to learn everyone's name, but it can be time-consuming unless you combine it with another activity, such as a workshop "status-of-the-class" check (see Chapter 5, "Conducting Class Workshops") or a brief written response to a reading. You might also take attendance silently, noting who's present during workshop or group activities. Some instructors ask students to sign an attendance sheet at the start of every class, making the point that if their name isn't on the attendance sheet, they'll be considered absent. This method puts the responsibility for taking attendance on the students, rather than on the instructor, and produces a paper trail of student attendance—or lack of it. A variation relies on simply collecting something from each student every day—a draft, a piece of in-class writing, a report of group work that all group members sign—and using it as evidence of attendance. The virtue of the daily assignment is the emphasis not merely on attending, but on doing the work of the class.

Structuring class time. Most of the time, instructors feel that class periods aren't long enough, no matter the number of minutes in each one. Here are some suggestions for using your class time wisely:

- Take attendance as part of another activity, as described above.

- Begin each class promptly on time with a brief writing activity. If you do this every day, students will get to class and out of their coats in time to do the activity, rather than straggling in and getting themselves arranged while you try to start class.

- Maintain a schedule for each class that includes an estimate of the time each activity will begin and end. Even if you can't keep to this plan—students are engaged in a good discussion or workshop, they have more questions than you anticipated, a piece of technology you're using stops working—you can adjust the schedule by shortening an activity, moving it to the next class period, eliminating it, or turning it into an out-of-class activity.

- Have some activities on hand that you can insert if, for some reason, you have time on your hands that you didn't anticipate. A couple of minilessons, an engaging group exercise, even an essay or a couple of children's picture books relating to the assignment that you might read to them can help you fill extra time with a worthwhile activity. Although dismissing class early will seem like a treat, most students, especially those who are working to pay their own way, will object if classes are abbreviated with any regularity. Experienced instructors are good sources of backup plans and activities, and they are usually happy to share, so don't hesitate to ask.

- Hand back papers while students are working in groups. As you circulate, returning their materials, you can monitor the groups' work.

- End each class with a writing activity. If you do this every day, students will be less likely to start packing in anticipation of the end of the class period.

Motivating Students

Some students want to do well and consistently come to class prepared, having read and written what you've assigned. Other students are less inclined to work without prodding, motivated more by their sense of how their peers will see them than by their desire to please you or to earn a good grade. You can help those students by creating class activities that ask them to perform for other students. A traditional approach is to ask questions and call on students at random for the answers, but that method is hard on shy students and isn't often appropriate to a writing class. A better way is to build in occasions for students to present their work to the rest of class. Ask students to read parts of their drafts aloud within small groups and to the class. Require that groups report their work to the class, alternating the role of speaker. Have students read in-class writing to start, refocus, or conclude a discussion. Alternate various methods of asking for student performance: go around the room, asking each student to read or respond; ask for volunteers; call on a few individuals at random; require postings on an online discussion board. The key is to use class activities that demand everyone's participation and don't allow students to become unengaged, invisible, or mute.

Observing Other Classes

While reading about and discussing how to design class meetings is useful, the best way to come to an understanding of how classes work is to experience them. Ideally, you should sit in on several veteran instructors' classes in order to watch them as they teach. Observe how they structure their time, establish rhythms, move the class from place to place, and deal with surprises or unanticipated issues. Some tips on visiting include the following:

- Ask permission first. Some instructors are hesitant to let other instructors observe their classes, or they may want you to visit when certain activities are planned.

- Arrive on time, even a bit early. You want to disrupt the class as little as possible, and already being seated when students arrive is one way to do that.

- Ask the instructor where you should sit. Remember that you're a guest, and, more than that, your mere presence changes the dynamics of the entire class, at least at first. Once the students get used to you, they'll ignore you, but during the first ten minutes or so, they'll be aware that you're there.

- Take your cues from the instructor. Some instructors will introduce you to the class and explain why you're there; others won't. Some instructors will want you to participate as much as you'd like, sitting in on groups, speaking up during discussions and contributing during lessons; others will want you to sit quietly and apart from the class to minimize the effects of your presence.

- Take notes—lots of notes. Take notes on whatever you see and hear—eavesdrop on students' conversations to one another or in groups, look over students' shoulders (if you can) to see what they're writing, describe what the instructor is doing when he or she's moving around the room or sitting at the desk in front. If you vow to yourself that you'll take notes more or less continuously, you'll force yourself to pay attention to the class so you'll have material to write about later. Jot down the time in the left-hand margin every few minutes, so you'll know what happened at what time. Divide your notes into three columns: one for the time, one for the notes you take as you observe, and one for additional observations, comments, and responses that you add later.

- Focus on students as well as the instructor. In a workshop class there's a lot of activity going on, whether or not the instructor is talking: Students are working in groups or individually, the instructor is conferring with individuals, modeling desired behavior, or preparing for the next set of class activities. Remember that a classroom is a rich milieu filled with twenty or twenty-five people engaged in a common enterprise: Things are happening, even when the room is silent and everyone is working quietly at their desks or computers.

- Expand on your notes as soon as you can after the class meeting ends. Add additional details and your reactions while you still remember them.

- Offer to share your observations with the instructors whose classes you observe. Most will welcome the opportunity to see their classes through the eyes of another instructor.

A Sample Observation

Chris Massey, a first-year graduate teaching assistant at Wright State University, wrote this report of his observation of a class taught by Catherine Crowley, an instructor in the English Department. He notes the time periodically to help him remember the pacing of the class, and he intersperses his reflections (in italics) with his report of his observations.

I sat in on two classes taught by Catherine Crowley, an instructor at Wright State University. The two classes met on Wednesday and the following Monday during the 6th and 7th weeks of the 10-week fall quarter, as students finished writing an analysis of a text and began working on a profile. Each class period lasted 65 minutes and took place in a classroom equipped with networked computers for each student. Students have access to Microsoft Office applications as well as the Internet and courseware that includes WebCT and Turnitin.com.

Wednesday, October 13, 2004

1:30 pm. Professor Crowley returns papers and passes around the attendance sheet. While the students review their graded papers, Professor Crowley reviews the lesson from Monday and connects Monday's activities to the students' objectives for today. Here, she accomplishes two tasks at once—she gets "housekeeping issues" out of the way while, at the same time, bridging the gap between Monday's lesson and today's lesson. *I like the way she accomplishes this task: effortlessly. The students are not even aware of the teaching taking place.* Upon successfully transitioning from Monday's assignments to those scheduled for today, Professor Crowley asks the students if they are ready to submit their rhetorical analyses as final drafts. As you might expect, the entire class responds with a resounding "no." She then agrees with the students and tells them that they can have the weekend to polish their papers. *I hope I have this same connection with my students. I also need to realize that the goal is to get a set of well-written papers. Who cares about the deadline? I hope I have enough foresight to make changes to due dates when necessary.* She then gives the class the plan for the day: She will visit each student and discuss topics for the upcoming paper, the profile. While she is visiting with each student individually, the rest of the class is to begin researching the topics for the profile paper using the Internet. While talking, she begins passing out the assignment; she has posted it to WebCT and has printed them each a copy. *I wonder if I should use hard copies for my students. I always put the assignments on WebCT, but I never give them a handout. I do this to keep from wasting so much paper, but I wonder if it helps to reinforce the assignment if the students have a paper copy to refer to later on.* Moving from the next scheduled assignment, she asks her students to recall specifically what they observed on Monday: "Stephen, what did we do Monday?" Stephen answers that they went outside and observed activities in the Quad. At this point, she links their individual responses ("rustling leaves" and "the hot chick with the pink book bag") to the assignment: observing behaviors and places. *Here, the questions serve to reinforce the assignment from Monday and allow the students to link both* *assignments. It serves as a review of sorts. . . . I need to remember to do this. I tend to move too quickly. Take the time and review prior assignments.*

1:36 pm. At this point, Professor Crowley mentions that students who use a MacIntosh computer need to review their font choices before submitting assignments to web sites. She gives this information because the sheet she passes out is from her computer, a Mac. *This information is not related to the assignment, but it serves to link Professor Crowley to her students; they see her as one of them. She becomes human. I thought this was nice of her—students appreciate any information their instructor gives them that helps them out in the real world.* Next, she tells the students that, "We need to make a plan, man." Here, she relates the observation in the Quad to the assignment: to come up with topics for the profile paper. She calls on individual students to relate their observations to their topics—Ryan wants to observe the Dayton mall, and she warns that malls can be generic; Pam wants to observe a football game from her old high school, and Jessica wants to observe a homecoming. Professor Crowley gives constructive criticism here—some topics are good, others too general. *Going around the room serves to make the assignment real-the students get to hear each other's ideas, and it cements the profile topics in their minds. I sometimes back away from having my students share their ideas publicly, but I see now it can work to the students' advantage.*

1:43 pm. At this point, Professor Crowley gives the students pointers for getting started on their plans. She tells them to take notes on a piece of paper, type it, etc. She then writes on the board: "What is your topic? How will you take your observation notes (laptop, pictures, video, etc)? Remember to include the date, time, and specific place. Who do you plan to interview (may not know yet)? How will you make your interview (live, contact)? Write down possible questions. Create a survey?" *This allowed her students to have a starting point (they took notes and made their own lists) to think about what they wanted to do.* She then asks her class, "How will you find published sources about your topics?" She responds to their answers and advises them to look on the internet for possible sources. She also reminds them to identify and document their sources.

1:51 pm. Here, a student—Katie—asks a question: "When researching soccer, do I research soccer in general or soccer about my high school?" Professor Crowley responds and compliments her student on a good question. She tells her entire class the question and responds that they should research specific topics, not general ones. She even responds to one student by telling him to ask his grandparents about his topic. *She has a good connection with her students . . . they respect her and value her opinion.* Professor Crowley then logs onto the main computer console and pulls a website up: "St. Anne's Hill," a website for the community where she lives. She informs her students that many Web sites are themselves profiles. She shows them the community homepage and the information located on the Web site, such as the demographics. She reminds her students that you can put opinions in a profile; and, she clues in the class that their main job now is to get information—concentrate on detail, detail, detail. *I like the way Pro-*

fessor Crowley demonstrates how to utilize a Web site—I would have never thought of this. Good idea. Sometimes the simple ideas are the best.

1:55 pm. She reminds them that their textual analyses are due Monday. She tells them have plenty to do this weekend. She tells them to use their fellow students as sounding boards: use each other to come up with ideas and comment on each other's.

1:56 pm. Professor Crowley begins individual conferences with students; other students are working on gathering information—she encourages them to talk to each other, to utilize the class time. *I really like the idea that she encourages her students to talk to each other. It seems so simple; yet I have never used this. Good mix between individual time and group time. This approach allows Professor Crowley to spend time with each student while, at the same time, allowing students to work on their papers.* Some students are typing answers to questions. Others are searching the Internet and discussing ideas with their peers. One student asks, "Is first person OK?" She repeats the question to the class and answers yes to the class. She reminds the sports people that they don't want just a play-by-play account; they need to interview players, cheerleaders, whatever will make the account realistic. She reminds them to zero in on the hometown event. *Professor Crowley maintains excellent control of the room even when talking to students individually. I noticed several students who wandered from the assignment, but they only did so momentarily.*

2:16 pm. Professor Crowley continues to consult with individual students. She asks the class: "Is everybody working on something here?" *Again, nice control of the room—this one statement reels in those students who are not working on the assignment.* She responds to one student's question about chat rooms, that you can use quotes from these sources. She also responds to a student who asks her about Turnitin and tells her to ask at the helpdesk. She reminds her students that they are going into this assignment as reporters and need to be as objective as possible.

2:27 pm. Professor Crowley reminds the students that there is no class on Friday and tells them that she wants their topic choices. Dismisses class.

Useful Readings

Elbow, Peter. "Collaborative Peer Evaluation by Faculty." *Embracing Contraries: Explorations in Learning and Teaching.* NY: Oxford, 1986. 179–205.

Frank, Carolyn. "Classroom Observations." *Ethnographic Eyes: A Teacher's Guide to Classroom Observation.* Portsmouth NH: Heinemann, 1999. 82–93.

Conducting Class Workshops 5

Workshops play an important role in most writing courses. In fact, workshops are often the predominant use of class time. Most simply, a workshop includes any activity in which students write or respond to others' writing, providing them the opportunity to give and receive focused response to their writing in order to revise it. When students confer with their instructor, they also receive focused response leading to revision.

Getting Started

You may offer workshop time as a regular feature of your course, so that during a workshop your students are engaged in various activities at once: generating ideas and text, drafting, conferring, evaluating, revising, editing, or proofreading. You may want to structure workshop times to focus on a single set of activities, such as editing final drafts before submitting them or on collaborative activities such as analyzing a text in groups. However you use workshops in your course, here are some guidelines to help them run smoothly:

Define workshop tasks clearly. Students should know what you expect them to do during workshop time and what to produce by the end. You may begin the workshop with a brief lesson outlining the tasks and

the reasons for doing them as well as provide structure for the activities, as appropriate. If students are writing during class, clearly define what writing activities are acceptable and how they should carry them out. If you expect a certain product (a draft, a worksheet, a report to the class by a group), provide clear instructions.

Establish rules of behavior. At a minimum, you should expect students to come to workshops ready to do the assigned tasks. If you want students to follow specific rules (when responding to one another's drafts in groups, for example, or when editing one another's essays), state them clearly and enforce them.

Hold students accountable for their workshop time. If students are working independently, you might take a few minutes to conduct a quick "status of the class" check by asking each student to declare orally what they will be working on during the workshop. As they do, jot down their intended focus. Then you can use the notes to determine who might need help, who should work with another student—in other words, individualize your workshop instruction. Many instructors create simple forms that allow them to record students' workshop intentions quickly. Here's an example.

Status of Class		Section _____ Week _____	
Student's Name	Monday	Wednesday	Friday
Abendroth, Kim	Work on draft		
Bender, Joe	Peer conference		
Cathcart, Ashante	Editing conference, work on draft `		

You can require each group to present a report to the class on their achievements, or ask each group to produce something in writing—a worksheet or an informal report—that each group member signs.

Allow for some chit-chat. Students forming groups often need to establish a social connection before they can get down to work. To do that, they may talk informally together for a few minutes first. Also, if the group discussion becomes more serious than group members can handle, they may cool off by diverting the discussion away from the topic at hand. If they don't return to the main topic, you may need to nudge them or give them a followup task.

Circulate and monitor. Workshops work best when students are given tasks that they complete independently, using you as a resource when necessary. Give them space to do that by staying at your desk for a few minutes after getting them started. Then circulate around the room, pausing to answer questions or listen to groups as they work. Students will ask questions if you're in their vicinity, and you can glance over shoulders and initiate impromptu conferences as students work. Your presence may also keep students or groups on task, at least while you're in the area. If your classroom layout permits it, sit at a student desk in the middle of the room. You'll be able to hear all the groups as they work without seeming overly intrusive.

Model writers' behavior. Just as students benefit from seeing your writing, they benefit from seeing you write and share your writing. You might spend classroom workshop time working on a draft of something you're writing—a piece you're asking students to write, a professional essay, a personal piece—and at some point share it with them, perhaps showing your revisions and describing your own process. Ask students to respond to your draft, using the same techniques you want them to use when responding to one another's writing. Your students can be perceptive readers, especially in helping you explain concepts clearly.

Conduct conferences or small-group mini-lessons. You may schedule individual conferences during workshop time, speaking softly to students at your desk while the rest of the class works independently. If several students are having a similar writing problem, you might use workshop time to work with that group while the students who don't share their problem work on their own.

Selecting a Format for a Workshop

Here are some common formats for writing workshops:

Independent workshops. In these workshops, students work on their own writing assignments, so in a class of twenty-five students, ten may be writing drafts, eight may be revising, five may be doing research on computers, and two may be editing a final draft. Have students declare their intentions through a status-of-the-class check; circulate and be flexible, nudging students when they finish one task to begin another. For example, a student who finishes a draft may need to get you or a peer to respond to it and then begin revising. A few minutes before the end of a workshop class period, it's useful to stop students and ask them, either orally or informally in writing, to review what they did and what they plan to do next.

Whole-class response workshops. In these workshops, the entire class discusses one or two students' drafts. Establish rules: The writer provides a draft a couple of days ahead of time, either bringing copies for everyone or posting it online, where the other students must read the draft before coming to class. In class, the writer reads the draft aloud while the class follows along and the writer provides background by describing the rhetorical situation and the stage of writing (rough draft, revision, final draft). Classmates respond to the draft, offering suggestions and guidance, orally or in writing or both. Students should be reminded of their need to balance honesty and tactfulness.

Group response workshops. Students work in groups of three or four in these workshops, responding to one another's drafts. In one method, students take turns. The writer reads his or her draft aloud, while the other group members listen, taking no notes. When the writer finishes, the others write a brief response. The writer reads the draft again, and this time the others take notes on what they liked, what they didn't like, and what they had questions about. When the writer finishes, each group member describes his or her response while the writer takes notes. The writer does not engage in conversation or debate with the others, since they are simply reporting their reactions to the draft, which are not arguable. The writer then decides how to revise based on the various responses. Here are some variations:

- Students trade drafts and read them silently before responding as described above. If left to themselves, some groups will decide to follow this procedure to avoid reading aloud. Encouraging reading aloud helps students hear both their own voice and potential trouble spots in their writing, but if you encounter a group of students who are very reluctant to read aloud, consider offering this silent option.

- Students read their drafts aloud to a group, which listens but does not respond, except with applause (which may consist of finger-snapping, to keep the noise level down). Especially early in a term, students may need to get used to the idea of sharing before they can work up the courage to give or get response.

- Students respond to one another's drafts based on specific criteria, such as the Key Features of genres defined in the *Field Guide*. In this sort of workshop, have individual students or groups fill out a worksheet that outlines the criteria to ensure that students address everything you want them to.

Focused-activity workshops. The instructor defines a particular task for individual students or groups of students to complete. These tasks might include asking students to work individually on any of the processes of writing as part of their work on their own drafts; to analyze their own drafts or the drafts of classmates, answering specific questions about the writing; to collaborate to complete a writing task; or to choose one group member's essay for oral publication to the entire class.

Useful Readings

Murray, Donald M. *A Writer Teaches Writing.* Revised 2nd ed. Boston: Heinle, 2003.

Garrison, Roger H. "One-to-One: Tutorial Instruction in Freshman Composition." *New Directions in Community Colleges* 5 (1974): 55–84.

Working One-on-One with Students 6

Individual conferences with students to discuss their writing are time-consuming but can be very effective. If your school has a writing center, you can also refer students to work with the tutors there, but in fifteen or twenty minutes, you yourself can establish a personal relationship with a student and offer focused, detailed advice to help the student write and revise. While you may have specific goals for some conferences (for example, you may hold conferences solely to help students settle on a topic for an essay), you can use conferences for a number of purposes:

- Provide one-on-one help
- Listen and respond respectfully to students' writing, working with the text they have—or discussing the text they don't have
- Offer whatever help students need, such as generating ideas and text, organizing a draft, working on various writing strategies, or exploring research options
- Help students understand their own writing processes and identify areas for further work
- Answer students' questions

Whatever you do, avoid taking over the draft or telling the student what to write. Most of the time, instructors and tutors make no marks on students' drafts, leaving that job to the students themselves. The best conferences consist of conversations between two writers who are trying to improve one writer's work. You should remind students that it's up to them to interpret and enact, modify, or reject the advice they've been given. Here are some common questions instructors ask about conferences.

How often should you schedule conferences? The simple answer is, as often as possible; working one-on-one with students allows you to tailor your instruction to each student's needs, making conference teaching "the most effective—and the most practical—method of teaching composition," as Donald M. Murray says in "Conference Teaching: The Individual Response." In that essay Murray outlines approaches for turning an entire course into a series of conferences. Before you structure your course that way, however, you need to know your school's policy on canceling class periods for conferences, and you need to gain experience conference teaching. Although it's rewarding, it's also challenging, because you need to think on your feet, which can leave you mentally exhausted at the end of a day of conferences. Typically, instructors schedule one mandatory conference for each major assignment, usually two or three per term.

How long should a conference take? Conferences can vary from five minutes for a very focused conference on a limited topic to a half-hour or more. If you're teaching writing for the first time, schedule twenty-minute conferences the first time, and see how they feel. Then adjust the length for subsequent conferences.

How should you schedule conferences? If you're holding twenty-minute conferences for twenty-five students, your conferencing time totals eight hours and twenty minutes. You should schedule four conferences in a row, followed by a twenty-minute break, to allow for conferences that run long (some will) and to give you time to use the bathroom, eat, and recharge. So you'll need a day and a half or so, with most conferences taking place on a day you cancel class. Setting a timer can help you keep to your schedule—both you and your student will wrap up your conversation once the bell rings.

What if students can't meet during the times you've scheduled? If attending a conference is a course requirement, you have the obligation to make the requirement possible to complete. You may have to negotiate with some students for a special time or, if a meeting isn't possible, a telephone or online conversation.

How can you hold conferences without spending so much time on them? You can schedule briefer conferences of ten to fifteen minutes each. When you're crunched for time, you will need to be more focused, but most instructors find that it's possible to get all the work done. Another option is to hold small-group conferences, scheduling three or four students for one thirty-minute conference—in essence, establishing a workshop of which you're a member. If your class periods are lengthy, you can set aside the last fifteen to twenty minutes for conferences, meeting with three or four students each day.

At what point in a sequence of assignments should you schedule conferences? The glib answer is, anytime you want. Students will benefit, no matter when they have a conference with you.

What should students bring with them to a conference? Depending on the nature of the conference, in general it's useful to ask students to bring something in writing: a thesis statement, a rough draft, an introductory paragraph, a set of questions. That writing gives both of you something concrete to work with. Since few students will have had conferences before, it's a good idea to let them know what to expect, as teaching assistant Ozlem Wierzbicki did: "I gave them a minilesson on one-on-one conferences, which made a big difference in terms of their expectations for the conference. This minilesson was basically an outline explaining to them how the conferences would be conducted."

Should you read students' drafts ahead of time? Inexperienced instructors who haven't read many student essays may feel more confident in their ability to give good advice if they collect drafts and read them ahead of time. Most instructors, though, find that they can answer students' questions or deal with the conference's main issue after quickly skimming the essay at the start of the conference—or after having students point out the parts of the essay that concern them. Also, the time spent reading first and then conferring can double the time you spend with each student.

What if students come unprepared? Some instructors turn away students who come to a workshop without a thesis statement or a draft. I believe, however, that if students come unprepared, they're genuinely stuck: They can't think of anything to write, they're blocked, or they have personal problems that prevent them from doing the work. So I work with what they have, helping them get caught up so they can progress toward success in the course.

How do you start a conference? What do you say? Invite students to sit, and make them comfortable with a few words of welcome. As Murray points out, you may not need to say anything, or you may begin the conference with a question like, "Well? What questions do you have?" For students

who don't know what to say, ask some general questions like these:

- What's the strongest part of your draft? What makes it good?
- What's your purpose for writing?
- Who's your audience?
- What gave you the most trouble as you wrote?
- Where do you think you need more information?

If students come without a draft, these questions won't work, of course. Then you need to shift gears with questions to generate ideas for topics:

- What interests you?
- What do you do for fun or relaxation?
- What makes you mad?
- What puzzled you in the reading we did? What made you uncomfortable?
- If you *could* write about _____ [fill in with the topic], what would you write? This "fill in the blank" approach is surprisingly effective, useful in many situations.

How can you use The Norton Field Guide effectively as you confer with students? The *Field Guide* is organized for easy reference, so you can quickly find the advice you need at the time you need it. When you hold a conference, you might keep the *Field Guide* open to the glossary/index. As you work with students, you—or, better, your students—can go quickly to the advice they need. In the process, you'll be teaching them how to use the textbook as a reference tool.

What should students do while you're reading their drafts? You might give students something interesting to read while they wait. You can also ask them to bring two copies of the draft and read it while you do, so it's fresh in their minds when you start discussing it. Here's what teaching assistant Holly Gilbert discovered:

> I had the students bring two copies of their draft to conferences with them. I found it to be extremely helpful because we both were not trying to flip through the same document at the same time. While I read through each draft, I had the students find specific points in their drafts that they wanted to talk about and star them; some even jotted down little notes in the margins to explain to me what they think works and what doesn't and why they think it does or does not. I really found this to be helpful. It helped those students who even after writing a self-assessment had no idea what to discuss in the conference. The students who took the time to reread their drafts and star specific parts really got into discussing how they wanted to make their draft better and where they wanted to go from this point. Instead of staring at me and fearing what I was going to say about their drafts, they had something to do that kept them engaged and refreshed their memory about certain aspects of their drafts that they may want to discuss in conferencing. Our conferences started to have the tone of a conversation (as Murray would say).

How should the conference end? Each student should leave the conference with a clear sense of what to do next. It's a good idea to ask students to state their plans in writing before leaving the conference, as the act of composing it together forces both of you to be specific and clear. You might ask if they have questions about any other aspects of the class or about their progress in the course.

How should you handle students who don't show up? I usually count a conference as the equivalent of two absences because I value my time. Since I've canceled a class period, replacing 50 to 100 minutes of group instruction with fifteen minutes of individual attention, I want students to take the conference seriously. As teaching assistant Chuck Holmes notes, there's also a personal dimension when students don't come to conferences:

> The most powerful response I had to any of my first conferences was the way it felt when students didn't show up. I was pretty indignant about that. The vast majority of the students did attend the conferences and I think we all got something worthwhile out of it, so I have made myself a promise that I won't say anything in the next class about how it made me feel, being stood up that way. As a matter of fact, now that I think about it, being stood up is exactly what it felt like.

How can you use your campus writing center to best advantage? First, make sure your students know the writing center exists and encourage them to seek help there with their writing, whether they're seeking a topic or polishing a final draft.

Include writing center information on your syllabus and on each assignment handout. You might contact the center's director to ask for brochures or other material describing the center's services to give your students. Some writing centers will send tutors to classes to describe its services to students. You could give students a bit of credit toward their grade for attending a tutoring session. Send a copy of your course syllabus and assignment descriptions to the writing center, and make sure they have copies of *The Norton Field Guide to Writing* available for tutors. The more tutors know about your course and expectations, the more they can help your students. You may be able to require some students to get help at the writing center, but check with the center's director first since some centers have limited scheduling ability.

Useful Readings

Boynton, Linda. "See Me: Conference Strategies for Developmental Writers." *Teaching English in the Two-Year College.* May 2003: 391–402.

Murray, Donald M. "Conference Teaching: The Individual Response." *A Writer Teaches Writing,* 2nd ed. Boston: Houghton, 1985. 147–175.

7 Using Writing Activities in Class

Writing is a form of learning. As we write, we generate thoughts we wouldn't have had if we hadn't put pen to paper or fingers to keyboard. In our own writing as well as our students', we can see that thinking improves as drafts evolve. More than once a student of mine has exclaimed, "I didn't know this essay would head in this direction!" Because writing helps us generate ideas and clarify our thinking, the act of writing is a useful tool for teaching. This chapter explores some ways you can use writing to both enhance your teaching and improve students' learning.

Freewrites

Chapter 22 of *The Norton Field Guide to Writing,* describes freewriting as "an informal method of exploring a subject by writing about it." Freewriting is a useful tool to help students pull thoughts out of their minds as they prepare to write essays, and it's also useful in class. Students may discover that freewriting helps them articulate their thinking whenever they prepare to speak or write. Having students freewrite on index cards often reduces their anxiety, because, after all, anyone can fill up a small card. Here are three times when you can use brief, informal freewrites as pedagogical tools:

At the beginning of class. Ask students to write questions they have about the assignment that's due or reactions to a reading. You can use their answers to start a discussion or to start the class with a brief question-and-answer session, or you can collect the cards and skim them later to find out how well students understood the assignment—or if they did it. If students write on index cards, you can give them two assignments, one on each side. For example, "What's one question you have about this assignment?" and "What's one thing you liked about the reading for today?" Alternately, set aside the first ten minutes of every class for writing. Expect students to spend ten minutes writing whatever they want, an activity which settles them down and warms them up for the day's activities. Starting the class with a writing activity is a good way to let students know that they need to arrive on time and be prepared and gives you a way to take attendance: if students turn in the writing, they're present and on time.

At the end of class. Ask students to sum up the day's activities or what they learned during class. Ask them to relate the day's discussion to their reading, to ask questions about the assignment, or to predict what they'll do with their drafts after working on them in class. These end-of-class freewrites help students synthesize course material and think about how to apply it to their own writing. They also forestall students' tendency to start packing up several minutes before the end of class and let them know that you've planned their class time carefully.

During class. Brief writing activities can be valuable during class, too. When you finish one class activity, have students reflect on it before moving on to the next. If a discussion bogs down or becomes heated, ask students to stop and write briefly on the topic to get everyone on track (and give you a few minutes to regroup!). These brief freewrites may take as little as two minutes—just enough to give students a chance to think on paper.

Here's how teaching assistant Andrea Nay uses brief writing assignments on index cards:

> Every single class period, students must write on a topic I assign for the first 3–4 minutes of class. Some assignments are designed to be funny and simply serve as a means to capture attendance. Others are in keeping with the day's lessons. In advance preparation for Wednesday's mini-lesson on sentence breaks, for example, I had the students take the first few minutes of class Monday to write the longest grammatically correct sentence they could concoct on the front or back of an index card. The "winner" got a prize on Wednesday, and I used that sentence as a good example to illustrate the proper use of coordinating conjunctions.

Letters

Everyone knows how to write a letter. The form is simple, the stance and tone natural. As such, letters are a great way to communicate with your students. Sue Dinitz and Toby Fulwiler suggest that you require each student to write you a letter of at least 250 words—one page—each week. You might specify a topic, but I've found that simply requiring the letter and leaving the contents up to the students produce wonderful results. You might ask students to send you an email letter or give you a hard copy, or let them choose the medium they feel most comfortable with. Then read the letters quickly, highlighting or copying interesting passages or good questions. Respond with a "Dear Class" letter in which you use the passages you've chosen as the basis for your own remarks, sharing interesting thoughts they've expressed, answering questions, and exploring ideas with them. Give students credit for their letters.

You'll find that these letters have several good effects. Students will be doing more writing, always a good thing. They'll be writing to a real audience—you—on topics of importance to them. As a result, you'll learn much more about their interests, backgrounds, emotional states, and circumstances than you would otherwise.

You'll be able to tailor your instruction to meet their needs and answer their questions promptly. And through your exchanges of letters, you'll get to know one another far better than students and instructors normally do. In colleges and universities where young people may be living away from home for the first time, this personal connection between students and faculty can be crucially important to the students' success, not only in your class but in making it through their first year. Besides, learning about your students' lives and thoughts is at turns touching, interesting, sad, and funny—but thoroughly rewarding.

Consider, too, asking students to write letters to one another, perhaps providing a copy for you. After several rounds of letters to and from you and each other, discuss the effects of varying audiences on the letters' form, content, and stance.

Online Discussion Lists

You can use online discussion lists to engage students in conversations about any topics you might otherwise use class time to discuss or to extend discussion that begins in class. You can post a specific topic or question for students to discuss, or you could also ask students or groups of students to create discussion topics. It's best to require students to post responses; otherwise, participation will likely be spotty. Most colleges and universities offer you the ability to set up a group consisting of members of your course through a Web site portal, email, or online courseware. For more advice on online discussions, see Chapters 13 and 14 in this book.

Journals

Journals—also known as daybooks, logs, or personal notebooks—have been popular with high school and college English teachers for many years because they give students practice in writing and thinking on paper or online without the pressure of crafting polished prose. Some instructors focus their journal assignments on practice, simply requiring a certain amount of writing, such as a page each day or five pages each week. More often, though, students are given more direction, so that their journal writing contributes to the overall goals of the course. The sorts of assignments you might ask students to complete in a journal include the following, adapted from a list of characteristics described by Toby Fulwiler in *The Journal Book* (2–3):

- *Questioning.* Students can explore questions about their assignments, their research material, or class activities. They can also work out conflicts between what they've previously thought or learned and new information.

- *Responding.* Students can play with ideas or react to aspects of the course, giving them a chance to work out their thinking and giving you a window into their difficulties.

- *Consolidating and connecting.* Students can explore the ways that the various course activities and assignments interrelate, or how your course relates to their writing in other courses.

- *Analyzing.* Students might reflect on their own processes of writing, explaining how their activities helped (or didn't help) them write an assignment. Periodically, they might also analyze the course itself: What's been helpful so far, how the course differs from or matches their expectations, what might be done differently to help them learn better.

- *Playing.* Students might use journal entries to play around in a safe environment: write parodies or poems, draw cartoons, or explore hypothetical situations that they or you create.

- *Conversing.* Dialectical journals (also discussed in Chapter 8, "Using Readings to Teach Writing") give students an opportunity to reflect on their own earlier journal entries. The technique is simple: students write journal entries on one side of a notebook page, leaving the other side blank, or they fold a page in two and write only to the left of the fold. Later, they read their entries and, on the other page or right-hand side of the page, they comment on those earlier entries. If students keep class notes, you might ask that they follow the same procedure.

Tips for assigning and evaluating journals. If you ask students to use a three-ring binder for their journals, they can use the same binder for all course materials and you can collect only the entries you want, rather than having to lug two dozen spiral notebooks around. Make sure students date each entry and begin each entry on a new page. Alternately, set up a system that allows students to post their entries online. Designate a minimum word length for entries; often, writers' best insights appear near the end of an entry. To manage your work load, consider collecting the journals from half the class each week, so you'll see each student's journal every two weeks.

When you evaluate journals, remember that they are places for students to play, experiment, and explore. You should respond to their content as a reader. To evaluate the journals, you might give credit based on quantity, for example, journals with lots of writing earn high grades, journals that meet the minimum requirements get a C. Or combine quantity with quality: Doing the minimum earns a C, and higher grades depend on such qualities as elaboration, thoughtfulness, and playfulness.

Weblogs: Blogs (short for "Web logs") may be used as online journals. Blogs, which at their simplest are personal Web sites built upon a template, are easy to create and allow writers (or *bloggers*) to include photos, documents, links to other Web sites, and even video as they explore ideas. One significant difference between a traditional journal and a blog, of course, is audience; instead of an audience of the writer and the instructor, the blogger's writing is posted on the Web, where it can be accessed by classmates and people all over the world. As a result, students may avoid certain topics that they might write about in a more private journal. For more information on how to set up a blog, visit www.blogger.com/.

Useful Readings

Bean, John. "Informal, Exploratory Writing Activities." *Engaging Ideas: The Professor's Guide to Integrating Writing, Critical Think-ing, and Active Learning in the Class-room.* San Francisco: Jossey-Bass, 1996. 97–118.

Dinitz, Sue, and Toby Fulwiler, eds. *The Letter Book: Ideas for Teaching College English.* Portsmouth, NH: Boynton/Cook, 2000.

Emig, Janet. "Writing as a Mode of Learn-ing." *College Composition and Communica-tion* 28 (May 1977): 122–28.

Fulwiler, Toby, ed. *The Journal Book.* Ports-mouth, NH: Boynton/Cook, 1987.

Using Readings to Teach Writing 8

Maureen Daly Goggin

Like reading, writing is not a natural act; it's a learned activity. Because there are many genres in writing, readers attend to these genres in different ways. Reading, then, is not a single act but multiple practices that vary with the purpose, context, and kind of text. As the first readers of their own work, writers need to anticipate other readers' needs, concerns, and levels of knowledge about a topic. Writers must predict readers' expectations for the genre and relationship to the writer. In other words, writers need to learn to read as well as write rhetorically: They need a strategy for reading a text for its purpose, audience context, expected conventions, and style. Using *The Norton Field Guide to Writing* with its sample readings in the genres you're teaching offers you an important opportunity to show students how to read a variety of genres rhetorically. This chapter offers strategies for assigning readings and using them in the classroom.

Writing teachers assign readings for many reasons. As Wayne Booth so powerfully observes, embedded in readings of all kinds are world views and values: "To teach reading (or viewing or listening) that is both engaged and actively critical is central because it is in stories, in narratives large and small rather than in coded commandments, that students absorb lessons on how to confront ethical complexity. . . . It is in stories that we learn to think about the 'virtual' cases that echo the cases we will meet when we return to the more disorderly, 'actual' world" (48).

To become critical citizens and consumers, students need to learn how to make sense of ethical complexities and to understand multiple perspectives. Readings you assign can support this critical thinking at the same time they demonstrate the key features of a genre, explore a topic or an issue, and initiate research in an area of interest for the class. Most important, readings teach students how to read other writers rhetorically so they can read their own writing rhetorically.

Regardless of your purposes for incorporating readings into your writing class, make your reasons clear so students will understand how the readings relate to their own writing. The suggestions here are by no means exhaustive but are meant as examples that may spark additional ideas.

Preparing Students to Read

Let students know why you have assigned the readings, either by including your purposes in the assignment or by giving a brief lecture or minilesson before they begin the reading. You might save the last five minutes of class to prepare students for the following class's reading assignment by giving them a focus or a series of study questions. You can also prepare them for any unfamiliar vocabulary by playing a version of Balderdash: you say and spell one or more of the words you suspect will be unfamiliar, then have students write impromptu definitions. They pass the definitions to you or a chosen speaker in the class to read aloud. Students then vote on the most likely definition. The writer of the definition chosen gets a point, and all those who defined it correctly get a point. Points can be accumulated throughout the semester in this manner. Here are some other ways to use readings effectively:

Models. Readings can serve as good examples of the genres being studied but *only* if students are taught *how* to look at them as models. In ancient Greece, Isocrates offered a caution against placing models in front of students and expecting them to know how to compose a similar piece, offering the analogy that it's like placing a row of shoes in front of novice cobblers and expecting them to understand how to make a shoe. How would the would-be cobblers know what raw materials were needed and where to get them? How to prepare those materials even if they could

locate them? How to fashion the shoe? In writing as well, students need to be taught how to look at models.

It's worth spending class time early in the term going over at least one essay in depth to demonstrate how to read it for its rhetorical features. Students can then continue this process on their own, guided by questions or perhaps by keeping a reading journal. You might ask students to write out their understanding of the essay's rhetorical situation:

Purpose: What is the writer's purpose? To entertain? Inform? Persuade readers to think something or take some action?

Audience: Who is the intended audience? Are you a member of that group? If not, did you need to look up unfamiliar terms or concepts or run into assumptions you don't necessarily share?

Genre: What is the genre? Is it a report? An argument? An analysis? Something else? What are the key features of this genre, and where are they found in this essay?

Stance: Who is the writer, and what is his or her stance? Critical? Curious? Opinionated? Objective? Passionate? Indifferent? Something else?

Media / Design: What is the medium, and how does it affect the way you read? If it's a print text, do you know anything about the publisher? If it's on the Web, who sponsors the site, and when was it last updated? Are there any design elements—such as headings, summaries, color, or boxes—that highlight key parts of the text?

Collecting their responses and reviewing them in class will help students take the readings and their responses to them seriously and will also help to show how reading is an integral part of writing. More advice on responding to reading may be found in Chapter 38, READING STRATEGIES in the *Field Guide.*

Reader's logs. You can ask students to keep a reader's log or journal where they record their impressions of assigned readings, focusing on their reactions to the lines of argument or the writer's position or the rhetorical stance of the readings. You can provide specific questions tied to each reading or provide a template of questions that students apply to all readings. If you ask students to bring their logs to class, their entries can be a starting point for discussing the readings. You can also ask students to reflect on their entries either during class or outside of class following discussions in class. At the end of the term, you might ask students to review all of their entries and write a reflection on that review.

Summarizing and outlining. You can ask students to summarize or create outlines of readings. These activities force students to read carefully and attend to the structure as well as the content of the text. They also allow you to see how well the students understand the reading, and offer a starting point for discussions of the reading. You can find advice on summarizing in

Chapter 42, QUOTING, PARAPHRASING, AND SUMMARIZING and advice on outlining in Chapter 38, READING STRATEGIES in the *Field Guide.*

Double-entry notebooks. Ann Berthoff developed the concept of a double-entry reading notebook. As she explains:

> What makes this notebook different from most, perhaps, is the notion of the double entry: on the right side reading notes, direct quotations, observational notes, fragments, lists, images—verbal and visual—are recorded; on the other (facing side), notes about those notes, summaries, formulations, aphorisms, editorial suggestions, revisions, comment on comment are written (48).

With a double-entry notebook, the opposing pages are seen in dialogue with one another. According to Berthoff, this kind of reading notebook helps students develop critical reading and writing skills because they are conducting a "continuing audit of meaning" (I. A. Richards, qtd. in "Curious" 42). Questions and observations that appear in these notebooks can launch vibrant classroom discussions.

Discussions. Discussions of readings can take place either face-to-face in class or in a synchronous or asynchronous online forum. The goal of these discussions should be to help writers advance their own writing. Unlike literature classes where the readings serve as the focus for literary analysis, in writing classes discussions of the readings ought to be tied directly to the aspects of writing with which your students are grappling. If, for example, you're teaching a unit on how to write a profile, you might have students analyze readings in this genre for rhetorical moves that would be useful for their own writing. Students might read the model in Chapter 16 of the *Field Guide* or a profile they find in a magazine or newspaper. Does the writer begin with an anecdote? What kind of information does the writer provide about the subject (person, place or thing) profiled? How did the author get the information she or he uses in the profile? How does the author end the profile? Also, to help students prepare for discussions, you might ask them to freewrite any questions, concerns or observations they have about the assigned reading. This task jogs their memory and provides a framework for discussion.

Small group discussions and activities. Small group activities help students practice collaborative work and are central to active learning. Variations on games students know can produce lively discussions. For instance, students can play a form of Jeopardy where they form groups and devise answers to questions relevant to the readings. They then challenge other groups by stating their answers and asking the other groups to form an appropriate question. Another strategy is to have student groups identify the rhetorical or content points they feel everyone should attend to. The small groups then share their recommendations with the whole class. Finally, students can be asked to select readings for the class and then lead the discussions either by themselves or in groups.

Quizzes and essay exams. Although some teachers assign quizzes as a way to make sure that students are doing the readings, an alternative and perhaps better approach is to use quizzes to help students learn how to write quiz and exam answers. Let students know that they will be taking periodic quizzes on the readings as a way to help them become strong quiz takers throughout their educations.

You may also want to help your students learn how to write essay responses to exam questions under pressure. A twist is to have students design a final exam on the readings and to write a rationale for their exam. Students find that they have to understand a whole lot in order to write good essay exam questions.

There are lots of valid reasons for incorporating reading into the writing classroom, and there are many creative ways for doing so. Still, a note of caution is in order: Because they often have a strong background as readers, some new writing teachers are tempted to spend too much time on the readings instead of the writing that should be the primary focus of the course. Keep your goal in mind: Use readings to help your students improve their writing.

Useful Readings

Berthoff, Ann E. "A Curious Triangle and the Double-Entry Notebook: or, How Theory Can Help Us Teach Reading and Writing." *The Making of Meaning: Metaphors, Models, and Maxims for Writing Teachers.*

Upper Montclair, NJ: Boynton/Cook, 1981. 48.

Berthoff, Ann E. "Is Reading Still Possible?" *The Sense of Learning*. Portsmouth, NH: Heinemann-Boynton/Cook, 1990. Rpt. *Composition in Four Keys*. Eds. Mark Wiley, Barbara Gleason, and Louise Wetherbee Phelps. Mountain View, CA: Mayfield, 1995. 45–49.

Booth, Wayne C. "The Ethics of Teaching Literature." *College English* 61 (1998): 41–55.

Foster, David, "Reading(s) in the Writing Classroom." *College Composition and Communication,* 48 (1997): 518–39.

Roth, Audrey, "Students Collaboratively Choose Reader Selections." *Teaching English in the Two-Year College,* 20 (1993): 298.

9 Responding to Student Writing

You've just collected twenty-five students' essay drafts and have promised to return them at the next class meeting. You also have several assignments to complete for the graduate courses you're taking. You want to give your students as much help as you can because you want them to succeed in your class—but you also need to get your own work done and, you hope, cook an occasional meal and get some sleep. Ways to respond helpfully to students' work and still manage your own time is the subject of this chapter.

Responding and Grading

First, remember that responding and grading are two different activities. When you respond to students' writing, your goal is to help them improve their writing of the draft at hand and in future writing. For that reason, you should respond in greatest detail to drafts that will be revised. Grading, on the other hand, ranks the writing's overall quality in relation to standards you or your writing program has set. You'll find advice on grading in Chapter 12 in this book, "Grading." Once a grade has been assigned to a piece of writing, students are likely to see the writing as finished. At that point, detailed responses are more often an attempt to justify the grade and function primarily as an autopsy. Here is advice on responding usefully and efficiently to students' writing.

Developing Criteria for Response

Since most students have been taking English in school for many years, they may have some definite ideas about what makes good writing. However, their ideas may not match one another's ideas or your criteria. So a good first step in preparing to respond to students' writing—and a good way to help them understand what you want—is to describe, as clearly as possible, the criteria you'll use when you respond to their writing. Here are a couple of ways to do that.

Use rubrics and checksheets. Checksheets and rubrics are excellent tools for responding to students' work in progress. They spell out as clearly as possible your expectations and provide detailed response to as few or as many characteristics as you want students to be responsible for. Students can use them to evaluate their own and one another's work. And they control your response by reminding you what to look for as you read students' work. On page 54 is a sample checklist for an essay that argues a position. To respond, you would simply place a check mark along the continuum from 3 (very well) to 0 (poorly or not at all).

You could substitute "well," "acceptable," "poorly," "not at all" or "early," "middle," "late"—whatever method of response you choose. Having an even number of response levels prevents grouping checks or credits in the middle. Why not use numbers or letters? For one thing, students will expect you to tally them up to create a precise grade for the whole rubric, increasing your workload. For another, the criteria on the rubric are not equal in value and, in fact, may change in value from draft to draft. For example, you may not want to weight "mechanics, usage, grammar, and spelling" as much as "adequate and appropriate source material," but if the mechanics are flawed enough that the writer's credibility comes into question, those problems will likely outweigh other criteria. And absence of a grade reinforces the idea that this checklist is a response to a work in progress.

Develop evaluation criteria collaboratively. Students understand and accept evaluation criteria more readily when they participate in developing them. You'll find, too, that students know and can articulate standards very well; they know what makes for good writing, even if they have trouble achieving it. (Here's a useful analogy: you may know what qualities characterize a good tennis backhand, guitar lick, or pastel drawing technique but still be unable to do it.) Here's a way to work with your class over one or two class periods to develop a checklist of evaluation criteria collaboratively:

1. Ask students to jot down a list of the criteria on which the type of writing they're currently working on should be judged.

2. Place them in groups of three to six students. Each group's task is to share their individual lists and come up with a single list on which they can agree.

3. Ask one member of each group to write the group's list on the board, which you have divided into sections for each group's list plus one in the middle that you've reserved.

4. Once all groups' lists are on the board, ask the class to find common criteria. If, for instance, every group's list contains "focused topic," write that term on a class list in the middle section. As students find common criteria, they'll note that groups use various terms to describe some criteria. Discuss possible differences in the terms and help the class decide on a single term that everyone agrees will be used to mean one criterion. This discussion will help students understand the criteria and develop a common language for discussing their work.

5. After the groups' lists have been merged into a single class list, you may find that criteria important to you are missing. Now is the time to add them, explaining what they mean and why they're important.

This procedure results in a class-specific set of criteria on which you can base check-

Taking a Position: Response Criteria

	very well	well	some- what	poorly or not at all
THE ASSIGNMENT				
The essay presents an argument				
Required drafts and other related assignments are present				
THE RHETORICAL SITUATION				
The essay accomplishes its PURPOSE				
The essay meets the needs of its AUDIENCE				
The essay fulfills the demands of its GENRE				
The essay's STANCE is reasonable and fair with an appropriate tone				
The essay's DESIGN is appropriate and effective (readable, clear)				
THE ARGUMENT				
The position is stated clearly in a THESIS statement				
The position is appropriately qualified				
Reasons are clearly stated				
Reasons are adequately supported				
Supporting evidence is accurate, current, appropriate, and sufficient				
Counterarguments are addressed, acknowledged, refuted				
The draft is clearly organized				
The argument is presented logically throughout				
Writer works to build common ground with AUDIENCE				
Transitions help reader move from idea to idea				
USE OF SOURCE MATERIAL				
The essay includes adequate and appropriate source material				
Sources are introduced and identified				
In-text citations are present and correctly formatted				
Summaries and paraphrases are accurate and avoid plagiarism				
The Works-Cited section is correctly formatted (MLA)				
IN GENERAL				
Sentences are consistently correctly phrased and punctuated				
The language is precise, the wording exact and accurate				
Mechanics, Usage, Grammar, and Spelling are correct				

lists and rubrics that you and the students will follow in responding to and evaluating their work. You may want to extend the exercise by comparing the class criteria with generally accepted criteria from your school's writing program documents, your textbooks, and other sources. For example, share with students three or four checklists or rubrics that define criteria for the kind of writing you're working on. (The WPA *Outcomes Statement*, reprinted in chapter 1 of this book, is a good starting point.) As out-of-class work or in groups, have students compare their class criteria with these other criteria and then discuss the comparisons: What does the class list contain that these others don't? What do they include that ours doesn't? Should we consider adding these other criteria or changing our criteria to match theirs more closely?

Responding to Drafts

Don't. Many writing teachers think that if students write something, they need to respond in detail. That's not true. If a student writes in a journal or does in-class writing as part of class work, a check or date stamp to acknowledge that it's done may be all that's needed. Much other informal writing may only require a brief comment on some part of the content—"Really? That's interesting," "I didn't know that," "Is this always the case?"—to show that you've read it.

Ask students to respond first. If you ask students to write out an assessment of their writing (as described in Chapters 24 and 27 of the *Field Guide*), your job will likely be easier, because you can then respond to their assessment, which is often exactly right or even excessively harsh. It's pleasant to engage in a written dialogue with students over the merits of their drafts in which you can affirm their evaluation rather than having to point out problems yourself—and even more pleasant to point out strengths they may have overlooked.

Respond as a reader. Respond to students' writing as an interested reader, and you'll provide them with a lot of useful information on which to base revisions. Respond to content with reactions ("Really?" "Wow!"), personal responses ("That happened to me once, too." "I'd like to know more about this."), questions ("How do you know this?" "Do others have the same opinion?"), and suggestions ("What if you . . . ?" "Consider moving this to . . . ?").

Highlight strengths as well as weaknesses. Research suggests that we learn best when criticism is balanced with praise—when our strengths as well as our errors are pointed out. Frequently, however, praise for what students do well in writing has been far outweighed by "correction" of their errors. Look for ways to respond positively and show that you're taking their writing seriously, itself a positive gesture. Note interesting ideas, well-organized paragraphs, graceful turns of phrase, and striking words and images; sprinkle the margins with smiley faces and stars when something strikes you positively.

Look for patterns. Many students' errors result not from ignorance but from their attempt to create order by inventing rules that are consistent but wrong. If a student consistently links two closely related sentences with a comma, for example, that student needs lessons in editing for comma splices in the context of showing how one sentence follows logically from the previous one. Unlike random errors, which suggest a lack of editing skills, patterns of error can be identified, after which you can help students learn the correct rules. You can show students such patterns in several ways. Once you identify two or three patterns, you can mark only those patterns by underlining the problem, circling it, or putting a notation in the margin next to the line on which the error appears. You might draw lines connecting each instance of a pattern to show that the same problem occurs several times. If you're commenting with a word processing feature, you might highlight each instance of a pattern in a certain color: yellow for comma splices, green for a certain type of misspelling, and so on. Or you can mark one example and ask the student to locate others as a way to recognize and eventually edit that error.

Limit your responses. If you're having a tennis lesson and the coach criticizes your stance, your grip, your swing, your serve, your racquet, and your clothing all at once, you're more likely to walk off the court in frustration than to improve your game. The same is true with writing, so concentrate on a small number of issues on any given draft and ignore the rest—for now. If you're reading an early draft, pointing out errors in sentences that may well be changed or deleted as students revise is wasted energy. As a rule of thumb, comment on issues in students' drafts according to a hierarchy, dealing with the biggest issues first:

- *Focus.* Does the student have a workable topic? Is it appropriately narrowed or focused?

- *Development.* Does the draft say enough? Does it cover the topic in appropriate depth?

- *Organization.* Does the draft have a clear beginning, middle, and end? Are the paragraphs in the best order? Are the paragraphs themselves organized appropriately?

- *Coherence.* Can the reader follow the logic throughout the draft? Does the writer include transitions and other signposts to help the reader?

- *Sentences.* Does each sentence contribute to the whole? Is each sentence correct? Is there appropriate variety in sentence construction?

- *Phrasing and tone.* Are phrases idiomatic? Is the tone consistent? appropriate?

- *Editing, proofreading, and design.* Is the draft correct? Is the design appropriate for the genre and the audience's expectations?

As you read the draft, try to identify strengths, the areas most in need of improvement, and strategies to suggest to the student for revising.

Recognize the stages in the writing process.
One way to encourage students to see their assignments in terms of work accomplished and work yet to be done is to respond at stages in the process. Edwina L. Helton and Jeff Sommers have described a useful method: E-M-L, or early, middle, and late. A draft marked early is early in the process: it may lack a clear thesis; it may be unfocused and underdeveloped. A middle draft likely has a clear direction but needs significant work on development and clarification. A late draft may be almost finished, needing only editing and proofreading.

Use minimal marking. Students, like the rest of us, often know more than their writing shows; they make mistakes that they know are mistakes but simply don't see as they put together a draft. To place the responsibility for finding and fixing errors on the students, consider this method, first described by Richard Haswell: Note errors in grammar, spelling, mechanics, and usage by a check mark in the margin next to the line on which the error appears. Students then must identify and fix the errors. Problems that remain after they've gone through the draft are probably problems they need assistance with in conference, through lessons in class, or in a visit to the writing center.

Respond to errors in context. Many of us are good at seeing errors; in fact, marking formal errors is the easiest part of responding to writing. Although there's no question that errors in a piece of writing can seriously undermine its effectiveness and its writer's credibility, a resolute focus on error leads student writers to the conclusion that what they have to say doesn't matter as long as they write error-free prose. Let students know that errors are like bee stings: a few are an annoyance, but too many can be fatal. It's not useful to create a rigid policy on errors, such as "Three errors and your paper automatically fails." Your role is to teach, not punish, and if student work has errors, it's likely that the student didn't know they were there; otherwise he or she would have corrected them. You can teach students how to edit and proofread, what to look for, and where to get additional help, whether from computer spelling and grammar checkers, handbooks, classmates, or the school's writing center.

To respond to error productively, remember that correctness is one of a constellation of goals. Here are some questions to help you think about errors:

- Which errors are most serious? Problems involving sentence structure and boundaries, such as sentence fragments, comma splices and run-on sentences, are usually seen as more serious than misspellings or nonstandard verb forms.

- Do the errors interfere with the reader's ability to understand the text? If so, the writer needs to know.

- Do the errors affect the writer's credibility? Rightly or wrongly, readers often judge the writer's intelligence by the correctness of his or her prose.

- Do the errors form patterns? A pattern of errors can be corrected through instruction; random errors are most likely the result of poor proofreading.

Making Specific Comments

When you respond to students' drafts, you should consider these questions: What response will help the writer at this stage of the writing? What does the writer need to know—and what does the writer not need to know—right now? How should this response be given? Your response will vary, depending on your knowledge of the student and the student's needs, the timing of the draft (rough, revised, or final), and the text of the draft. For example, consider the following responses to two drafts of a student's argument essay on the dangers of the Atkins and other low-carbohydrate diets. Here's the student's first draft; the comments were made using Microsoft Word's Comment function:

Atkins Diet, Good or Bad?

first draft

[With the general population in the United States being obese and constantly more and more people becoming obese,] many consider the Atkins diet. This diet is simply [low to no carbohydrates and a great intake of protein.] This diet has been around for many years, but is currently getting more publicity and many people are starting to consider it. [The main focus now is, is the diet really healthy for ones body?]

    [The Atkins diet is broken up into stages.] The first stage is where the weigh becomes off the fastest because it is predominately water fat, but [after this stage] is when the weight loss slows. Constantly eating protein everyday is not merely the healthiest way to remove those unwanted pounds. There are many health risk involved with this diet.

    Studies reported that weight loss was associated with the length of time being on the diet and not the reduced intake of carbohydrates (PCRM pg7). Low carbohydrate diets induce a chemical known as ketosis which is an abnormal state that occurs in starvation. [In the long

> **Comment:** It's good to explain the context for your topic, as you do here. In fact, I'd like to know more about why Americans are diet-crazy!

> **Comment:** Good, brief summary of the diet.

> **Comment:** Is this your thesis? Can you restate this as a statement? "The Atkins diet is _____." (See FG on Thesis Statements)

> **Comment:** I like the idea of discussing the stages—it's a good way to show the effects of the diet.

> **Comment:** I'd like to know more about these stages. Are there more than 2?

run| this chemical can effect ones body physically, having calcium

Comment: Wow! This sounds serious! I like this specific information.

loss, a high risk of osteoporosis, and a high risk of forming kidney stones. Your body can also be in high risk of problems dealing with bones, the cardiac system, and the liver. Food containing a high count for protein usually lack important healthy ingredients such as fibers which results in problems with the body.

Many people don't look at the risk factors for this diet, but their focus is primarily on, Am I going to lose weight, how fast, and is it easy? The Atkins diet fits these three questions and that's why many people decide to go on it. This diet is said to burn your fat for energy. This attracts the so called "busy" people fast. Those always on the go can lose pounds fast because they need the energy and their fat is their supplier. [Research found this diet to be top notch over almost any other diet.| Low fat diets, Weight watchers, and many others were

Comment: This seems to contradict the first part of your paper. How can it be harmful and yet the best?

compared to the Atkins diet and more results were viewed in favor of Atkin. More pounds were shed and blood pressure, glucose, and other body problems in question were all in normal range.

I guess depending on the person Atkins might be for you, but for those concerned with their body in the future may take more consideration into what diets they partake in.

Comment: You'll need more sources than this one, and your sources will need to be documented accurately. See FINDING SOURCES & MLA DOCUMENTATION in FG for help

Work [Cited]

PCRM: http://www.pcrm.org/health/reports/pdfs/
HighProteinReport.pdf

This draft has several problems, ranging from its lack of a clear thesis to problems with sentence structure and wording. Since it's a rough draft, however, your goal in responding should be to give advice to help the student revise it. You may have a checklist or rubric for the assignment that moves from more global issues (focus, development, organization) to more local (coherence, sentence structure, mechanics, editing and proofreading). Generally, when you respond to early drafts, emphasize global issues first. Marking errors in sentence construction, wording, mechanics, and spelling is inappropriate because at this point your response will advise the student to rewrite much or all of the essay, eliminating the material you've marked. Here's how this student's instructor responded in a summary comment:

> I think this topic is really interesting; I tried the Atkins diet once and couldn't stand how I felt after just one day! Your information is troubling; it sounds as if you don't think Atkins is a good diet. Try to make your position clearer in a thesis statement. Then organize your ideas so you can discuss one at a time, completely. You need more information in the essay: What is the Atkins diet and how does it work? What are the benefits in the short term? What are the worst effects in the long term? Look in more sources for answers to these questions.

The student then revised the draft twice, eventually submitting the following final version in her midterm portfolio for a grade. In this situation, your response can be more comprehensive, covering all the requirements for the essay; however, if you allow students to revise throughout the term, you can still urge improvement, as this instructor does, both in the comments and through minimal marking of errors.

Atkins Diet, Good or Bad?

With the general population in the United States being obese and constantly more and more people becoming obese, many consider the Atkins diet. This diet consist of little to no carbohydrates and a high ✓ intake of protein. This diet has been around for many years, but is currently getting more publicity and many people are starting to consider it. The main focus now is, whether or not the diet is really healthy ✓ for ones body? In my opinion [this diet is too risky and unhealthy to ✓ partake in just to lose a few pounds.]

> **Comment:** Much better statement of your thesis!

The Atkins diet has [four stages:] the induction phase, ongoing weight loss, pre-maintenance, and lifetime maintenance. The induction stage last for approximately two weeks. This switches your body ✓ into ketosis [where] your metabolism begins to burn fat for energy. In this stage you are consuming protein and vegetables. [Ongoing weight loss] is where more vegetables, nuts and berries are included in your diet. This is where you are changing the ratio of carbohydrates to protein and fats (atkins.com). Stepping into the pre-maintenance stage is the crucial change. This is where you begin to change your eating

> **Comment:** You explain the four stages much more clearly in this draft. Good work!

> **Comment:** All 4 stages start with "this is where." Vary sentence structure

> **Comment:** Another stage?

habits to something you will stick to for the rest of your life. During this stage your weight loss will slow. The last stage is where you are controlling your intake of carbohydrates and focusing on the future. This stage refers to your permanent eating habits. [The Atkins diet is broken up into stages.] The first stage is where the weight comes off the fastest because it is predominately water fat, but after this stage is when the weight loss slows. What makes the fat come off so fast ✓ the first stage of this diet is because eating fewer grams of carbo- ✓ hydrate results in fewer spikes in blood sugar, resulting in less insulin output. Insulin makes the body retain sodium, which makes your body retain water. When you are not producing as much insulin, the cycle slows and the effect is like taking a diuretic which is a drug that ✓ increases the output of urine. After a few days, that's when you will also begin to lose body fat. [Young men and people who have a lot of weight to lose are more likely to lose weight more rapidly at the start of the Atkins program] (Atkins FAQ).

> **Comment:** You already outlined the 4 stages; why not combine that discussion with this one—don't repeat yourself

> **Comment:** Why?

Supposedly many health benefits are to come out of this diet. [It is suppose to lead you into a way where you can control your ✓ eating habits and stay slim for the rest of your life, maximize your carbohydrate intake and staying within three to five pounds of ✓ your ideal weight, prevent you from getting caught up in those foods that cause severe weight gain, help you to make healthy food choices, reduce risk factors for various disorders including diabetes, and give you a sense of accomplishment.] However, these health benefits are not clearly what you are going to get out of this diet in the long run. Constantly consuming protein for several weeks is not nearly the healthiest way to remove those unwanted pounds. There are many health risk involved with this diet. Studies reported that weight ✓ loss was associated with the length of time on the diet and not the reduced intake of carbohydrates (PCRM pg7). Low carbohydrate diets induce a process known as [ketosis] which is an abnormal state that

> **Comment:** A long sentence—break into at least 2: one on weight benefits, one on health benefits

> **Comment:** You discuss ketosis more below. Keep discussion together

occurs in starvation. The increase of this and uric acid can lead to severe headaches. It also has said that people on this diet have bad breath odors, maybe causing halitosis. Many experience [weakness, drowsy and having a lack of energy.] Others have also experienced the case of hair loss. Food containing a high count for protein usually lack important healthy ingredients such as fibers which results ✓ in constipation and chronic bowel disease.   ✓

> **Comment:** These 3 terms should be parallel in form

   This diet doesn't even fit the guidelines for the American Heart Association. These guidelines include: eating fruits, grains, drinking milk, limiting food high in saturated fats, eating less than 6 grams of salt, exercise, and drinking no more than one alcoholic drink a day for a woman and two for a man (AHA). In the long run this keto-sis can effect ones body physically leading to having calcium ✓ loss, a high risk of osteoporosis, and a high risk of forming kidney ✓ stones. Your body can also be in high risk of problems dealing with bones and the liver. The cardiac system can be effected also because of the high counts of animal fat consumed on this diet. Animal fat leads to cardiac disease and/or high cholesterol. Many case studies ✓ show many people to have dealt with high cholesterol even though this diet is said not to have any effects of an increase of cholesterol. Many people don't look at the risk factors for this diet, but their focus is primarily on, Am I going to lose weight, how fast, and is it easy? The Atkins diet fits these three questions and that's why many people decide to go on it. This diet is said to burn your fat for energy. This attracts the so called 'busy' people fast, those always on the go can lose pounds quicker because they need the energy and their fat is their supplier. Research found this diet to be one of the top sellers right now. Low fat diets, [Weight watchers, and many others were compared to the Atkins diet and more results were viewed in favor of the Atkins diet. More pounds were shed and blood pressure, glucose, and other body problems in question were all in normal range.]

> **Comment:** Who did this comparison? Can we trust them? Seems to contradict the rest of your argument. Maybe it belongs with the earlier section on "Many health benefits."

Unfortunately it is still putting your body in a higher risk of health problems in the future (atkins.com).

Many studies done came to the conclusion that the Atkins diet is good for a short period of time, but not a lifelong thing. I feel short or long, you will still be in a higher risk for health problems either ✓ now or in your future. Some how this diet will effect your body, by ✓ not just having you lose weight. It has proven to help lose more ✓ weight in a six month period, but after about one year 1/3 of the weight is regained (diets nutrition). Though this diet may work in ones favor for a few months it still has its share of serious disadvantages. ✓ I guess depending on the person Atkins might be for you, but [for those ✓ concerned with their body in the future may take more consideration into what diets they partake in.] I see it as the only healthy way to lose weight is to change ones eating habits and exercise. Not only are ✓ you losing weight, but it's healthy for the body and you don't have to worry about what future side effects may occur due to your early years of dieting.

> **Comment:** You lose control of your sentence structure here—rework

Works Cited

Physicians Committee for Responsible Medicine. "Health Advisory."
Atkins Diet Alert. n.d. 11 February 2004. <http://www.atkinsdietalert.org/advisory.html>.

"Why Atkins Works." Atkins.com. 19 September 2003. 2 February 2004.
<http://atkins.com/index.html>.

This draft shows many improvements over the first draft, but it still has problems with organization, wording, editing and proofreading, and accurate documentation of sources. The instructor said as much in the summary comment:

> You've improved this essay considerably. You take a clear position on the Atkins diet and provide a lot more information on it—just what it needed! I like the way you describe the four stages of the diet and how you rebut the Atkins claims. It still needs work on organization, however: you discuss 3 different topics in two different places in the essay, so the essay seems to repeat itself. For example, discuss the benefits of Atkins all at once, and discuss the aspects of each

stage as you introduce it. Your reliance on only two sources, both from the Web, is worrisome, too—getting additional support in some academic sources and getting help from a reference librarian would strengthen your argument. Also, look through each sentence to make sure it works grammatically, and proofread carefully—spell checkers won't pick up on "effect" when you mean "affect," for example.

Marking Student Writing

Respond in pencil. If you're responding to printed drafts, pencil is less intimidating to students than ink, red or otherwise. Also, I've learned that occasionally I make a comment that I want to reconsider, and comments in pencil can be erased without making a mess of the student's draft. Of course, if you're responding using computer or online programs, you can change or delete comments easily.

Comment electronically. Another way to write comments that you can revise or reconsider is to comment electronically on drafts students submit electronically. Some courseware programs, such as Turnitin.com, offer the ability to insert comments wherever you want, simply by mouse-clicking on a word in the document. Microsoft Word's Reviewing toolbar offers a Comment feature that works the same way—and even allows you to record a voice comment. These tools offer the advantage of legibility, since you don't have to worry whether students can read your handwriting.

Respond on a separate sheet. Marginal comments offer the benefit of being visually tied to the text to which they are responding, and patterns can be marked easily. If you need to say more than a few words or a phrase, however, the margins can become crowded and your comments hard to read. For that reason, consider making up response sheets that you can attach to each draft. On the sheet, you can print any rubric or checksheet you're using, or you can simply provide space for comments. When you want to comment on a student's work, simply place a number near the passage on which you want to comment. Number and write your response on the attached sheet. As an alternative, compose a response as a letter to the student; if you use your word processor, you can save a copy of your feedback.

Use correction symbols or abbreviations sparingly. Handbooks traditionally provide a list of correction or revision symbols that instructors may use to save time. Unfortunately, students seldom know what those symbols mean and too often they are too vague to be helpful. (AWK, for example, usually means, "There's something wrong with this sentence, but I can't tell you what it is." X, for "obvious error," suggests that the error is obvious to you, but if it had been obvious to the student, he or she probably wouldn't have made it.) If you use such symbols, use only a limited number and explain to students what they mean. I've found that the slight increase in time spent identifying the problem in plain English benefits student understanding.

Useful Readings

Blumner, Jakob S., and Francis Fritz. "Students Using Evaluation in Their Writing Process." in Stephen Tchudi, ed. *Alternatives to Grading Student Writing*. Urbana, IL: NCTE, 1997. 233–242.

Elbow, Peter. "Ranking, Evaluating, and Liking: Sorting Out Three Forms of Judging." *College English* 55.2 (February 1993): 187–206.

Haswell, Richard H. "Minimal Marking." *College English* 45.6 (1983): 600–604.

Helton, Edwina L., and Jeff Sommers. "Repositioning Revision: A Rhetorical Approach to Grading." *Teaching English in the Two Year College*, December 2000. 157–164.

10 Teaching with Writing Portfolios

Take a good look at the snapshot on your driver's license. How well does it capture your looks? When you read a draft of a student's writing, you see a snapshot of their writing at a particular time, in response to a particular prompt or assignment. And, like any snapshot, it's not clear how well that draft represents the student's overall writing ability. For that reason, many writing teachers ask students to create and submit portfolios of their work during a course. Portfolios allow instructors to examine several samples of students' writing for patterns, trends, strengths, and weaknesses—and, depending on what the portfolio includes, to see the students' processes as they researched, drafted, and revised the texts in the portfolio. Portfolios also provide students the opportunity to create written reflections on and evaluations of their own work to help them see what they've accomplished and what they need to work on in the future. This chapter offers advice on creating a writing course that will foster the creation of writing portfolios along with tips on managing student portfolios.

Self-Assessing Writing Portfolios

Many writing teachers who require portfolios see the students' written assessment of the contents as the most important element because it moves students toward independence through the ability to assess their work themselves, instead of relying on teachers. This reflective self-assessment may be written in the form of an informal letter or a formal essay asking students to use the materials in the portfolio as the evidence on which they base thoughtful examination of their writing and their work in the class. Chapter 27 of *The Norton Field Guide to Writing* offers guidelines on reflecting on a writing portfolio that can help students compose a useful self-assessment letter or essay. Bonnie Sunstein's essay, "Be Reflective, Be Reflexive, and Beware: Innocent Forgery for Inauthentic Assessment," offers additional guidelines and questions for students as they self-assess.

If you ask students to include all drafts and revisions as well as in-class work and research materials, you can evaluate how diligently they worked, and usually that diligence will result in good final products.

Some students will use their self-assessments to argue that their grade should be based on their effort, rather than on the writing they produce. Also, some students will use the self-assessment to try to flatter you. Emphasize the goal of focusing their attention on their writing and observable class performance, not on evaluating the course or instructor. Let students know that flattery will not persuade.

Assigning Writing Portfolios

What should go into a portfolio of writing? In its barest form, a portfolio is simply a folder in which students keep their writing. If you assign, collect, and grade individual assignments and then ask students to submit them again in such a portfolio, they can write an assessment of the contents before submitting it at term's end. More often, however, instructors ask for a portfolio of students' work once or twice during a term and evaluate the contents as a whole, looking for patterns and trends that persist over several pieces of writing. However you design your portfolio requirements, explain them to students clearly, preferably on the first day of class, because they'll need to know what writings to keep in order to have a complete portfolio. Here are some suggestions for what portfolios might include:

Polished, final drafts of assigned essays. You may ask for every assigned essay or offer students a choice among their assignments, since every writer drafts some texts that don't work out. Or, you might require some and make others optional. For example, if students work on a literacy narrative, a text analysis, and an evaluation, they must include in their portfolio the analysis plus either the narrative or the evaluation. To prevent students from assuming they don't need to write the essays they will exclude from their portfolios, you might insist that at least one complete draft of those omitted essays be included. Their self-assessment can then address the reasons why they were abandoned.

All drafts of assigned essays. Drafts are useful for seeing the progress students make from first to finished draft and for jogging your memory if you've seen an earlier draft. Ask that students label and date each draft and place them in order from finished on top to first on the bottom.

Cited source material. It's easy to check the accuracy of summaries, paraphrases, quotations, and citations if photocopies of the sources are in the portfolio. Again, ask students to label each source; consider asking students to highlight or underline the passages in each source that they used in their own essays.

Student assessment of the contents. Some instructors ask for an informal letter that discusses the strengths of the contents and the writer's plans for improvement in the future. Others assign a lengthy self-assessment essay that includes quotations from and references to the essays the student is assessing, treating this essay as an additional sample of the student's writing or the equivalent of a final exam.

Other materials. Other course-related writing, such as collaborative work or in-class writing and tests, may be included. Also, some instructors allow students to include other writing—essays from other courses, fiction or poetry, work-related writing—that shows aspects of their writing ability that the course writing does not.

The portfolio itself can be a simple two-pocket folder. Ask students to place pieces to be graded in one pocket and drafts and other materials in the other, to simplify your reading. Insist that they write their names on the outside of the folder, again to make record-keeping easier. If, of course, you allow or require students to create online portfolios (as discussed in Chapter 27 of the *Field Guide*), their work must be organized through links or other means, depending on the computer programs available to them. What's important is that their work be organized so that you don't have to wade through it to find what you need to respond appropriately. Also, organizing their selections helps students review their own evolution as writers.

Organizing Electronic Portfolios

If you ask students to submit their work in electronic portfolios, you need to create ways for students to organize their essays and files. Courseware programs such as Turnitin allow you to create specific assignments to which students post their drafts, so you may set up portfolio assignments like "Position essay portfolio draft," "Evaluation portfolio draft," and "Self-assessment." If you're relying on email, you might require students to attach their final drafts to a single message. If students create online portfolios on Web sites or blogs, you need only visit each site to read their work—though you may need to respond to their writing in an email, since commenting within the body of the text may not be possible online.

Reading Portfolios

The guidelines presented in Chapter 9 of this book on responding to students' writing apply to portfolios of writing, too. A significant difference is that instead of or in addition to evaluating individual pieces of writing, you may evaluate students' overall performance for your course as well as their self-assessment. Here, for example, is a list of the qualities writing program faculty at Wright State University look for in course portfolios in the second course of its two-course sequence:

Content

- Defines the issue and its context
- Enters a debate (engages the issue, not just a literature review or detached analysis of the argument: "One might argue . . . ")
- Shows awareness of the audience and needs of that audience

- Is focused (appropriately chosen and limited topic)
- Is developed (uses sources but doesn't create a collage of quotations or paraphrases; creates and sustains a line of reasoning; covers topic appropriately; explains thoroughly and clearly)
- Is convincing or reasonable
- Presents differing arguments
- Bonus: Displays passion in arguing

Evidence

- Evidence is present
- Evidence relates to point
- Evidence is properly cited and documented
- Evidence shows synthesis of ideas with multiple citations

Form

- Coherence and cohesion (at the essay and sentence level: transitions, signal phrases, repeated words, integrated quotations)
- Thesis statement or equivalent

- Satisfying conclusion
- Control over sentence construction
- Subject and verb agreement
- Mechanics, usage, grammar, and spelling (don't distract or cause credibility problems)

Assessment

- Critical assessment of own work, supported by evidence from portfolio

You might combine criteria common to each individual essay's rubric to develop a single rubric for the portfolio as a whole, separating out only those criteria that apply only to a single assignment. You might also combine the rubrics for each individual essay with a rubric for the self-assessment or reflection, such as the one below:

Delaying Grades

If you design your course to include portfolios, you may assign grades much less often than if you grade each assigned essay separately. As a result, some students will

REFLECTION	3	2	1	0
Analyzes work habits from invention to polished work				
Analyzes strengths & weaknesses of each item in portfolio				
Analyzes strengths & weaknesses of overall writing ability				
Discusses how writing has changed over time				
Analyzes performance in this class				
Offers evidence from portfolio papers to support assertions				
Avoids argument from effort or undue flattery as persuasive techniques				

express anxiety over not receiving frequent grades, as they did in high school or other classes. To allay their fears, make this offer: "Any time you want to know your grade as it stands at this point in the course, schedule a conference with me. Bring your portfolio with the work you've done so far, and I'll go over it with you and tell you what your grade would be if I had to give you one at that time." Interestingly, almost no students will take you up on your offer. Although they are disoriented at first by the lack of grades, students quickly realize that they are now free to concentrate on their writing, which they can work to improve over a much longer time span than they're used to. Portfolios encourage multiple revisions precisely because students have not received grades, which they consider the mark of a finished assignment.

At the same time, students do need some indication of their standing in your course before the very end. To provide that progress report, ask students to submit a midterm portfolio that contains the work done through the first half of the term, along with their self-assessment of that work. They'll get practice in compiling, organizing, and assessing a body of their work as well as an indication of their grades so far. To maintain an incentive for continued revision, you might consider weighting the portfolio grades unevenly. For example, make the midterm portfolio worth 20% of the final grade, while the final course portfolio (which might contain some or all of the contents of the midterm portfolio in addition to the work done in the second half of the course) is worth 50%. You might offer students an additional incentive to continue working hard (or start working harder!) by offering them a choice: If they wish, they may drop their midterm portfolio grade and add its weight to the final portfolio. In the example above, the final portfolio would then be worth 70% of their final grade.

Useful Readings

Conway, Glenda. "Portfolio Cover Letters, Students' Self-Presentation, and Teachers' Ethics." *New Directions in Portfolio Assessment: Reflective Practice, Critical Theory, and Large-Scale Scoring.* Ed. Laurel Black, Donald A. Daiker, Jeffrey Sommers, and Gail Stygall. Portsmouth, NH: Boynton/Cook, 1994. 83–92.

Electronic Portfolios. Washington, D. C.: American Association for Higher Education. 17 May 2005.< http://www.aahe.org/electronic portfolios>.

Sommers, Jeffrey. "Bringing Practice in Line with Theory: Using Portfolio Grading in the Composition Classroom." *Portfolios: Process and Product.* Ed. Pat Belanoff and Marcia Dickson. Portsmouth, NH: Boynton/Cook, 1991. 153–164.

Sunstein, Bonnie S. "Be Reflective, Be Reflexive, and Beware: Innocent Forgery for Inauthentic Assessment." *The Portfolio Standard: How Students Can Show Us What They Know and Are Able to Do.* Ed. Bonnie S. Sunstein and Jonathan Lovell. Portsmouth NH: Heinemann, 2000. 3–14.

Yancey, Kathleen Blake, ed. "Special Issue: Electronic Portfolios." *Computers and Composition* 13.2 (1996).

Managing the Paper Load **11**

Consider the situation described by Chris Massey, a TA: "My students are constantly writing, and that means I am constantly reading what they are writing. Even though I am not marking every piece of writing they submit to me, I am reading each piece and responding to their writing in some fashion. My students are writing and writing well; the only downside is that I am spending a great deal of my time reading." The problem Chris describes, responding adequately to students' writing while not overburdening the instructor, is common among writing teachers. Fortunately, there are ways to teach writing that can make responding and grading manageable, including the techniques described in Chapter 9 in this book on responding to students' writing. Here are some more suggestions.

Don't read everything. Just because you assign it doesn't require you to read it, let alone respond to it. Some things you read carefully (drafts); some things you skim and, maybe, respond with underlinings, stars, exclamation points, and question marks (letters, some in-class writing); and some things you simply put a check on or stamp, record if they did it, and move on (much daily work). The more writing you assign, the more you need to beware overextending yourself.

Read all the drafts first. We evaluate things by comparing them with others, and student drafts are no different. To get an overall sense of how your students did on an assignment, read quickly through all the drafts you collect, perhaps sorting them as you read into three groups: strong, middling, and weak. This process helps you see the criteria by which you'll read each draft in concrete terms and gives you choices of what to read: some instructors like to read some strong drafts first to establish what's possible, while others like to save some of the best for last.

Set a schedule. As a new instructor, you're likely to spend thirty minutes reading and responding to each draft of an essay; in a class of twenty-five students, that totals $12\frac{1}{2}$ hours. Establish a schedule for responding and keep to it. If you collect drafts late in the week and keep them over the weekend, spread out your responding sessions over three or four days. Include time for breaks to rejuvenate yourself, because reading and responding is taxing work. Use a timer set at thirty-minute intervals to keep yourself disciplined. If you're teaching more than one course at a time, consider establishing a regular, daily schedule: every afternoon from 3 to 5, you read student writing.

Use rubrics. If you clearly articulate the requirements of an assignment, you can create a chart-style rubric that lists them in the form of a table. The rubric helps you maintain discipline over your reading, forcing you to pay attention to the features of each student's writing in similar ways. It also provides a clear, descriptive response for students to use as they revise or contemplate their grades. Make copies and do most of your responding on the rubric sheet, placing a check mark at the appropriate place on the right-hand side. Other comments may be written below the table. An example using statements of desired criteria is printed in Chapter 9 of this book. Below is another example that phrases criteria as questions. If you provide space between each question for comments, you can provide a summary response as well as commentary.

Have students evaluate their drafts. Before students give you their drafts, have them write a self-assessment, pointing out strong elements, parts that need to be improved, and questions they have. You might also have them fill out the same rubric you'll use when you respond. When you respond to their drafts, you can then respond to their assessments, continuing a conversation they've already begun. You'll be surprised at how much easier it is to write comments.

Argument Draft Assessment: Author_____Assessor_____

Circle one: First draft   Rewritten draft   Further revision

Answer each question on a scale of 1–5, 5 = very well, yes indeed; 1 = no, not at all
Comment below the question.

1. Is the thesis clear and appropriately qualified?   5   4   3   2   1

2. Are the reasons plausible? Do they make sense?   5   4   3   2   1

3. Does the writer provide enough appropriate support for the reasons?   5   4   3   2   1

4. Can you follow the steps in the argument's reasoning?   5   4   3   2   1
   (If not, identify where you lose track.)

5. How well does the argument deal with potential objections or counter-arguments?   5   4   3   2   1

6. Is source material documented carefully, w/in-text citations and works cited?   5   4   3   2   1

7. Does the writer use signal phrases to introduce information from sources?   5   4   3   2   1

Avoid over-responding. If you identify a few strengths, problems, and patterns and use minimal marking, you'll avoid the trap of making too many marginal and in-text comments that take time and energy (and overwhelm many students). Also, avoid a too-long end comment; some instructors' comments end up longer than the student's draft. Work toward a single paragraph that offers a couple of positive comments, a couple of suggestions or goals for the next draft, and a helpful strategy or two—and then stop.

Don't worry about originality. Several students' drafts will have similar problems, so responding with the same comment can save you time—and they're unlikely to compare their comments' prose style. If you respond using a computer, you can even program certain comments to print with a single keystroke.

Stagger due dates. If you're teaching more than one section of a course or more than one course at a time, create course plans with due dates that don't coincide. Making one syllabus for multiple sections may save time up front, but you might have fifty drafts or portfolios to respond to during one weekend, a task that will not be to your or your students' best advantage.

Keep good records. Be sure to keep records of your students' work as you read so you don't have to go through the stack one more time to record grades or other marks. Many instructors use a "received—date" stamp to show that assignments, especially those that don't require much attention, have been received. If the papers are stamped, they earn full credit when presented in the student's portfolio. If papers are presented but not stamped, they get half credit (for doing the work but turning it in after the due date). And, if the papers are not present at all, they get zero credit.

Useful Readings

Ketter, Jean S. "Using Rubrics and Holistic Scoring of Writing." *Alternatives to Grading Student Writing.* ed. Stephen Tchudi. Urbana, IL: National Council of Teachers of English, 1997. 291–295.

White, Edward. "Using Scoring Guides to Assess Writing." *A Sourcebook for Responding to Student Writing.* Ed. Richard Straub. Cresskill, NJ: Hampton, 1999. 203–212.

12 Grading Student Writing

If you've developed good assignments and responded to drafts of students' writing, grading will be less onerous. If you clarify expectations up front, students will know what you want and will usually have a fairly good idea of how well they performed. Still, grading is often difficult work for experienced and inexperienced instructors alike, so the following advice can help you as you face a stack of essays or portfolios to grade.

Developing a Method

Preview your students' work. Avoid the temptation to jump in and start reading with an eye to a grade. First, reread your assignment to remind yourself what you asked for, and then read quickly through the whole stack (if you're new to teaching) or a random sample (if you've given the same assignments before) to give yourself a sense of how students did. You may find it helpful to create three stacks as you skim: good, poor, and middling. Simply dividing students' work into those three piles helps you internalize your criteria and how those criteria translate into various letter or number grades.

Use rubrics. Rubrics help you maintain your focus on the criteria for evaluating students' work. Even if the rubrics are fairly general, they also provide a vocabulary to help students understand why they earned the grades they did. See Chapter 9, "Responding to Student Writing" and Chapter 10, "Managing the Paper Load," for sample rubrics and advice on creating your own.

Write a final comment. Whether or not you use a rubric, it's helpful for students when you sum up the strengths and problems in an essay or portfolio as a guide for their future writing and as an explanation for the grade. A good final comment offers an overall assessment of the work, discusses how well it meets the demands of the assignment, and briefly outlines the work's strengths and weaknesses. The final comment should be an occasion for you as a serious reader to discuss the writer's work honestly and respectfully. At the same time, it shouldn't be overly long or detailed—about 100 words is enough.

Use the full range of grades. After working with a group of students for ten or fifteen weeks and getting to know them and their work, we all have difficulty assessing that work fairly. Most often, we give higher grades than an objective grader who doesn't know the students. You should resist the temptation to give most students grades of B and a few grades of A or C, reserving the D or F for students who didn't do the work or disappeared but didn't drop the course. Why? Because your credibility and your writing program's credibility in the university will suffer if students leave your course having earned a high grade and then do poorly in a subsequent writing course. Conversely, if your writing program includes a sequence of courses, you could end up with students whose grades in the first course mask their lack of preparedness to do the work of the second—and that's no favor to the students. The hardest part of grading is giving students (especially students who have worked hard) the low grades they have earned and that reflect your and your school's expectations. It's advisable to discuss grading criteria with other writing instructors, to get help in understanding and applying the writing program's and university's criteria to your own students' work.

At the same time, don't expect the grades in your classes to form a bell curve. Writing classes are relatively small, so the group of students you have in any one class may consist of many strong writers, many weak ones, or a mix, depending on how courses are scheduled, whether or not students register by major, or even time of day. You may well have a class in which more than half the students earn Bs and As—and in your next course, the reverse may be true. Remember, though, that few instructors consistently attract only the best writers, so monitor your grades over several courses to see how they average out.

Ask for second opinions. All writing teachers encounter student work that they have trouble grading. No matter what the reason, ask another instructor what grade they would give to a troublesome portfolio or essay. Your conversation about the merits of the work and the reasons for your grades will not only help you grade that student's work fairly; it will help you understand your own grading better. If you share grading with several other instructors, you'll also develop a clearer sense of the standards held for student work at your institution and have to worry less about whether you're grading too high or too low.

Don't grade every revision. Once expectations have been established, offer the option to revise for a higher grade, but don't fall into the trap of regrading every draft a student submits. Some students will change exactly what you point out, with the expectation that if they follow your instructions, they will earn a higher grade. A few will resubmit several times, assuming that enough incremental changes will turn a C paper into an A paper. As the grader, you, too, will feel pressure to add points or raise a grade on a draft that a student submits repeatedly. Better to offer a deadline for resubmitting work for reconsideration of the grade along with an offer to help students improve their drafts at any time before that deadline—but refusing to put grades on each successive draft.

Don't assume that grades motivate. As you teach, you'll find that some students are motivated only by a grade and will ask,

"What do I have to do to get an A in this course?" Many of us who pursue advanced degrees and teach in college were motivated as undergraduates by the desire to excel, not just by earning high grades but by working hard to learn. As statistics show, though, we are a distinct minority of the population. As you teach, you'll encounter students who are happy to earn Cs, even if they could do better, and occasionally you'll run across students who are trying, for one reason or another, to flunk out. These various students create a rich mix that you may find alternately frustrating and delightful, and you'll need to find various ways of reaching them; grades alone won't do it.

Keeping Records

It's important to keep students' grades organized so that you can calculate their final grades without difficulty. One way to lose credibility as a teacher is to lose students' work or fail to record their grades accurately, and for good reason: students' grades are their record of having done the work of a course. Here are some ways to keep track of students' work and grades.

Note cards. Many instructors ask students to list information on index cards on the first day of class. Those same cards can then be used to jot notes about the students' work: goals framed in conferences, ongoing progress in drafts, and various other assessments that might not lend themselves to a letter grade or number of points.

Three-ring notebooks. If you ask students to sign an attendance sheet, using three-hole-punched paper that you can slip into a three-ring notebook simplifies maintaining attendance records. In fact, you can organize your entire course—syllabus, assignment sheets, daily class plans, handouts, and student records—in a single notebook that you can bring to class and keep with you as a ready reference for whatever questions students might have about the course.

Gradebooks, online gradebooks, and spreadsheet programs. To keep track of students' grades and attendance, you should have a means of identifying each assignment and noting students' performance—a system that won't take too much time. The traditional gradebook offers a grid, but its spaces tend to be very small and uniform, forcing you to abbreviate assignment titles and, at the same time, providing far more spaces for grades than you're likely to need. Online gradebooks provided with some courseware packages can be flexible and useful, even tallying up grades automatically. A third alternative that can meet your specific needs is a spreadsheet program like Excel. Not only can you create a customized grade sheet that you can program to figure grades automatically, you can create a color-coding scheme for such things as attendance and daily work assignments: if a student was present, you simply color the appropriate square, so that absences are visually obvious. You can also color graded assignments, making them easy to find. Here's a simple example, showing one month's class attendance:

	A	B	C	D	E	F	G	H	I
1	Eng 102 Fall 2005 ATTENDANCE						Present		Absent
2	Name	1/4	1/6	1/11	1/13	1/18	1/20	1/25	1/27
3	2 A. Joseph								
4	2 B. Emily								
5	2 B. John								
6	2 B. Jerri								
7	C. Elizabeth								
8	2 D. Nick								
9	2 D. Carly								
10	2 G. Elizabeth								
11	2 H. Tyler								
12	H. Amanda								
13	2 H. Bret								
14	J. Jennifer								
15	2 K. John								
16	2 L. Doug								
17	L. Nathan								
18	2 M. Nicole								
19	P. Christopher								
20	2 S. Erica								
21	2 S. Stephany								
22	T. Mindy								
23	2 T. Matt								
24	2 T. Amanda								
25	2 W. Brad								
26	2 W. Elizabeth								
27	2 W. Daniel								
28									

Returning Students' Work

The final step in responding to and grading students' work is returning it to them. Here are a few hints on doing that effectively.

During the term. Strive to return students' work as quickly as you can; within a week or ten days is reasonable. If you bring a stack of essays or portfolios to class, resist the pressure to hand them back at the beginning; wait until the end, when you can briefly discuss the class's overall performance after completing the day's agenda. When you return the work, let students know that you'll be available for conferences, but not right after class. Give them time to review the paper and your comments before you meet. Also, asking students who wish to dispute their grades to write out a response rather than present an oral argument will help defuse emotions that might get in the way of a fruitful discussion.

At the end of the course. Most writing instructors schedule the due date of final portfolios or essays during final exam week. As a result, students often cannot pick them up until the following term or until the next fall term. If your school has no policy on keeping or returning student work, the easiest way to deal with these portfolios or essays is to tell your students that they may pick up their work in your office during your office hours in the first five weeks of the following term. Place them in a box in your office and give them to students as they show up. Students who want their work before the next term may provide a self-addressed envelope with sufficient postage, so you can mail it to them. If students do not plan to pick up

their work, having saved it on their computers, ask them to write "Discard" on it so you don't need to keep it. Don't place student work outside your office door or in an unguarded room—doing so invites theft and plagiarized essays.

Useful Readings

Adkison, Stephen, and Stephen Tchudi. "Grading on Merit and Achievement: Where Quality Meets Quantity." *Alternatives to Grading Student Writing*. Ed. Stephen Tchudi. Urbana, IL: National Council of Teachers of English, 1997. 192–209.

Carbone, Nick, and Margaret Daisley. "Grading as a Rhetorical Construct." *The Theory and Practice of Grading Writing: Problems and Possibilities*. Ed. Frances Zak and Christopher C. Wheeler. Albany: SUNY, 1998. 77–94.

Haswell, Richard H. "Minimal Marking." *College English* 45.6 (1983): 600–604.

Teaching in a **13** Computer Classroom

You walk into your classroom and find, not rows of desks, but long tables holding computer monitors and keyboards. The desk at the front of the room—now called the "teacher's station"—holds a computer, monitor, keyboard, and mouse, and possibly also a remote control for a projector in the ceiling or a panel of buttons that control the projector, a motorized projection screen, the classroom lights, and various other electronic functions. This is not the kind of classroom where you were taught to write. So what do you do? This chapter will offer advice on teaching writing in a classroom equipped with computers for you and your students. In addition, check out the activities and advice in Chapter 14 of this book, "Teaching Writing Online."

Getting Started

The availability of technology always implies an imperative that we use it. When you teach in a computer classroom (I prefer that term to "computer lab," because a lab implies that students will work there mostly independently, doing experiments, rather than learning together in an electronically enhanced environment), you may feel pres-sure to use whatever is in the room, every day. Resist that pressure. Instead, use the equipment and software as you feel comfortable and as they support writing instruction. After all, you may be teaching for the first time, and you have a lot to get used to; there's no need to increase your anxiety by struggling to master the principles and practices of effective teaching as well as hardware, software, and courseware. You can always increase your use of technology as the term progresses, or use a few, simple tools (such as email) one term and add a few more tools to your repertoire each term. It's more important that you use a technological tool effectively than that you use every tool that you can.

Using the Tools in Computer Classrooms

The configuration of electronically enhanced classrooms varies from school to school. Typically, the following tools are available for your use, but before you start teaching, go to the classroom where you'll be teaching and find out exactly what's available and how each piece of equipment works as well as how to get technical support.

Networked computers for each student.
When your students arrive in class, they sit in front of a computer at a workstation or get out their laptops. Typically, they'll need to log into your university's computer network just as you do, with a username and password. While most students master this procedure easily, there are always a few students—usually students new to the university—whose password doesn't work or who don't remember it. Find out how to assist these students, usually through your school's Help Desk, so they can gain access as quickly as possible. Beware the temptation to become so embroiled in helping one student that you lose significant class time; you can always suggest that students look on their neighbor's screen or do the day's work with paper and pencil during class, and find the answers to their computer problems after class.

Once students are logged in, you can immediately give them tasks on the computer such as creating a writing sample, sending you an email (to which they can attach a writing sample, if you ask for one), finding your course syllabus if you posted it online, or registering for courseware you'll be using. Provide complete, step-by-step instructions on the board, projected onscreen, or on a handout and be prepared to circulate, offering help and making sure students' screens show the desired destination.

When you want to engage in a face-to-face discussion, lecture, or some other activity, some students will keep working at the computer. Computers are compelling, after all, and one way classes using computers differ from other classes is that the presence of the computers forces instructors to find ways to divert students' attention away from the machines and toward the instructor or one another. Have students move their chairs toward the front of the room, if possible, or ask students to turn off their monitors or place a sheet of paper over the keyboard.

Another difference that you may need to take into account is the noise of the computers. Most computers contain one or two small fans to dissipate heat, and the low hum generated by twenty-five computers running at once can add up to a level of noise that makes hearing speech across the room difficult. If you can't hear students, they probably can't hear you, either, so students and you may need to project your voices more than usual. Students may need to stand up when they speak so they'll be seen and heard.

A printer is usually available, either in the classroom or in a central location nearby. If students have to pay for printed copies, they may prefer to use their own printers, so it's a good idea to reserve in-class printing for special occasions or leave it up to students whether or not to print in the classroom.

Instructor's station. Familiarize yourself with the instructor's station: how to log onto the computer, how to raise and lower the projection screen, how to turn on the projector and show or hide the image being projected, how the other available features work. Your school's computer services office may offer sessions to teach faculty how to use this equipment; if so, you'll find it time well spent. If not, you may be able to enlist the aid of a Help Desk employee or an experienced teaching assistant or faculty member.

Your room will probably also be equipped with a white board, rather than a chalk board (to eliminate chalk dust, which can harm computers), so find out what kind of markers you should use—usually, water-based and erasable—and take several with you. These markers dry out quickly, so having your own supply is a good idea, and if you want several students to write on the board at once, you'll know you have enough for everyone. Electronic whiteboards are the latest in technological advances, and if provided, you'll need special markers and training to use them. Your room may not contain such items as an overhead projector, television monitor or VCR/DVD (unless built into the computer in the instructor's station). Find out how to request such equipment well before you need to use it.

Access to the Internet. If your students have Internet access on their classroom computers, you can use it in several ways, from providing examples from various Web sites to asking students to do online research.

Library resources. So much academic material is available online through academic libraries—the catalogue, hundreds of databases and online scholarly journals, even librarians available to answer research questions—that students can do substantial library research in class while you circulate, offering help and instruction in the research avenues available through the library. At some schools, research librarians will visit your classes to introduce the library's resources and help your students start searching for information on their topics—a service worth taking advantage of.

Courseware. Courseware is sophisticated computer software that is available at many universities and accessed on the World Wide Web. These programs allow you to post course materials, including readings, lessons, your syllabus, and photographs; to create links to various Web sites, such as your school's library and writing center and other sites you want students to have easy access to; and to create discussion boards where students can post responses to questions you pose or topics you specify and then follow threads of postings, responding to one another. They also include course management features, such as the ability to email all students at once as well as individuals or groups; to sort students into collaborative groups, either randomly or by your choice; and to track students' attendance and grades. Many courseware programs are available through a university-purchased license, so your choice may be limited to the program supported by your school. As with other aspects of a computer classroom, you may find the easiest introduction to be a workshop presented by your school's computer services department.

Making Choices about Technology

You can use courseware to effectively reduce or eliminate paper in your classroom, as you make assignments, collect drafts and comment on them, and even have students compile portfolios of their work, all online—but you don't have to. You can select the features of the courseware that you feel comfortable using and ignore the rest. If you like the idea that students have access to the course syllabus and all the assignments whenever they have access to a computer, post those materials online. If you prefer to read students' drafts on paper, ask students to present you with printed copies. If you'd like students to send you drafts as email attachments instead of posting assignments on courseware, that's okay, too. It's better to teach effectively using technology to enhance your teaching and students' learning than to struggle with technology with which you aren't familiar or that you aren't convinced improves students' writing or learning. See Chapter 14 in this book, "Teaching Writing Online," for activities adaptable to the computer classroom.

Useful Readings

Computers and Composition: An International Journal. Elsevier, Ireland: Elsevier House.

Selfe, Cynthia L. "Technology and Literacy: A Story about the Perils of Not Paying Attention." *College Composition and Communication* 50.3 (Feb. 1999): 411–436.

Yancey, Kathleen Blake. "Made Not Only in Words: Composition in a New Key." *College Composition and Communication* 56.2 (Dec. 2004): 297–328.

Teaching Writing Online 14

Adrienne Cassel

In July 2003, the U.S. Department of Education reported that more than three million people were enrolled in online classes during 2001 (http://nces.ed.gov). By 2006, they have projected, that figure will double. Accompanying this increase is the need for more faculty who can effectively and efficiently teach online classes. Thus, whether you are a TA teaching for the first time, an adjunct faculty member, or a full-time faculty member who has considerable teaching experience, you are likely to be given the opportunity to teach in a virtual learning environment. This chapter aims to help you successfully meet that challenge.

As an online teacher, you will share in the conveniences that attract students to online classes. Like your students, you can log on anytime day or night at any computer that has an Internet connection. You can avoid the hassles of driving to campus, finding a parking place, and designing and maintaining a schedule that requires your physical presence at a certain time or place. However, you also share in the frustrations of the online learning environment. Computers crash, programs fail, support is not always available, and it is often difficult to create and maintain a community that supports and fosters successful learning.

Further, all of the challenges of teaching in a face-to-face classroom are present in the online classroom as well. You still have to motivate students who don't know why they need to learn to write, communicate standards and concepts to students who are new to the academic community and unfamiliar with university methods and requirements, and figure out ways to help each student improve his or her ability to successfully conduct research and write essays in an academic environment. So, how do you do that?

Preparing to Teach Online

You don't have to be a computer expert to teach online successfully. Similarly, your students do not have to be computer experts to learn online. However, you do need some basic knowledge of computers. In order to succeed in an online learning environment you should be able to do the following:

- Set up folders for organizing files
- Use word processing software properly
- Handle email communications, including attachments

- Use a Web browser to access information on the Internet

Although you can teach online without course management software (courseware), many teachers and students prefer access to reliable, user-friendly courseware and both training and technical support from the university. If you are being asked to teach online by administrators, the course management software and technical support most likely are already in place. Your job is to find out what is available to you and also to find out the technical capabilities of your students.

In order to develop the best course design, you need to gather some information about the students and the institution where you are teaching. Find out the following:

- Does your institution already provide courses online? If so, which courses?
- Who teaches them?
- Which course management software package do they use? (The three most common are WebCT, Blackboard, or Angel, although new ones are springing up daily.)
- How are the courses put together? Who sets up the course? Does the course need to be approved before it is offered? If so, by whom? Who populates the courses with students?
- How long does developing an online course usually take from start to finish?
- Who coordinates the development, delivery, and support?

Once you find out the answer to these questions, visit with some of the faculty already teaching online. First-hand information from them will be some of the most valuable information you can collect. Contact any support organizations available to you. Many colleges provide workshops and help you set up your course and keep it running smoothly. If your university does not offer faculty support in this area, contact the company that provides the course management software. They can often answer questions and provide materials to make your transition to online teaching easier and more effective.

Give yourself ample time for design, creation, and testing of materials before you offer a course online. The most successful courses offered online have been offered first as Web-enhanced courses with students in face-to-face classes. If that is not possible, at the very least ask five people with varying technical skills to complete at least one of the assignments you have designed for your course to see how well they understand your instructions. You may need to utilize the technical support staff or instructional designers for some materials. Find out the turnaround time for these services when you are planning your course. If you are able to use Web development software instead, you'll have more versatile documents. Make sure to save backup copies of all the materials you have created for the class in several places before you upload them to the Web or courseware. Most course management software programs work best if files are uploaded in HTML format, and most word-processing programs provide an easy way to convert documents to HTML files, usually with a simple save-as command.

Once you find out about support services for yourself, check into the support provided for students. Does your university have a help desk for students? What information is available concerning the technical literacy of students at your university or the students who will be targeted to take your class? Is there an orientation for students who are taking online courses? Do they have computers at home? Or will they be visiting a library or campus to complete their work? All of these factors will affect how you set up and manage the course.

Developing an Online Course

Planning the course. As with preparing to teach in a face-to-face classroom, begin by determining your goals and objectives. (See Chapter 1 in this book, "Designing a Writing Course.") Then determine the assignments and assessment tools for helping students meet those objectives. This last step, determining assignments and assessments, offers the greatest challenge to teaching online. You won't be able to simply transfer your syllabus, assignments, instructions, and lectures word for word to an online format. Instead, you'll need to identify new approaches and new techniques that take into account the limitations and opportunities of learning online. You might begin with a list of four or five techniques, strategies, or specific abilities that you would like your students to achieve by the end of the term. Here is a sample list of outcomes for a course on research and academic writing:

- Students will be able to formulate research questions that really matter to them.

- Students will know where to go to get credible research materials for an academic paper.

- Students will know how to evaluate research resources to determine their reliability, authority, currency, and relevancy.

- Students will be able to summarize, synthesize, and demonstrate an understanding of the information they have read from scholarly, credible sources.

- Students will be able to write and document research essays that demonstrate higher-level thinking skills and knowledge of one of the documentation methods used in academia (such as MLA or APA).

Generally, it's a good idea to work through the objectives individually, brainstorming about the learning activities, assignments, and assessments that will help students reach each goal, but often as you begin to work through the objectives in this way, you'll discover that many assignments and learning activities can fulfill multiple objectives. For instance, for the class outcomes mentioned above, an inquiry-based learning project utilizing topics selected by each individual student seemed the best approach for accomplishing the goals. Allowing students to choose their own topics engaged students in the process, and step-by-step instructions on how to complete the project gave students confidence in the online environment as they worked toward meeting the objectives for the course.

Presenting Materials and Activities Online

Most activities and assignments for teaching online will fall into one of the following general categories:

Instructor presentations. Online instructors have many of the same options as instructors teaching in traditional classrooms when it comes to presentation methods. Faculty can give online lectures, present online simulations, and conduct online demonstrations with PowerPoint and other multimedia software. Power-Point is the most commonly used presentation method because the slides are easy to create and post. Moreover, the slides can be accompanied by audio files which contain instructor explanations of course materials. Most universities have multimedia labs that can help with the development of PowerPoint presentations, but keep in mind two guiding principles: First, online learners do best with small chunks of information rather than huge blocks of text. Slides should provide a simple outline of the information students are to learn. For more detailed information, it is best to direct students to texts they can read offline. Second, because PowerPoint presentations can take a long time to load, especially from a dial-up connection, pro-

vide links to Web sites that offer the same information with faster load times or design a one-page summary sheet for students to review. If you are working in Microsoft Word or Corel Word Perfect, you can save the file as HTML and upload it into the courseware. It will open within the course frames, making it easy for students to read, and will load more quickly than a PowerPoint show. Another option is Web pages on a Web server or uploaded into courseware. Web development software is increasingly user-friendly and Web pages don't depend on specific software for display.

Simulations and demonstrations. Simulations and demonstrations can best be provided on Web sites. If you give students a link to information instead of actual files, loading times will be exponentially quicker and frustration levels much lower. One of the best resources for online simulations and demonstrations can be found at <http://www.merlot.org>. MERLOT, a free open resource center designed primarily for faculty and students in higher education, offers links to online learning materials that have been peer reviewed. Sample assignments and annotations are provided with each interactive activity.

Discussions. Discussions are one of the best ways for students to demonstrate understanding of course material, and discussion tools are included with all of the course management software packages. Current research has shown that counting discussion postings as part of the grade for an online course is an excellent way to encourage student engagement in your class (Hannafin, Land, and Oliver 1999). Interactive discussions demonstrate students' understanding of particular readings, allow them to summarize and synthesize information from various sources, and, if students post drafts in the discussion area, provide opportunities for peer review. Two basic types of discussion formats are available in most course management software packages: the chat room, which is synchronous—meaning students meet at a designated time—or the discussion board, which is asynchronous—meaning students can log on and post anytime that is convenient for them. In online learning environments, asynchronous discussions are often more successful than synchronous discussions because students taking a class online often have schedules that prevent time-constrained meetings. That said, synchronous discussions (chat rooms) can be valuable for office hours. You can designate times that students can find you in a chat room; students can log on and ask questions that require some back and forth discussion. Chat rooms can also be valuable for student group projects, as they are most effective when used by four or five people at a time rather than large classes.

Group work. All types of group activities, from peer review to cooperative learning projects, are possible in the online environment. However, for group projects to be successful, pacing and organization are crucial. Consider the following as you design the group work for your course:

- Incorporate nongraded activities that allow students to get to know each other and develop working relationships before you require them to submit work that will be graded. Include activities that will allow them to become familiar with the technical skills needed to share and post information.

- Consider how, when, and where students will meet and how you will evaluate individual contributions alongside group contributions. Make all of this information available to students from the beginning of the project.

- Provide group members with as many ways of communicating as possible. Set them up with a chat room, a discussion area, a place to share files, email contact information, and if possible phone numbers. If all students are on campus, you may encourage face-to-face meetings; however, do so only if ALL students are on campus. Otherwise, students who are off-campus will feel slighted.

- Determine ahead of time how groups will be formed. It is not a good idea to allow groups to evolve organically, nor is it a good idea to determine groups arbitrarily. Groups formed around common interests are the most successful online—as they are offline.

- Clear and well-articulated guidelines for group work are imperative if the group assignments are to be successful. Also, clear assessment criteria must be given before the work is under way. Providing rubrics for online group work and discussion postings is an excellent way to help students successfully meet learning objectives.

Research. Much of learning to write in college involves learning how to effectively and efficiently conduct research. Fortunately, much of the research needed for first-year composition courses (in fact, for most university courses) can be effectively completed online. University libraries are on the forefront of developing online research tools and access to those tools. Many libraries provide online tutorials on how to find and evaluate sources that can be used for research projects, and often the tutorials are geared toward online students.

Assessing Online Classes

Every well-designed course—whether online or face-to-face—includes well-designed assessment measures. In fact, since the feeling of isolation is one of the biggest challenges for online learners, students have cited immediate and ongoing feedback as one of the most essential characteristics of a successful online course. Chapter 9 in this book offers several options for responding to students' writing, many of which can be adapted for online courses, as can the advice in Chapter 12 on grading.

Ensuring Academic Honesty

Although concerns have been raised about the reliability of online assessment, in first-year writing courses many of those concerns can be assuaged with assignments that require students to submit multiple drafts that you review or by group projects. For more information on teaching to avoid plagiarism, see Chapter 29 in this book, "Teaching Research and Documentation."

Designing a Syllabus

The next step after determining the design and structure of the online course is to create a syllabus. Generally speaking, the syllabus for an online course includes the same elements as the syllabus for a face-to-face course: course information, course requirements, grading, and scheduling as well as information on how to contact the instructor for individual concerns or problems. However, in an online course, the syllabus needs to include more information than in a face-to-face course. Make sure that the syllabus is visible on the entry level of the course so that students can easily find the information they need to get started.

In face-to-face courses students obtain additional information about course policies by asking questions as they come up, but in an online course, you must anticipate some questions. Moreover, assumptions that students and faculty make about some course policies might not fit in online courses. Many students take online courses because they expect that they will be easier or take less time. Others expect a self-study approach where they move at their own pace. Some may even expect the instructor to be available twenty-four hours a day, seven days a week. Be sure your syllabus specifies the exact nature of the course: hours a week devoted to class (typically nine for a three-credit hour class), type and frequency of student participation, availability and response time for instructor (online equivalent of office hours). Class participation is another aspect of the online course that will require additional information for students. You may require that students log on a certain number of times each week or that they make a specific number and type of postings each week. Just make sure they know what you will be looking for to determine adequate participation.

Provide students with adequate and detailed information about policies and procedures for using the online tools. Step-by-step written instructions for turning in assignments, completing tests and quizzes, participating in discussions, and contacting you or other individuals who can provide technical support when needed are crucial to a successful online learning environment. Slide shows, screen shots, and short movies can illustrate some of the processes and can be linked to or referenced in your syllabus.

Useful Readings

Bauer, John F. and Rebecca S. Anderson. "Evaluating Students' Written Performance in the On-Line Class." *Principles of Effective Learning in the On-Line Class: New Directions in Teaching and Learning, No. 84.* Ed. Renee E. Weiss, Dave S. Knowlton, and Bruce W. Speck. San Francisco: Jossey-Bass, 2000.

Bean, John C. and Dean Peterson. "Grading Classroom Participation." *Changing the Way we Grade Student Performance: Classroom Assessment and the New Learning Paradigm: New Directions in Teaching and Learning, No. 74.* Ed. Rebecca S. Anderson and Bruce W. Speck. San Francisco: Jossey-Bass, 1998.

Hanna, Donald E., Michelle Glowacki-Dudka, and Simone Conceicao-Runlee. *147 Practical Tips for Teaching Online Groups: Essentials of Web-Based Education.* Madison, WI: Atwood Publishing, 2000.

Hannafin, Michael J., Susan M. Land, and Kevin Oliver. "Open Learning Environments: Foundations, Methods and Models." *Instructional-design Theories and Models.* Vol. 2. Ed. Charles M. Reigeluth. Mahway, NJ: Erlbaum, 1999. 115–140.

Hewett, Beth L. and Christa Ehmann. *Preparing Education for Online Writing Instruction: Principles and Processes.* Urbana, IL: National Council of Teachers of English, 2004. Includes an excellent bibliography.

Kairos: Rhetoric, Technology, Pedagogy. Available at <http://english.ttu.edu/kairos/>

Palloff, Rena M. and Keith Pratt. *Lessons from the Cyberspace Classroom: The Realities* of *Online Teaching.* San Francisco: Jossey-Bass, 2001.

———. *The Virtual Student: A Profile and Guide to Working with Online Learners.* San Francisco: Jossey-Bass, 2003.

Reeves, Thomas C. and Patricia M. Reeves. "Effective Dimensions of Interactive Learning on the World Wide Web." *Web-Based Instruction.* Ed. Badrul H. Khan. Englewood Cliffs, NJ: Educational Technology Publications, 1999. 59–65.

Creating and Sustaining a Teaching Persona

15

Scott Geisel

If you've never taught before, or if you find yourself in new teaching situations, you're probably going to have a period of adjustment. Getting used to your new territory won't happen overnight. No one is going to hand you a script with every line of dialogue you'll deliver, provide you with a wardrobe and make-up, explain your character's motivation, or coach you when to emote and when to be stoic. Getting comfortable with yourself as a teacher is a much more fluid process than that.

You might think of your new teaching context less like a play and more like the first time you went to a movie with a date and held his or her hand in the dark. You want to hold hands, and it feels nice, but there are worries: Do I hold the hand the whole time? What if my palm starts to sweat, or I have an itch? What if my date starts to sweat? What if my arm goes numb and I feel like I'm going to pass out?

Don't worry—you'll deal with the things that come up as you're getting used to teaching, just like everyone adjusts to new circumstances.

Teaching as a Writer

You're in a writing classroom because you're a writer. You know how to write, and you've done it successfully. Your experience as a writer should inspire both you and your students. As someone who's been where they are, you can serve as an example. Writing along with students can be a powerful teaching tool and can help remind you why you're there and what you have to offer your students: a passion for writing and an ability to show how to work through the challenges and difficulties they'll encounter in your class and as college writers. The ability to write is your strength and can help you find your comfort zone. Don't be afraid to use it.

Teaching as an Expert

Start by reminding yourself who you are not: You are not another student in the class. Your students shouldn't expect you to act like one of them, and you shouldn't suggest that's what you're trying to do.

91

Think about it this way: You've got a lot of jobs that your students don't. Among other things, you have to prepare materials that are current, useful, engaging, and productive for each class day; manage the pacing of daily activities and the course overall; keep students on task and move students productively both in and out of class; and pay attention and be prepared to adjust when students' needs don't fit as well as you'd like with what you've planned. Your students will look to you to model activities, answer questions, explain concepts, and keep control of the classroom.

At various times as a teacher, you'll feel that you're acting as a writer, scholar, mentor, coach, friend, authority figure, organizer, manager, mediator, grader, and more. You can be the voice of good news and positive feedback to students, as well as the reality check they don't want to hear. And your responsibility as grader can often feel like it's in conflict with your other roles. Your teaching persona may be all encouragement while the course is getting under way, but if you're unprepared or haven't prepared your students, there can often be a change in the feel of the classroom when you hand back that first set of graded papers.

Tell your students your expectations up front. Let them know that you'll grade their work fairly and accurately when the time comes, but that grades aren't personal. You can help to clarify this new role by developing a set of grading criteria, soliciting additional input and revision of those items from students, and applying the criteria to a sample piece of writing to demonstrate how your grading process will work. You'll be giving your students the opportunity to begin to interpret the comments you'll put on their papers. Make sure to include characteristics of good writing in general as well as qualities specific to a particular assignment. Prioritize so students will know the greatest impediments to achieving the goals of an assignment and don't spend the majority of their time worrying about less important features like headings and margins. When students are aware of your expectations and know how you're going to grade their papers, you'll feel more confident in that role. Once you've squarely faced the reality of the balancing act that teaching can sometimes be, you'll be on your way to feeling comfortable and to making your students feel comfortable with your teaching style, too.

Balancing Your Roles

At the same time you're juggling your various roles in your classroom, you'll have a whole other life outside of the classroom and your responsibilities as a teacher. Your students will, too. Their lives are their own, and yours is your own, but there are bound to be points of intersection and common experience that come up in the activities and discussions and writing that you share. How you handle those intersections will depend mostly on you, but keep in mind that you'll want to maintain the ability to keep control of the course while still trying to show you're a real person. A key here is relevance. The class you're teaching is about your students much more than it is about you. Act honestly in the relationship you want to have and can afford to have with your students, but don't lose track of your responsibilities. You don't need to withhold personal information or remain distant and untouchable, but you also shouldn't deliberately work in or reveal details about your personal life without some reason for doing so.

At the same time, don't be afraid to think like a student—like your students. What questions might you have or would you want to know if you had to complete the assignment you've just given? What is its value and goals, and what would be your motivation to work hard and try to do well? What's likely to be difficult, and where would you start? What processes might you use to get everything done? Then remember that your students will have a range of experience, skills, and confidence about college writing. They won't all respond the same to everything you ask them to do, and some are likely to find more value in a particular activity than others.

Dressing Like a Teacher

Dress codes in an academic environment are often arbitrary, self-imposed, or even nonexistent. Look around you—what are other people wearing, and why do you think they dress that way? And do they look comfortable? If the people you're noticing have been teaching long enough, their appearance and demeanor probably reflect themselves as teachers, and that's what you'll be projecting, too, once you find your comfort level. It can be tempting to wear a new power suit, a jacket and tie, or even jeans and an old button-down to pro-

ject an image, and sometimes when you're starting out, dressing nicely may help you establish authority in the classroom (or at least feel like you are).

Consider, too, a balance between fashion and appropriateness. Short skirts or oversized baggy shorts may distract students from reading and writing tasks in class. Many teachers are comfortable in a similar wardrobe day after day; others dress in a variety of ways to suit their mood, what's happening at any given time in the course, and even the weather. It's useful to look around at what other English teachers and people in different departments are wearing, too. Your colleagues may not feel compelled to wear a tie every day, but faculty in the business college may put on a jacket to teach. You might want a rack of ties or skirts you can choose from on days you teach and a drawer of jeans for when you'll be on campus but not in the classroom. And then you'll probably want to start mixing it up. The point is that you should feel relaxed in the way you present yourself to your students, and comfortable that they accept you in a way that you're happy with.

Having Fun

Teaching can be serious business, but if you're not enjoying yourself, too, then why are you here? And if you're not enjoying yourself, how must your students feel? Doing some things for fun (especially if they have some inherent value or relate to what's happening in your course) can set everyone more at ease and help create a comfortable, positive learning environment.

I like to throw things like little chocolate bars or a soft, rubbery ball that we can toss up over the lights and off the walls to each other during a discussion without hurting anyone or anything. Getting students to smile once in a while eases the tension in the classroom and helps students relax and open up. I've seen students perform skits in class with more energy and fun than I could have imagined. Ask students to perform a draft of a paper or to draw their thesis as a cartoon. Assign groups to attend and review a film or play or restaurant. And serving popcorn while you show a movie in class can make the whole experience more worthwhile.

But don't force fun. Starting class every day with a joke that you think is funny will probably be about as enjoyable for students as you can imagine it would be for you if one of your teachers did that. You don't have to be funny; you just want to get to the point where you feel relaxed. Being prepared and knowing what you want to accomplish and what you want your students to accomplish on any given day will help you find opportunities to relax. Even a smile or a willingness to indulge a minor diversion into an amusing side trip during class can go a long way to making it a more enjoyable experience for everyone.

you may feel more confident for those days when technology fails you or students just don't respond as you'd hoped. If you'd like to do more than there is time for in the term, have some of those other activities ready as alternatives: a field trip to practice observation and the power of details, an activity with magnetic poetry to explore new boundaries with language, a writing day when students simply work on their assignments with you there to answer questions and offer input, an editing sample for students to work on and present in class, a provocative reading, or a workshop day when students can work on their own, in groups, or with you. Knowing you've got options can help you to feel confident and to take charge of your classroom in the ways you want to.

Outside pressures can also influence your attitude in the classroom: a restless night of sleep, the stress of other responsibilities, your love life (or lack thereof), or a dead car battery on a cold January morning. You'll know you're getting somewhere when you appreciate the good days and don't dwell on the bad—just keep moving forward. And remember that gaining confidence is a key to becoming comfortable with yourself as a teacher. You're here because you've got something valuable to offer your students.

Gaining Confidence

When you first start teaching, some plans will work better than others, and some activities you may do once and vow never to repeat. If you have a backup plan, or several,

A Useful Reading

Greinke, Russell. "What I Learned about Teaching from Observing Stand-Up Comedians." *The Teaching Professor* 18:5 (May 2004): 1.

Balancing Graduate Studies 16 with Writing Instruction

Melissa Faulkner and Melissa Toomey

Most of us speak and behave differently in a gym than a church or a neighborhood pub. We've had ample time, an entire lifetime, to learn the social norms of familiar places, and we recognize that there's an already established social hierarchy where we know our role. In a church, for example, we know that the priest or pastor stands at the front, behind the pulpit, and we sit in a pew facing the front. It would be highly unusual for a member of the congregation to walk straight to the front and take over the pulpit. Yet, as new graduate teaching assistants, that's what we feel we're doing.

Most of us have about seventeen years of experience learning how to be a student, from kindergarten through undergraduate school. On the first day of kindergarten we didn't know to raise our hands before we spoke. Through observation, practice, and reminders from the teacher, we learned to do so. High school teachers prepared us for college by saying, "When you get to college . . . " and the expectations gradually became clear.

The transition to graduate school, however, is usually abrupt, and the transition from student to teacher feels even more sudden. Most graduate programs provide some type of teacher preparation in the form of a crash course, but rarely do graduate teaching assistants feel prepared to deal with their dual roles as both teacher and student. As graduate teaching assistants ourselves, first in an M.A. program and now as Ph.D students at another institution, we would like to offer advice on how to wear both hats, that of student and teacher, simultaneously. We hope to ease your mind, to assure you that nearly all graduate teaching assistants feel the same apprehension and fear you are feeling, and to encourage you. You have the experience and the knowledge—all you need now is the confidence.

Teaching First-Year Composition

Before you ever step into the classroom, you can prepare yourself for teaching writing. Meet people. Introduce yourself to the other teachers in your program, the professors in your department, and—perhaps one of the most important groups of people to know—the office staff, who usually will help you make copies and assist you with scheduling questions, technological issues, and other logistical concerns.

As you prepare to enter your classroom, think about how you want to physically represent yourself to students. Dress nicely. Business casual is often appropriate. Dressing in slacks or a skirt and a nice top or a jacket and khakis can set you apart from your students and create a professional tone from the start, as well as make you feel more confident when you walk in on the first day. Consider how you and the students will address each other. Also, take a bottle of water or a can of soda with you, both to quench your thirst and to have something to hold in your hand. See Chapter 15 in this book, "Creating and Sustaining a Teaching Persona," for more ideas.

Once your class gets going, don't feel that you can't vary your routines. In fact, you should try different pedagogical approaches in order to keep the students and yourself interested and refreshed. Don't hesitate to ask students for their views on new activities. In doing a midterm assessment one semester, Melissa Toomey discovered that students wanted more collaborative work where they talked in groups, went back to their seats and freewrote about the peer workshop, and then discussed the results as a class. In trying their proposed technique, Melissa found that students were energized by the new use of class time. Reflecting on this activity, students commented that they like for teachers to "move things around so we don't get bored," and several others stated

they were "surprised and happy [the teacher] even took their ideas into consideration." Giving students a voice in designing your course can keep them personally invested in what they do.

Cultivating Good Habits as Teacher and Student

Developing sensible practices as both a writing teacher and a graduate student is vital to your success in both roles. In order to manage your busy schedule, it's useful to create systematic records of what you are teaching and reading. Here are some tips for keeping records.

Be organized. Try constructing a basic or detailed lesson plan for each class that you can place into a binder or folder. Include key points you want to address in class, and write down any information you will want students to note. As soon as possible after you teach, reflect in writing on what you taught and on your students' reactions: How successful were the class activities? Why did they succeed—or why not? How should you change them next time? Completing such a metacognitive activity helps you organize and track your personal experiences as a new teacher, gives you a chance to think about your students' reactions and needs, and helps you improve your teaching in later courses.

Keep your work for each class you're teaching and taking in a separate folder or binder so you can locate information both during the term and later, when you want to use a handout from your fall section of English 101 or cite from an article that you can find easily in your folder marked "English 700: Research Methods—Spring 2004."

Manage your time wisely. Staying ahead of your students in the coursework is crucial. When you've gained some experience teaching, you'll be able to plan several class periods ahead of time, but the first time through, you're likely to be figuring out what to do as you teach. If possible, keep at least two classes ahead in your lesson plans to reduce your stress level and allow you to alert students about challenges they may face as they do what you assign.

If you walk into class without students' homework or class assignments ready, you quickly can lose credibility, so make copies of handouts or put information on reserve several days before you'll use or assign them. Unanticipated problems—broken copiers or scanners, delays in the library—often arise, and you want to avoid scrambling for an alternative to your planned lessons. You can then review the readings, copied handouts, and lesson plans just before your class.

It's equally important to manage your time wisely as a graduate student. Schedule time to write. We write in our planners (another good way to stay organized) that from nine to five on Mondays we will do nothing else but write. Schedule specific times to read, research, and revise. The more papers you write, the better you can estimate how long the process takes you. Melissa Toomey always allots herself five days to get through the initial researching,

notetaking, and drafting process for a paper. Melissa Faulkner gives herself the same amount of time but writes into her schedule that, for example, she will do the research notetaking while at her son Brandon's basketball game and finish it up at her daughter Chelsea's cheerleading practice. Because it is important for her to spend time with her family, she made the decision to talk and laugh with her kids on the way to and from practices and games, but while she's at practices, she'll do schoolwork—when she isn't cheering.

You may often feel overwhelmed when you think about dealing with your students, your own work as a student, and your family. Do whatever it takes for you to maintain your balance and sanity. Melissa Toomey only recently decided that she should take an entire day off each week from doing any schoolwork whatsoever. She believes she has made herself a better student; knowing she has a day off coming up soon, she works extremely hard to get there, and after that day off, she feels revived and rejuvenated. If you can't schedule a regular day off, consider a private holiday. When Rich Bullock was in grad school, he and his wife periodically declared "Januarius McGahan Day," and took the day off in honor of the liberator of Bulgaria.

Read actively. Being a busy student and teacher, you need to find ways to read that will help you understand material and remember it long after you have read it. Generating good reading notes is crucial to initial readings of texts and gives you a way to review the information later. Ask other students in your program to show you how they take notes, and after viewing as many examples as possible, find a system that will work for you, given your learning style. Some students write summaries of text in the margins as they read, some create double-entry notebooks (described in Chapter 40 of the *Field Guide*), while others create a form on which they record basic information about each text they read. Such a form might include the following:

- Summarize the chapter read.
- What two questions do I have?
- What three terms should I remember based on the content of the chapter, and what are their definitions?

Whatever strategy you use, it's important to remember that you are building a system that you can consciously change and renegotiate as your learning habits and skills are modified.

Help students manage their time. The syllabus is a key element in any classroom, especially in a writing classroom where assignments are due regularly, so use the syllabus to your advantage by spelling out assignments and rules in detail, making it a place where students can go for quick and concise answers to many of their questions. Students also appreciate having a detailed document to lead them in the right direction when they are experiencing difficulties. Sequences and deadlines help students manage their time. Outlining assignments on the syllabus before the course starts will also save you valuable time because you will have already planned the fundamental parts of your course. Chapter 2 in this book provides detailed advice on what to include in your syllabus. Go over the syllabus with your students, ideally on the first day of class, and discuss exactly what you mean by each item and your purposes for creating such a structure. Leave room for updates, and perhaps even include students in the decision process when making changes.

Although you may change some of your assignments as the term progresses, follow through with whatever policy you have stated. Inconsistency can foster student irresponsibility and reduce your credibility. For example, Melissa Toomey's syllabus states that she does not accept assignments by email. Yet students have sent her their work with notes attached stating that their printer is out of ink or that they forgot to give the assignment in class. Accepting papers after saying she wouldn't do so would undermine her authority as an instructor, and her other policies could also be called into question.

Succeeding as a Graduate Student

Here are some concerns we've encountered, with some advice for dealing with them.

Relating to faculty. As a graduate student, your relationships with faculty are different than they were when you were an undergraduate. Your professors may ask you to call them by their first names. They will probably begin to ask you how things are going. Don't be shocked if they offer suggestions or even offer to help. Take advantage of it! Your professors know the pressures you face and want you not only to survive but to succeed, because your success reflects their own. If you've been admitted into a graduate program, faculty assume you have what it takes to succeed and are interested in helping you do so. In addition, the reputations of universities are formed in part by the quality of the graduate students they produce. Faculty members want to be associated with institutions with excellent reputations. Therefore, they have a vested interest in your success.

Relating to your fellow grad students. Grad school does not have to be competitive. Next to faculty, your fellow graduate students can be your greatest resources and your best sources of support. You have all proven your academic ability by being accepted into your graduate program, so you don't need to compete to see who can be the best of the best. Form alliances, share useful sources, and help one another. Write together. We teach collaboration in the classroom, so why not practice what we teach? This very chapter is the result of an on-going collaboration between peers. As grad students, first at the same M.A. institution and now with the same Ph.D. program, we have written together, workshopped drafts together, presented papers together at conferences, and even co-taught together. Although this sort of partnership is not the norm, it's important to find or build your own support system. Even hanging around the teaching assistants' offices or grabbing a beer after class has real benefits: You can build friendships that might lead to collaboration, now and later when you're working in your chosen field, and the act of discussing your course content and your teaching with other graduate students will deepen and enrich your understanding of both.

Publishing. We don't intend to downplay the importance of building your credentials, and we recommend you not feel overly pressured to publish and present at conferences. However, attending conferences even without presenting is an invaluable learning experience. You get to learn about exciting new research and ideas as well as meet people who are important in your field—and they get to meet you. If possible, attend several conferences to learn their routines before you attempt to be a presenter. Seek advice from experienced presenters on how to write a proposal. Investigate which conferences are most respected and well known in your area of interest, whether it is creative writing, literature, TESOL, or composition and rhetoric. Be aware, though, that presenting papers not only adds stress to your already tired psyche and busy schedule but also can get expensive. Even with a student discount, some conferences can cost hundreds of dollars in registration fees, food, and lodging. Some institutions offer financial resources for graduate students' professional development, so be sure to inquire about assistance at your institution.

While publishing is an honor and a desirable goal, concentrate first on writing successful seminar papers; focus on completing your degree. Do not be afraid, however, to submit your work to appropriate journals for publication, especially work that may grow into something larger like an M.A. thesis or Ph.D. dissertation. These submissions can help you develop an area of expertise or specialization and can help to link your name with a very specific topic. Even if your work is rejected, the comments of referees can help you understand what publishable work in your field should contain and may improve your writing just as your comments help students improve their writing. While publication is certainly not impossible for grad students (plenty of us have done it), it is also not mandatory.

Useful Readings

Deen, Rosemary. "Notes to Stella." *College English* 54.5 (1992): 573–585.

Fulkerson, Richard. "Four Philosophies of Composition." *The Writing Teacher's Sourcebook*. Ed. Gary Tate, Edward P.J. Corbett, and Nancy Myers. New York: Oxford Univ. Press, 1994. 3–8.

Hall, Donald E. *The Academic Self: An Owner's Manual*. Columbus: Ohio State Univ. Press, 2002.

Interacting with Students 17

Jimmy Chesire

You are about to enter a college composition class, maybe for the first time. You might be nervous. Good, you should be: I don't think we can do anything well without worrying at least a little. We need a bit of adrenalin to get us going, to keep us going. But we don't want to panic. One reason new teachers worry is that they're adopting a new role, teacher rather than student, and don't know how to act: Should I try to act "professorial," whatever that means? Should I try to be formal, laid back, distant, a confidant? How do I interact with my students, who so recently—or not so recently—were my peers? Here are a few ideas and suggestions that might help you relax a bit and be yourself—and as a consequence, become a better and more effective teacher.

Being Honest

Be as honest with your students as you can be. Tell them the truth about yourself and the subject at hand. This approach does not mean telling your students everything you feel, think, believe, or desire, nor does it mean telling them your life story. You should, however, try to be open. Often we are so close-minded, so closed off from one another, and why not? As Brenda Ueland says in *If You Want to Write: A Book about Independence and Spirit*, we're well advised to be careful who we trust and open up to. But in your classroom, you have great power and authority. You can afford to take risks, you can dare to reveal yourself, because it is your turf.

If you want to connect with your students, if you want them to trust you, if you want them to do the things you direct them to do, then take some chances to let the real you appear. Be silly if there's a silly moment in class. Be loving and complimentary when you feel like it. Be wise-crackery if that's your bent, but if it is your bent, be sure to make clear to your students that you're joking. When making wise cracks, let them know you're playing and trying to be funny. Let students know if and how and when they can be wise-crackers, that they can crack wise about you.

Are you scared? Are you lost some of the time? Admit it. Tell your students you're new, that this is your first class, your first year teaching, that you're just learning. They'll appreciate your honesty, and most of them will be relieved because they already know it (or intuit it) and feel embarrassed and uncomfortable when you're embarrassed and uncomfortable. So if you own up and express your concern, they'll understand while being flattered to have been trusted. Then you can both relax.

If you allow it, students will help you and care for you and protect you, too, especially if you tell them you believe they can teach you a thing or two—and that you're open to learning from them. When they do teach you something, and they will, let them know, thank them, and then use that learning in front of them, giving them credit as you do. When your students witness this sort of openness and humility, this sort of graciousness and self-assurance, they'll relax and try harder to do all the work you ask them to do.

Doing the Work

I learned as a TA that one of the most effective teaching techniques was to do the homework assignments you give your students. Do the work you ask them to do. Tell them you are doing it, and tell them why. Explain that you want to keep in close touch with just how complicated and difficult many assignments can be; because when you have trouble doing the work, or can't complete the work in the allotted time, then surely you can understand their challenge—and be sure to give credit to those who are able to do what even you could not.

Early in my TA career, I did every assignment with my students but stopped because it seemed like too much work (which is the whole point—to realize just how much work we're asking them to do).

I started again doing all the assignments I give my students, and students appreciate that the teacher is doing the work, that I know exactly what I'm asking them to do, and that I know how hard it is. And they like the forgiveness: "I couldn't get mine typed up, so I'm not going to insist that you type yours up." But mainly they are very impressed, reassured, and wonderfully appreciative of how close I am to the pain and intellectual challenge of the homework I've assigned.

Caring

Look for ways to let yourself really care for your students and learn how to be compassionate toward them. There is a tremendous pressure, in my opinion, to belittle and ridicule our students, to make jokes at their expense, to laugh at their weaknesses and deficits—as if we teachers are so much more wonderful human beings because of our love of reading and writing. If you witness denigrating stories in your offices, lists of students' mistakes on email, and complaints at faculty meetings, don't be sucked into this morass. Don't make fun of your students, put them down, or laugh at them. Don't get me wrong. I love funny people, I love comedy, I love witty, clever, hilarious people. But there is a big difference between telling funny stories and stories that make the student the butt of the joke.

Try instead to understand how and why your students fell so far behind, why they don't read. Check out John Holt's wonderful essay, "How Teachers Make Students Hate Reading." Decide to care about your students and their deficits. Decide to be good and kind. Offer them condolences, understanding, and a second chance. They may have been chastised along the way by a reading or spelling teacher, and it only takes one such teacher to put a child off. Many of my students have told me so.

I love my students and tell them so, especially in the opening days of the term when talking about my university's many strengths. I say things like, "I learn a lot from my students and will probably learn a lot from you all." I respect my students and show it by paying attention to them, by taking them seriously, and by looking for reasons to praise and honor them as often as I can for their wit, for their humor, for their compassion, for their kindness to me and to others, for their fine writing, for their clear, incisive thinking, and for their willingness to work hard. I compliment them a lot, only saying things I really mean and believe. I tell my students I like them, that I'm glad they're in my class, that I'm lucky to have them in my class.

Observing Yourself

Discern how you are most effective in the classroom. Perhaps being open, honest, and willing to reveal your vulnerabilities won't work for you. Find out what does. Notice the things that really get your students reading and writing, and then do more of those things. A number of my peers bring sweets to their classes like donuts or little candies. Their students love the treats and then work harder.

Conferencing one-on-one with students (discussed in Chapter 6) is hard work, but you might love it and students say even ten-minute sessions are valuable. When I discovered how much I enjoyed conferencing, how much my students and I could cover, how much they grew as writers and readers, and how they blossomed as people because of our conferences, I expanded my conferences to thirty minutes per student.

If you discover an approach that works with one class, use it with another. Don't be afraid to do the same thing over and over again. It'll be new to your students, and with the repetition, you'll get better and better at it. If something you find exciting bombs, try it again before abandoning it. Sometimes the idea is good but the term, the students, or your delivery aren't right but will be another time.

Setting an Example

If you want to be the very best teacher you can be, then make a conscious decision to grow, both personally and professionally. Dedicate yourself to learning—the best teachers believe in teaching, which means we value learning. Actively learning and having a lot of fun in the process will show by your demeanor, and students will see it. They will be excited by your enthusiasm for learning and will be encouraged to follow your lead. Besides, learning is the richest thing, the most long lasting pleasure, and the most life extending thing you can do for yourself. You and your students will benefit more from your classes as you take risks and learn and teach together.

Useful Readings

Holt, John. "How Teachers Make Students Hate Reading." *The Underachieving School*. Holt Associates, 1994. Rpt. *The Norton Reader*. 11th Ed. Linda H. Peterson and John C. Brereton. NY: Norton, 2004. 420–428.

Nathan, Rebekah. *My Freshman Year: What a Professor Learned by Becoming a Student*. Ithica: Cornell UP, 2005.

Ueland, Brenda. *If You Want to Write: A Book About Independence and Spirit*. St. Paul: Graywolf, 1997.

Teaching for Inclusion 18 and Diversity

Adrienne Cassel

Students who feel comfortable sharing their ideas and experiences with their instructors and other students in their classes will learn more and stay in college longer than students who find their learning environment and their interactions on campus awkward and uncomfortable. But creating a classroom in which all students feel included, comfortable, and respected regardless of physical abilities, learning styles, sex, age, ethnicity, sexual orientation, socioeconomic background, or religion can be challenging, whether you are a graduate student teaching for the first time or an experienced faculty member who has taught for many years. This chapter aims to help you meet the challenge by introducing four key elements of inclusive design and providing ideas for integrating them into your writing course.

Understanding Four Key Elements of Inclusive Design

Simply put, *teaching for inclusion* means you teach so that each student's individual learning needs are met. Sometimes called *culturally responsive* teaching, this approach calls for instruction that honors each student. Inclusive courses, no matter what the subject, contain the following key elements:

1. The instructor demonstrates awareness of his or her own attitudes and biases.
2. Course content reflects various world views and perspectives.
3. Assignments are varied to engage students with different learning styles and students with learning disabilities.
4. Materials are accessible for everyone regardless of any physical or cognitive disabilities.

Appraising Your Attitude and Awareness

To create culturally responsive classrooms, begin with an honest appraisal of your own attitudes and biases. Sometimes we think we are encouraging multiple viewpoints and world views, but unless we have examined our own beliefs in light of the dominant culture within which we live and

105

work, we may be unconsciously replicating and encouraging the same frames of reference we are trying to avoid.

To begin to discover your own biases, ask yourself: What values do I hold that are consistent with the dominant culture? Sociologist Robin M. Williams (Wlodkowski and Ginsberg 11–12) has identified themes that generally reflect the basic values and beliefs held by the dominant culture in the United States. These themes are presented here as questions you might ask yourself to begin examining your own attitudes. Although these questions provide polarized viewpoints, they are not meant to suggest that the only possible responses are "either-or" responses. They are meant instead to provide a springboard from which multiple perspectives and interpretations are possible. As you answer the questions, think about other perspectives that may be equally valid in other cultures or situations, and assess to what degree you allow for these alternative world views and approaches to learning in your classrooms. The first two questions include some analysis. Use these examples to help you create your own analysis of the other questions.

- *How do you define success?* In the United States there is an emphasis on "pulling one's self up by the bootstraps," or the rags-to-riches success story characterized by large financial gains achieved by working hard or by being "rescued" by a well-to-do relative. An alternative viewpoint might be that the highest human value is generosity, that "conspicuous consumption represents greed and self-interest". Also, the rags-to-riches story overlooks the influence of privilege and ignores the social, political, and economic factors that favor certain groups in succeeding in this way.

- *What do you believe about work?* In the United States we generally believe that working hard is a virtue; however, that belief devalues the importance of taking time for others and for contemplation and leisure. We often fail to recognize the value of other types of discipline besides the discipline of the workplace.

- *What are your humanitarian mores?* Do you believe people should come together to help the "underdog," or do you believe that people "get what they deserve"?

- *What is your moral orientation?* Do you believe in a definite right or wrong? Should right and wrong be defined in the context of particular cultures? Or, do you believe that "right" and "wrong" are subjective judgments meant to protect the more privileged members of society?

- *Which is more valuable, efficiency and practicality or the quality of the process?* Is it more important to make decisions and act on them or to make sure the opinions of everyone affected by such decisions are heard before a course of action is settled on?

- *What is your view of economic growth and "progress"?* Do you believe that the development of industry, roads, buildings, houses, shopping centers, and the like equals betterment for humankind or do you believe that honoring the natural world and the inherent cycles is a better way to live?

- *What constitutes "the good life"?* Do you see the good life as the attainment of things that can make you more comfortable, or do you believe the good life is about sharing and giving, even if it involves personal sacrifice?

- *Who controls the government?* Do you believe that every person has a voice in the political destiny of the country or that only those who hold power and its privileges influence politics?

- *Is freedom an absolute good?* Do you believe in freedom at any cost, or do you believe that limiting your own freedom may be a way to show respect for someone else's freedom?

- *What is more important, the individual or the group?* Do you honor being true to yourself, or do you believe the group should take precedence over the individual?

When you look at your cultural values through the various perspectives suggested by these questions from Wlodkowski and Ginsberg, you develop a better understanding of how your world view can subtly, but profoundly change the experience your students have in your classroom. For example, simply asking, "Where are you going on spring break?" may unnecessarily make some students uncomfortable. Students who travel on spring break are usually supported by their parents or guardians, giving them the freedom and financial means to make a spring break trip. Many students at the community college where I teach use their spring break to catch up on much needed sleep or other projects outside of school—or to work extra hours at a job. Taking a trip someplace exotic is not within their means. Instead of asking where they are going on spring break, which assumes that everyone is going someplace, a better question might be, "What are you doing over the break?" That question assumes nothing except that they are getting a break, a pretty safe assumption.

Although this variation might seem like a small thing, awareness of these kinds of implied values can have a huge impact on first generation students and/or students from underrepresented groups who often get through college only if they are lucky enough to find people who are willing to help them interpret, analyze, and maneuver through a system characterized by elitism, process, rules, and complicated traditions. By uncovering your own biases and beliefs, you become more sensitive to your students' biases and beliefs, allowing you to create a classroom environment that is more comfortable for more students.

Revisiting Course Content and Materials

Once you understand how your own values and beliefs shape your teaching, you will be better able to evaluate the content you present and the materials you use in the course. Wlodkowski and Ginsberg suggest first thinking about the course within its discipline. For instance, ask yourself what values are embedded in your discipline that may confuse or disturb some students. How can you encourage students to express alternative perspectives? For example, in writing classes, the focus on teaching traditional genres over alternative forms or genres reveals values embedded not only in the field of writing studies, but also in the entire institution of higher education. The ongoing debate about what authors and works should be included in the English literary canon is just one example of how embedded values shape education.

Another example is the debate over the teaching of a standard form of English and the acceptance of Ebonics and other dialects in spoken language in the classroom. Of course, students must understand and learn to write with the conventions accepted in the professional world, but it is also important that students understand that issues of diversity are inherent in any use of language. One way to honor various dialects and teach students about the discourse communities within their own sphere is to design some assignments that do not require "standard" forms of English. For instance, if you include a literature component in your composition class, you might ask students to write from the viewpoint of a character speaking in a particular dialect in a manner that would be comfortable to that character. You could ask students to write versions of their research or argument essays for various audiences, including younger siblings or friends. When you ask students to generate ideas and text that won't lead to a polished final draft, make it clear that you'll accept their writing in rough draft form, which may be influenced by various spoken dialects.

While it's important to allow students to understand and explore various ways of speaking and writing, it's also important to be aware of the various challenges that students face based on their ethnic background, the area of the country in which they grew up, and their preparation for academic work. If you can identify the challenges facing specific groups of students and learn to work with them beginning where they are—without judgment—you'll be more successful in creating classrooms where students feel comfortable to express themselves.

You should also review your examples. Are the examples that you use to illustrate key points both meaningful and sensitive to the students? Do the examples demonstrate that you value multiple perspectives and ways of viewing the world? One way to incorporate a variety of viewpoints is to first offer your own example and then ask students to supply theirs. Also, consider the models of writing and reading that you assign as part of the course. Do they include materials written by persons of differing backgrounds and ethnic groups? Do they too offer various world views? Do they address underrepresented groups in ways that do not trivialize or marginalize those groups?

Understanding Learning Styles

In addition to engaging a diverse student population by providing content that reflects multiple perspectives and experiences, you can also motivate students by designing assignments that appeal to various interests and learning styles. Students learn best when teaching addresses their preferred style. The writing assignments listed below provide additional ideas for designing course work that appeals to each of the four types of learners identified by David Kolb, an organizational researcher (in Sharp, Harb, and Terry).

- *Divergers* learn through interaction and discussion. Freewriting, peer reviews, personal reactions, and opinion papers appeal to this type of learner.

- *Assimilators* learn by observing and reflecting. They like to consult the experts but then discover new ways to tie the old ideas together. They like reading assignments, writing summaries, creating maps and trees, and they actually enjoy listening to well-organized lectures.

- *Convergers* prefer to take things apart and put them back together again. They learn by doing. The key to engaging convergers is to be sure they know why they are doing what they are doing. They like case studies, simulations and assignments that involve keeping track of problem-solving protocols.

- *Accommodators* learn best through self-discovery. They are risk takers who resent having to follow too many rules. They would enjoy assignments that involve teaching concepts to other students, solving "what if" formulas, and formulating problems.

One of my favorite assignments is for students to post their research projects on blog (Weblog) sites they have created themselves. Using blogs for both group and individual projects is an easy way to publish students' work, and blogs also provide an opportunity for students to gain computer literacy skills while participating in an activity that they consider trendy and fun. In addition, the blog assignment has a component that resonates with each of the learning types described by Kolb. For *divergers*, who like interaction and discussion, the blog provides instant access to both. *Assimilators,* who prefer consulting with experts as opposed to consulting with each other, can invite experts to post as part of their project or can cite experts from research. *Convergers*, who like to solve problems, can use the blog assignment as a problem to solve; and *accommodators*, who like to teach to other students, have a perfect venue for doing so. By mixing the types of writing assignments in your courses and providing students with several options for completing their assignments, you will enhance learning in your course and give students tools to succeed in their writing tasks in other classes as well. In addition, assignments such as these encourage authentic assessment: They ask students to perform real-world tasks that demonstrate meaningful application of essential knowledge and skills, the best approach to embracing a diverse student body.

Understanding Learning Disabilities

Complicating the issue of learning styles are students who come to us with diagnosed or undiagnosed learning disabilities. Keeping these students engaged requires going beyond respecting their world views, cultural backgrounds, and preferred learning styles. In order for students with learning disabilities to feel respected and comfortable in the classroom, they need to feel that they are able to successfully complete the tasks and assignments. The ERIC Clearinghouse on Disabilities and Gifted Education has identified three instructional interventions that consistently help students with learning disabilities to improve their writing abilities, and thus feel more relaxed and valued in the classroom.

1. Teach writing as a recursive practice. Show students that even the most accomplished writers do not create a successful draft on the first try, and require multiple drafts and editing sessions before they are satisfied with the written product.
2. Explicitly teach critical steps in the writing process and accompany each step with a series of prompts or questions to guide students through the writing task. For instance, in the planning stage, students might be asked to answer a series of questions such as, "Who am I writing for?" "Why am I writing?" What do I know?" "How can I group my ideas?" and "How will I organize my ideas?"
3. Provide frequent feedback based on the information explicitly taught. One way to do this is to give students rubrics that outline the strategies and components that you have identified as most important in their drafts. Students can use the rubrics as guides, and then you can use them to assess their success with the writing task.

Providing Accessibility

In order to meet the needs of all students, course materials need to be available to all students regardless of any physical or cognitive disability. Most campuses have an office of disability services that can help you critique your course materials with student accessibility in mind, but the five techniques listed below will help you get started:

- Provide equivalent print text versions of all materials that are presented as spoken or electronic components of the course.
- If you are using PowerPoint presentations, do not rely on color alone to convey information; also use text and shape. Choose high-contrast colors for text and background and test the presentation by changing it to black and white to be sure it can be easily viewed. Make handouts of the slides on request.

- Provide alternative versions of any material presented in class when students request it. For example, provide outlines of class activities and topics, or allow students to record lectures.

- Encourage students to let you know if they have any kind of disability and then work with students throughout the term to ensure that they are getting the support they need. Most universities have a disabilities office to support students and teachers; many require documentation for granting accommodations.

No matter which group of students you are working with, inclusive teaching means that you let students know ahead of time what criteria you will be using to evaluate their work. Part of teaching for inclusion is to make sure all students have clear and meaningful information for the course. Creating courses where all students feel respected and comfortable can be a challenge, but the rewards go far beyond the classroom. Students will be more engaged and motivated to learn as well as more likely to stay in college and succeed as writers and scholars. As a bonus, inclusive classrooms help to create a more just, equitable, and compassionate world for all of us.

Useful Readings

Corrigan, J. R. "Teaching Writing to Dyslexic Students: A Guide for the Composition Instructor." *Teaching English in the Two-Year College* 24.3 (1997): 205–211.

Sharp, J.E., J.N. Harb, and R.E. Terry. "Learning Styles and Writing Assignments." *The Teaching Professor*, Oct. 1997: 1+.

Wlodkowski, Raymond J. and Margery B. Ginsberg. *Diversity & Motivation: Culturally Responsive Teaching.* San Francisco: Jossey-Bass, 1995.

19 Teaching Second-Language Writers

Deborah Crusan and Carol Cornett

As you read through the stack of your students' first compositions, you may encounter some writing that stands out from the rest, but you can't quite put your finger on what's wrong. You can see that the writing doesn't flow; however, when you stop to decode, you aren't sure how to explain what you see happening on the page in front of you. You may see usages like the following:

- "Living in the cities is wonderful but it depends on how is your living standard."

- "For myself, The people who are college graduates it is better for them to live in the cities, because they will be able to handle that life of urban areas, because they will be getting enough salary to pay the bills and everyday expenses."

- "Teenagers and early twenty people always prefer living in crowded cities or where they can find some action."

- "There are lots of differents between living in cities and living in rural areas, and the most important different is the kind of people you see in each place."

- "My father always give me idea about what should I do."

- "There is not many roads and not many the gas station."

- "I am eighteen years old man."

- "So you can have a fun."

- "I came to the United States so many years but I still can not speak, write English well. Because I always stay at home, don't go outside, and we speak Chinese in my home. Many times I don't know how to speak English. So that shut my mouth."

You might encounter these usages randomly, in a single sentence, in one paragraph, or throughout a paper. If you do, you may well have a second-language writer in your class.

Writing in a second language is a challenging and complex process. Not only are second-language writers attempting to internalize the stages of the writing process, they also must contend with second-language processing issues. In some cases, this student should be placed in a class specifically designed for second-language writing. However, the student may well belong in your class, either through placement, promotion, or lack of alternatives. This chapter briefly describes some characteristics of second-language writers and their writing and offers practical advice on how to help your second-language writers succeed.

Understanding Second-Language Writers

There are no "typical" second-language writers. These writers defy generalization due to their different cultures, religions, ethnicity, language, economics, and development. In your class, you may find an eighteen year old with no college experience, a visiting professor doing post-doctoral research, or a student born in the United States who speaks English with peers and in school but speaks another language at home. These students do, however, have some common issues with writing.

Characteristics of second-language writers. Second-language writers differ from their native English-speaking counterparts in two important ways. Most significantly, they use rhetorical strategies from their first languages, often producing writing that seems redundant, repeating the same argument in slightly different ways in subsequent paragraphs. Second, while the stages in the writing process are the same, second-language writers approach each stage differently. Most noticeably, second-language writers are likely to have some or all of the following traits:

- Focus mainly on *what* to write rather than *how* to write

- Worry about vocabulary, constantly referring to a dictionary

- Compose more slowly and less fluently than native English speakers

- Don't proofread as much or as well as native English speakers

- Concentrate on errors at the sentence level to improve writing

- Make frequent errors, particularly with word usage

- May be unaware of expectations of readers in the United States

- May have little or no experience with or tolerance for peer review

- May have little or no experience with teachers' responses and response styles in the United States

- May be surprised by revision requirements

Common writing problems. Second-language writing may at first appear to be a jumble of errors, but close inspection reveals identifiable problem areas:

- Choice of word or word forms

- Article, pronoun, and preposition usage

- Verb tense, construction, number, and subject-verb agreement

- Sentence word order

- Countable/uncountable nouns and quantifiers

- Sentence boundaries: fragments, comma splices, and run-on sentences

Plagiarism. Even with awareness-building activities, plagiarism remains a problem for

ESL students for several reasons. First, what we call plagiarism in the United States is a practice encouraged in most Asian countries. For instance, Korean teachers give high grades when students imitate classic writers. In China, Confucianism still promotes the use of proverbs to communicate ancient messages about morality and universal truths. Thus, the second-language writer often grows up with a different perspective regarding ownership of text. An additional cause for plagiarism is the second-language writer's lack of adequate vocabulary to paraphrase original textual sources. Because of this lack of language proficiency, second-language writers may fear that they cannot express their ideas effectively in written English; instead, they tend to use what they have read without citing the source. Sometimes, as a last resort, a desperate second-language writer may ask someone else to write an entire paper.

Helping Second-Language Writers

Given what we know about second-language writers—who they are, what they need, and what they do—you can accommodate some of their unique needs, not as intimidating a task as it may seem. If your university offers English as a second language (ESL) courses, the specialists teaching those classes can help you plan writing activities. Writing centers and student skills centers can supplement your teaching. Your main focus should be on grammar errors and flawed rhetorical structure, since these represent the most troublesome issues inherent in second-language writing.

Grammar. You shouldn't be an editor, nor are you expected to be an expert in second-language grammar issues. Instead, encourage your second-language writers to take charge of their own learning. Helping them to analyze their errors and to understand why they make them will promote independent learning. Students can keep grammar logs to provide a structure for error analysis. Logs can be a simple table divided into three columns: error, correction, and the grammatical rule that applies to the error. Students record in their logs errors that you highlight in their drafts, either using electronic tools in a word processor or highlighting by hand. Marking drafts electronically allows the writers to paste errors directly into their log. Although this procedure adds extra work for them, second-language writers do need to keep track of their errors. This process will help them take a major part of the responsibility for analyzing errors and eventually move to self monitoring, where students independently discover and correct their errors.

You can also devote some conference time to grammatical concerns. However, you should require that students arrive prepared, bringing their draft with highlighted errors and their completed grammar logs. In addition, students can work with second-language writing specialists in university writing centers. Or, you can send them to online grammar resources to work independently on their specific errors. By completing grammar exercises and taking quizzes, writers test their understanding and their ability to apply grammatical rules.

Response. Second-language writers welcome feedback; in fact, they expect it. Sometimes they want to be told how to fix their problems. Strategies that work well with native English speakers often fail with second-language writers. For example, second-language writers fail to discover errors when reading their texts aloud; instead, they will benefit more from frequent conferences and more individualized attention. In general, second-language writers are helped by response

- in the middle stages of the writing process,
- on all elements of their writing—content, rhetorical structure, grammar and mechanics,
- in clear and specific language, and
- on grammatical errors that interfere with comprehension.

Being Flexible

Working with second-language writers may at first seem a daunting task. But don't forget that good teaching for your native English-speaking writers is also good for second-language writers. Yes, second-language writers may need more of every-thing, but you'll find them grateful for everything you do for them. You'll need to remain flexible, as each student will be unique, with different needs and abilities. One of the most important things you can do is to listen to them; they'll tell you what they need. Their writing will also tell you. As you get to know your second-language writers, you'll appreciate all the ways they enrich the classroom, providing outside perspectives along with linguistic and cultural diversity.

Useful Readings

"English as a Second Language (ESL) Resources, Handouts and Exercises." *Purdue Online Writing Lab.* 1995–2004. <http://owl.english.purdue.edu/handouts/esl/index.html>.

Guide to Grammar and Writing. Capital Community College Foundation. 2004. <http://webster.commnet.edu/grammar/powerpoint.htm>.

Leki, Ilona. *Understanding ESL Writers: A Guide for Teachers.* Portsmouth, NH: Heinemann, 1992, especially chapters 4, 5, and 9.

Silva, Tony. "Toward an Understanding of the Distinct Nature of L2 Writing: The ESL Research and Its Implications." *TESOL Quarterly* 27 (1993): 657–675.

Teachers of English to Speakers of Other Languages (TESOL). 11 May 2005. <http://www.tesol.org>.

part 2

On Teaching with *The Norton Field Guide to Writing*

Developing Course Plans **20**
Using *The Norton Field Guide*

The Norton Field Guide to Writing allows you to create various courses to meet your students' needs—and your own. This chapter offers an overview of some course plans commonly used in first-year writing programs and ways *The Norton Field Guide* may be used in their service. Because writing programs, courses, and term lengths vary from school to school, what follows are suggestions that you may wish to adopt or adapt to your own needs.

Using the Guides to Writing

If you're just starting your career as a teaching assistant or writing instructor, you may benefit from concentrating on the four detailed genre chapters: Chapter 6, WRITING A LITERACY NARRATIVE, Chapter 7, ANALYZING A TEXT, Chapter 8, REPORTING INFORMATION, and Chapter 9, ARGUING A POSITION. These chapters each provide a complete sequence of assignments, beginning with sample readings and followed by tasks that move students from thinking about a topic through drafting, revising, editing, and proofreading. Along the way, students are prompted to get response to their writing from others and to assess their own work. Color-coded links refer them to other sec-

tions of *The Norton Field Guide* for detailed assistance with various tasks if they need more help. This structure permits you to base your teaching activities on the structure of the chapters. Then, as you gain confidence and experience, you can modify your assignments and activities, bringing in lessons and activities from various parts of the *Field Guide* to suit your own purposes.

Creating Your Own Assignment Sequences

The Norton Field Guide also allows you to create assignment sequences to suit your own instructional goals and your students' particular needs. As a starting point, you may find it useful to show students how to navigate within the *Field Guide*. Show them the Key to the Book located on the front cover flap; each section of the book is listed, with the major topics covered within the section, so they can go directly to the colored pages to find the section they want. A brief menu of the contents is printed on the inside cover for students wanting to get to a specific chapter quickly. Cross-referenced material is screened in the color of the section in which it appears, and the page number where it may be found and an icon identifying the section are in the margin. Asking students to read "How to Use This Book" will help them see how they can use the *Field Guide* to get the answers to their writing questions; reading it yourself will help you understand how to help students navigate your own assignment sequences, which may require considerable moving around within the text. Here is a template for an assignment sequence using various chapters to help students compose a text:

1. *Introduce the genre, define key features, and discuss the rhetorical situation as it applies to the assignment.* Ask students to read the writing example presented in that chapter and then discuss it as a class. Introduce the Key Features of the genre as defined in the chapter and as applied to the reading. At this point, you will want to discuss the criteria for your writing assignment, asking students to think about their rhetorical situation. You may wish to assign Chapters 1–5 early in the term to get them thinking about purpose, audience, and the other components of any rhetorical situation. But each of the genre chapters, strategies chapters, and most other chapters include questions that help students focus on their rhetorical situation. You may at this point also want to ask students to read about media and design, in Chapters 47–49, to help them think about the medium they will be writing in and how their rhetorical situation will affect their design choices.

2. *Help students generate ideas and text, do research, and choose a topic.* Each genre chapter offers some guidelines to help students generate ideas and choose a topic to write about. You may ask students to do additional work in Chapter 22, GENERATING IDEAS AND TEXT. If students will be doing research, you might incorporate Chapters 39–46 as appropriate. For smaller projects, choose only the chapters that students need; for a larger project, you might assign students to use Chapters 39 through 43 as an assignment sequence.

3. *Teach students to organize, plan, and use appropriate strategies to write a draft.* Each genre chapter offers two or three typical ways of organizing a draft. You might ask students to create an outline (Chapter 22) and then use the advice in Chapter 23 for help with drafting. Along the way, they may need to consult chapters in Strategies for help with describing (Chapter 34), narrating (Chapter 37), dialogue (Chapter 35), and other writing strategies. If their texts include source material, they should consult Chapters 42 and 43 for help with quoting, paraphrasing, and summarizing.

4. *Show students how to assess the draft, get responses, revise, edit, proofread, and compile a portfolio.* Chapters 24–27 can be referenced or reviewed as needed and as time allows. These chapters include guidelines and questions which can be applied to any of the genre chapters. If your students will be compiling a portfolio, you will definitely want to spend time on Chapter 27.

Here's a quick reference guide for potential assignment sequences using the chapters in *The Norton Field Guide*. Ask students to read one or two chapters from each column as time and applicability warrant. Other chapters may simply be referenced or reviewed as needed.

A Menu for Designing Assignment Sequences

Introduce the genre, define key features, and discuss the rhetorical situation of the assignment:	*Help students to choose a topic, generate ideas and text, and do research:*	*Teach students to choose a topic, organize, and use appropriate strategies to write a draft:*	*Show students how to assess a draft, get response, revise, edit, proofread, design, and compile a portfolio:*
Chapters	Chapters	Chapters	Chapters
1–5. Rhetorical Situations	22. Generating Ideas and Text	23. Drafting	21. Collaborating
6. Writing a Literacy Narrative	38. Reading Strategies	28. Beginning and Ending	24. Assessing Your Own Writing
7. Analyzing a Text	39. Developing a Research Plan	29. Guiding Your Reader	25. Getting Response and Revising
8. Reporting Information	40. Finding Sources	30. Analyzing Causes and Effects	26. Editing and Proofreading
9. Arguing a Position	41. Evaluating Sources	31. Classifying and Dividing	27. Compiling a Portfolio
10. Abstracts	43. Acknowledging Sources, Avoiding Plagiarism	32. Comparing and Contrasting	44. Documentation
11. Annotated Bibliographies	45 and 46. Sample Research Papers	33. Defining	45. MLA Style
12. Evaluations		34. Describing	46. APA Style
13. Lab Reports		35. Dialogue	47. Print Text
14. Literary Analyses		36. Explaining Processes	48. Spoken Text
15. Memoirs		37. Narrating	49. Electronic Text
16. Profiles		42. Quoting, Paraphrasing, Summarizing	
17. Proposals			
18. Reflections			
19. Reviews of Scholarly Literature			
20. Résumés and Application Letters			
47. Print Text			
48. Spoken Text			
49. Electronic Text			

Sample Course Plans

First-year composition courses take many forms. Here are some typical first-year course plans that show how you might use *The Norton Field Guide*.

One-term courses. If your school requires students to take a single first-year writing course, you probably need to move students quickly through several genres. The following course plan begins by introducing students to the notion of the rhetorical situation and then creates a bridge between their past literacy and their current abilities through creation of a literacy narrative. Analyzing a text helps them to become critical readers, an ability they'll need for the next assignments, writing an essay that reports information and one that takes a position. The course ends by asking students to create and evaluate a portfolio of their work.

10-week Course

Week 1	RHETORICAL SITUATIONS
Weeks 1–3	LITERACY NARRATIVES
Weeks 3–6	ANALYZING A TEXT
Weeks 7–9	ARGUING A POSITION
Week 10	COMPILING A PORTFOLIO

14-week Course

Week 1	RHETORICAL SITUATIONS
Weeks 2–3	LITERACY NARRATIVES
Weeks 4–7	ANALYZING A TEXT
Weeks 8–10	REPORTING INFORMATION
Weeks 11–13	ARGUING A POSITION
Week 14	COMPILING A PORTFOLIO

Your writing program's requirements may require you to alter this outline. For example, if your program emphasizes argumentation, in a semester-long course you may need to replace REPORTING INFORMATION with a second assignment based on ARGUING A POSITION. In these circumstances, bringing in a GENRE chapter, such as EVALUATIONS or PROPOSALS, can provide variety for you and your students. Similarly, an emphasis on research may lead you to reduce the time you spend on earlier assignments and increase the time spent on REPORTING INFORMATION or ARGUING A POSITION, to make room for instruction in RESEARCH.

Two-term courses. If your school requires students to take two or three writing courses, you may either require students to write more essays or you may spend more time with each assignment, studying additional readings, asking students to write multiple revisions of their drafts, and including more group work and individual conferences with you. If your courses consist of 28–30 weeks divided among two semesters or three quarters, you can slow the pace even more, offering students additional opportunities to rewrite as well as revise their drafts and prepare lengthier and more detailed self-evaluations. You're likely to find, however, that the demands of doing academic research and creating acceptable arguments dictate devoting as much time as you can to these activities. Here's a two-course sequence based on a ten-week-long quarter:

First Course

Week 1	RHETORICAL SITUATIONS
Weeks 2–3	LITERACY NARRATIVES
Weeks 4–7	ANALYZING A TEXT
Weeks 8–9	EVALUATION
Week 10	COMPILING A PORTFOLIO

Second Course

Weeks 1–3	REPORTING INFORMATION, including RESEARCH and an ANNOTATED BIBLIOGRAPHY
Weeks 4–7	ARGUING A POSITION, including a TOPIC PROPOSAL and RESEARCH
Weeks 8–9	WRITING A PROPOSAL
Week 10	COMPILING A PORTFOLIO

Courses focusing on personal writing. If you'd like to teach a course that allows students to develop their personal voices and writing styles, you might design a course that combines several genres, including a profile, which requires a firsthand account and an interesting, often personal angle:

14-week Course

Weeks 1–2	PROCESSES of writing, focusing especially on GENERATING IDEAS AND TEXT
Weeks 3–4	LITERACY NARRATIVES
Weeks 5–8	writing a MEMOIR
Weeks 9–11	writing a PROFILE, including lessons on DESCRIBING and DIALOGUE
Weeks 12–14	writing a REFLECTION

Courses focusing on research. A course emphasizing research might use the RESEARCH chapters as a primary focus, moving students through the research process to an essay REPORTING INFORMATION or ARGUING A POSITION:

14-week Course

Weeks 1–2	Examining sample research papers, GENERATING IDEAS AND TEXT
Week 3	Writing a TOPIC PROPOSAL; choosing an appropriate GENRE
Weeks 3–4	FINDING SOURCES and EVALUATING SOURCES

Week 5	Writing an ANNOTATED BIBLIOGRAPHY
Week 6	Writing a REVIEW OF SCHOLARLY LITERATURE
Week 7	Considering appropriate STRATEGIES—ANALYZING CAUSES AND EFFECTS, CLASSIFYING, COMPARING, DEFINING, DESCRIBING, EXPLAINING PROCESSES, NARRATING, and so on; continuing RESEARCH as needed
Week 8–9	Considering appropriate MEDIUM AND DESIGN, BEGINNING AND ENDING, outlining and organizing; begin DRAFTING; GUIDING YOUR READER; QUOTING, PARAPHRASING, AND SUMMARIZING
Weeks 10–11	ASSESSING DRAFTS, GETTING RESPONSE AND REVISING; perhaps including additional RESEARCH
Week 12	ACKNOWLEDGING SOURCES, AVOIDING PLAGIARISM; DOCUMENTATION
Weeks 13–14	Further REVISING, EDITING AND PROOFREADING; may include presentation as PRINT TEXT, SPOKEN TEXT or ELECTRONIC TEXT

Courses focusing on preprofessional writing. A course for students looking for instruction in "practical" writing tasks might look like this one, where students might be encouraged to choose a single topic to research and report on, ultimately composing and presenting a proposal:

14-week Course

Weeks 1–4	Doing RESEARCH, writing a REVIEW OF SCHOLARLY LITERATURE
Weeks 4–8*	REPORTING INFORMATION, including an ABSTRACT—and some attention to the COLLABORATING or MEDIA/DESIGN chapters
Weeks 8–12*	Writing a PROPOSAL, including attention to COLLABORATING, PROCESSES, STRATEGIES, and MEDIA/DESIGN chapters
Weeks 13–14	RÉSUMÉS AND APPLICATION LETTERS

Courses focusing on textual analysis. If you are using *The Norton Field Guide* in combination with an anthology of literature, you might structure a course that combines analysis of literary texts with analysis of a nonfiction text. Such a course might build on students' familiarity with literary analysis and then move to the unfamiliar territory of textual analysis:

10-week Course

| Weeks 1–3 | Readings from the literature anthology, discussion, and informal writing using the chapters on GENERATING IDEAS AND TEXT |
| Weeks 4–6 | LITERARY ANALYSES, with appropriate chapters from PROCESSES and STRATEGIES |

*During the final week of each unit, students might present their findings to the class in the form of a SPOKEN TEXT or ELECTRONIC TEXT.

Weeks 7–9   ANALYZING A TEXT, with the chapter on READING STRATEGIES

Week 10   COMPARING the two analyses, evaluating their work

Courses focusing on a theme. If your course focuses on readings on various themes, such as work, the environment, civic engagement, and so on, you might want students to begin their writing by thinking about the theme, writing informally about readings as a basis for discussion, and then developing essays in response to the concepts they read about rather than writing in a specific genre. You might then ask students to begin by generating ideas and text and do research that leads them to a genre:

15-week Course or Unit

Weeks 1–2   Read essays and respond in writing as part of a discussion. For example, students may post ongoing responses to a discussion board, share comments at specified times in an online chat room, or just talk about their written responses in small groups. This method helps students respond not only to the text but also to other viewpoints and opinions. The READING STRATEGIES and COLLABORATING chapters may be helpful here.

Weeks 2–3   Have students explore topics in relation to the theme using the activities in the chapter on GENERATING IDEAS AND TEXT; and then do some research, first FINDING SOURCES and then EVALUATING those SOURCES.

Weeks 4–5   Students choose a GENRE they will use to approach their topic and refer to the appropriate GENRE, STRATEGIES, and PROCESSES chapters as needed.

Weeks 6–9,   Repeat this basic structure,

10–13   either with new readings on different aspects of the theme or on sub-themes of the main theme. If you're teaching a 10-week course, repeat only once.

Week 10   Provide time for GETTING

or 14   RESPONSE AND REVISING and helping students as they work on COMPILING A PORT-FOLIO.

Remember that your best resources for course designs are experienced instructors and graduate students in your school. You may also find useful ideas for course plans online.

21 Teaching about Rhetorical Situations

Students need to understand that they are always part of a rhetorical situation: Whenever they speak or write, they participate in a context that includes purpose, audience, genre, stance, and medium / design—and they need to address all those elements if their writing is to succeed. *The Norton Field Guide to Writing* offers a general introduction to the rhetorical situation in Chapters 1–5 and genre-specific questions to help students define the rhetorical situation they face when writing in any of the genres. In addition, each chapter in Part 6 includes questions to help students choose appropriate media and design their text to suit their own rhetorical situation. One way to teach rhetorical situations using *The Norton Field Guide*, then, is simply to ask students to respond to the questions as they prepare to write. You can also ask them to analyze the model essays in the chapters to see how the writers addressed their rhetorical situations. If, however, you'd like to do more, here are some ideas for teaching the rhetorical situation. Although each aspect of the rhetorical situation is considered separately, each one affects the others; each, in fact, cannot be considered apart from the others or emphasized too strongly without comparable consideration of the rest.

Purpose

In its most basic form, purpose in writing is simply the answer to the question, "What does the writer want this piece of writing to accomplish?" Usually we write to affect readers in some way: to change their minds, to get them to do something, to make them think or feel something, to share some thought or experience we've had. In fact, we often have several purposes when we write. You might ask your students to list their purposes before they write in order to give them a goal or after they've written a draft so readers can assess how well they achieved their purposes. These purposes might be listed as "primary" and "secondary." For example, a student might write an argument whose primary goal is to get readers to agree with the student's position, but the student may also want to entertain readers and demonstrate the ability to think clearly and do appropriate research.

It's also useful to remind students that their audience has purposes for reading, too: We read instructions to find out how to assemble a bookcase; we read op-ed pieces to understand the arguments over public policy; we read *The Onion* online to be entertained. When students write, then, they need to consider why their audience is reading their work. Again, having students identify their audience's purposes helps them see what they need to do to satisfy their readers' needs while meeting their own purposes.

There are questions focusing students' attention on purpose in the guidelines on "Considering the Rhetorical Situation" sections throughout the *Field Guide*.

Audience

The role of audience can be tricky for students because their writing in composition courses often must satisfy at least two audiences: the audience to which their writing is addressed (classmates, newspaper editors, scholars in various fields, informed but curious people, to name a few) and the course instructor, whose purposes in reading may differ considerably from the audiences the student writer is ostensibly addressing. A good way to deal with this potential conflict is to discuss it openly: Acknowledge the complexity of your students' tasks and point out ways in which your reading may differ from their chosen audience's. For example, if students are writing a report for an audience of their peers, that audience may well be very interested in understanding the concepts and information presented but forgive organizational problems or formal errors that you as instructor must take into account. If students are arguing a position in an essay for readers of a local newspa-

per, that audience will likely focus on the writers' perspectives and the force of their prose, while you will be on the lookout for gaps in their logic or misuse of source material as well as even-handedness in their presentation of differing arguments. Such explanations may not make students' jobs easier, but students will understand better how their writing must satisfy your requirements while meeting their other audience's expectations, too.

There are questions focusing students' attention on audience in the guidelines on "Considering the Rhetorical Situation" sections throughout the *Field Guide*.

Genre

Genre can be either a starting point or a destination. The Guides to Writing in each of the Genre chapters will help students write in a specific genre—NARRATIVE, ANALYSIS, REPORT, ARGUMENT, MEMOIR, and so on. Many writing instructors find it useful to teach specific genres: A body of information on the genre can be taught, genre-specific readings can be discussed by the whole class, and student activities and assignments can be coordinated. For example, students can easily work in groups to determine how well one another's drafts achieve the key features of a specific genre.

Sometimes, though, the genre emerges from the writer's needs. Students may study a subject and begin with a topic on which they want to write—but they don't know what they want to write until they've thought, generated text, and conducted research. At some point in that exploratory process they will choose a goal and with it a genre that will let them achieve it. So in a class of twenty, you might have five students arguing a position, six drafting memoirs or reflections, four writing proposals, and another five reporting information. This approach may seem chaotic, but it needn't be: Students working on similar projects can work collaboratively while you move from group to group, giving help as they need it. No matter what they're writing, they'll need to produce drafts, and at that point you can ask them to read and respond to one another's drafts, perhaps twice: once within the groups (where they can use their familiarity with the genre to assess one another's success) and once by other students (who, with fresh eyes, can respond to the content and clarity better than the students who have been working together).

Each genre represented in *The Norton Field Guide* is described in terms of its Key Features. These Key Features may be approached as textual features—what good examples of the text include or embody—or as features that audiences expect when they read a specific genre. For example, readers of evaluations expect that the object of the evaluation will be described for those who are unfamiliar with it and that the criteria on which the evaluation is based will be identified; if those features aren't present, readers will likely reject the evaluation as incomplete. This approach often motivates students more than the textual approach does, as students often see value in meeting audience expectations but have little interest in crafting a well-formed text for its own sake. The same holds true for the medium and design and stance of a text: Have students think about or do research on what audiences expect of texts in a specific genre so they can meet those expectations.

It's also good to remember that genres are seldom pure. Instead, genres are often combined; for example, someone arguing a position may well include a memoir as evidence, an analysis of a key text on the subject, and a proposal at the end. Therefore, you may wish to encourage students to consult additional Genre chapters in *The Norton Field Guide* for help as they write— or you could consider creating hybrid assignments, such as a combined evaluation and proposal or memoir and reflection. You might even explore multigenre papers, which Tom Romano defines as "composed of many genres and subgenres, each piece self-contained, making a point of its own, yet connected by theme or topic and sometimes by language, images, and content. In addition to many genres, a multigenre paper may also contain many voices, not just the author's. The trick is to make such a paper hang together" (ix).

There are questions focusing students' attention on genre in the guidelines on "Considering the Rhetorical Situation" sections throughout the *Field Guide*.

Stance

We can help students convey their stance in their writing by helping them think about their relationship to their subject and audience and by helping them create the appropriate voice to reflect that stance. Ask students to identify the tone they wish to adopt: serious? ironic? playful? cynical? scholarly? optimistic? neutral or self-effacing? Something else? Have them try out their chosen tone by writing a paragraph and then seeing if readers identify the tone for which they're striving. Or have students find a piece of writing that achieves the tone they wish to adopt and analyze it or imitate it to see how the author creates that tone. Consider having students rewrite a text several ways—either a passage you provide or one of their drafts—to attempt various tones, and then discuss with the class what they did to achieve them.

You can use similar techniques to help students develop voice in their writing. Scholars—like many writers—are split over the nature of voice in writing. In one view, the voice with which we write must be authentic and true to ourselves; in this view, voice can't be taught, but only encouraged. Many students begin with this first position. In contrast are those who believe that our selves, and thus our voices, are socially constructed and don't reflect a coherent self as much as they do our participation in a social group or discourse community. As Toby Fulwiler suggests in "Claiming My Voice," writers can and do move between these poles easily. Writers can learn to adjust their voice to suit both their desire to express their authentic selves and their need to adopt various voices to suit their purpose, audience, and genre. Doing so, however, requires awareness of how the various decisions they make as writers come together to create their voice. Here is a sampling of exercises, adapted from Dona Hickey's *Developing a Written Voice* (1993):

- Have students transcribe a short spoken text from television or radio. Then rewrite it for different audiences and occasions. They can also rewrite their own drafts in the same way.

- Have students write a paragraph using only one-syllable words and sentences one to ten words long. Share some aloud and discuss how the voices differ and what other genres they resemble: children's stories, parables, religious language. Examine some closely to see what features of the prose lend each a distinctive voice.

- Analyze texts that provide good examples of colloquial, informal, and formal voices. See what happens when students rearrange (without altering) the words in some of the sentences. How does the voice change as the word order changes?

- Then have the students write an imitation of one paragraph of the model, maintaining the sentence structure but changing the topic. Ask them to discuss the way they solved the problems of doing so and how the structure limited or enabled their writing.

There are questions focusing students' attention on stance in the guidelines on "Considering the Rhetorical Situation" sections throughout the *Field Guide*.

Media / Design

As students become familiar with addressing the rhetorical situation of any writing task, you will want to further their understanding by having them explore different text mediums. Students are generally more familiar with print text than with other forms, such as electronic or spoken text—but they may not understand how the design of a print text affects their rhetorical situation. You might present a brief text in several formats—handwritten on notebook paper, typed and double-spaced, printed in two justified columns—and ask students to explore the differences in rhetorical effect each design makes. Asking students to consider how a web page might be better suited for conveying an argument or how a speech might be more effective for a proposal will enable them to apply rhetorical situations to a broader spectrum of writing situations. See Chapter 30 in this book for more ideas and strategies for teaching about media and design.

There are questions focusing students' attention on media and design in the guidelines on "Considering the Rhetorical Situation" sections throughout the *Field Guide*.

Useful Readings

George, Diana. "From Analysis to Design: Visual Communication in the Teaching of Writing." *College Composition and Communication* 54 (September 2002): 11–39.

Ede, Lisa and Andrea Lunsford. "Audience Addressed/Audience Invoked: The Role of Audience in Composition Theory and Pedagogy." *College Composition and Communication* 35:2 (May 1984).

Elbow, Peter. "Closing My Eyes as I Speak: An Argument for Ignoring Audience." *College English* 49 (January 1987): 50–69.

Fulwiler, Toby. "Claiming My Voice." *Voices on Voice: Perspectives, Definitions, Inquiry.* Ed. Kathleen Blake Yancey. Urbana, IL: National Council of Teachers of English, 1994. 36–47.

Hickey, Dona J. *Developing a Written Voice.* Mountain View, CA: Mayfield, 1993.

Romano, Tom. *Blending Genre, Altering Style: Writing Multigenre Papers.* Portsmouth, NH: Boynton/Cook, 2000.

Literacy (and Other) Narratives **22**

Brady Allen

Narration tells a story, but narrative is not quite as simple as that. We tell stories many ways, and we tell stories for any number of reasons. A narrative could be a personal anecdote that sets up or that makes an argument, for example, a detailed account of paying too much for your auto repair to demonstrate that computerized engine diagnostics are not as valuable as mechanics who can roll up their sleeves and root around under the hood. We might narrate to relay information; a newspaper reporter might write a straightforward story about a new, technology based restaurant where customers order their food with a keyboard and monitor and have it sent from the kitchen on a conveyor belt. Or, we might use narration in a business letter such as a claim letter to that auto repair shop when its computer diagnosed a dead catalytic converter but the problem turned out to be bad spark plug cables or a claim letter to that techno-restaurant after your food was ruined by a diner with a cold because there was no sneeze-guard on the food conveyor. Narrative is flexible.

A literacy narrative tells a story about some event that was important to a person's development as a reader and writer. That event may be momentous or it may be fleeting, noticed only by the writer. It may have happened years ago or fairly recently. Whatever topic students choose, they have many ways of telling their story. Chapter 6 of *The Norton Field Guide* provides students with models and strategies. Here is some advice on helping students tell their stories well.

Sharing Stories

Narrative is the description of an event or series of events. So, while you're teaching narrative, tell your students as many stories as you can. Many of them might be writing-related. Walk into the room on the first day and tell a story—one incoming students will enjoy—about your experiences as a writer, teacher, or former student. You might describe the time your racy love note to the guy or girl you were dating in high school was intercepted by your health teacher—who then used it in her lecture about human sexuality. And ask students to tell their stories aloud in class, too. Ask your students to talk about their past writing experiences, and ask questions that prod them to reveal more detail and significance. This informal discussion is a great way to get you and your students in a storytelling mode together.

Writers write, and teachers should, too. Disprove that annoying old saying about how "Those who can, do, and those who can't, teach." Early on, share your work with them: memoir, fiction, simple narrative accounts. Or tell jokes; that's narrative, too. Point out choices you made and strategies you used in your own writing. It's only fair that you share with them, since they're going to be sharing with you. You'll get a chance to talk about the all-important need to focus on audience. You'll be telling your students that, although you wrote your pieces for yourself in a sense, it's important that the stance, purpose, details, and significance of your work are clear to them, too. Encourage them to discuss your work with you, and you'll all be a lot more comfortable when it comes time to discuss their narratives. You might let them respond to a draft of your writing (don't cheat and show them a revised and polished piece) in a whole-class response workshop (described in Chapter 5 of this book). Respond to their suggestions as one writer to another. Discuss your reactions to their comments. In other words, show them that you're not just the teacher, but a writer and a student of writing, too.

Using the Readings and Teaching the Key Features

You can use the readings in Chapter 6 of *The Norton Field Guide* to model key features of literacy narratives, which are also key features of any narrative. Each offers a well-told story, and you might point out what "well-told" consists of. In "All Over But the Shoutin'," for example, Rick Bragg offers a masterfully drawn unsavory character in the narrator's father and builds suspense as we wonder how the narrator will behave at this, their final meeting. Richard Bullock's piece can illustrate how vivid description might include such details as fuzzy African violet leaves, withering looks, and dialogue between a waitress and a snotty kid. And Bragg's piece also shows how significance can be conveyed by portraying past events through the filter of the present: The narrator sees, now, that by choking back an angry response to his father's questions, "I gave up the only real chance I would ever have to accuse him." You can bring in other narratives to share with your class and invite them to bring examples as well.

Getting Started and Choosing a Topic

So you've told stories to your students, listened to some of theirs, and read some good examples. Now how do you get them started writing in preparation for their own narratives? Narrative writing revolves around five things: people, places, objects, events, and "self." Here are examples of five exercises I give my students within the first week of class to get them thinking, somewhat indirectly, about possible topics for their narratives.

1. Who are some people from your past that impacted your life, taught you, "wronged" you, interested you, or, maybe, merely amused you? Write a short paragraph each for several of them. You may include one or two people that you're still in contact with or close to, but try to write about three or four that you haven't seen for a while or didn't actually know all that well. Try to touch upon a couple of traits, attributes, characteristics, or quirks for each person. Use specific details.

2. What/where are some of your favorite places? Write a short paragraph each for several of them. Focus on smaller places. (Instead of Pennsylvania, in other words, think of the Summit Diner off Exit 17 in eastern Pennsylvania. Instead of your parents' house, think of your mom's flower bed next to the front porch [where everything was always dead] or the cardboard box on the aluminum garage shelf where your dad hid [or thought he was hiding] his *Playboys*.) Try to recall at least five places. In fact, the places don't necessarily have to be your "favorite" places; think of them, simply, as places that you remember. Give specific details for each place.

3. Think of some objects/items/possessions from your past: Things you owned, things you borrowed, things you wanted but never got, maybe. What about things that were simply in your proximity sometimes? (Some examples: your first baseball glove, your dance shoes, your Britney Spears or Batman poster, a SAFE SEX poster in your school, a family photograph, a Husky pencil, those too-small sweatpants your neighbor always wore that revealed a little too much, your brother's KEEP OUT sign on his bedroom door, an ugly old chair in the living room—anything is fair game here.) List 25–30 things from your past. Now, choose eight of these things and describe them in detail, writing a short paragraph for each one, explaining what its "role" was in your life. How did it affect you? What was its purpose or use?

4. What event . . . ? Write a short line answering as many of these questions as you can. If it's something you don't want others to know, write it cryptically or "in code." What event . . . made you question yourself? made you question someone or something else? made you mad? made you laugh? made you nervous? scared you? scarred you? was your most forbidden? made you proud? made you feel guilty? made you happy? confused you? excited you? matured you? made you lie? taught you? made you curious? made you a little sad? made you question fairness?

5. So, who are you? Think first about "labels" that might be applied to you (girl, flirtatious, Asian, tall, geeky, upper class, Catholic, auto mechanic, etc.) and describe yourself by looking at yourself from the outside, perhaps through the eyes of another person. What stereo-

types are sometimes applied to you because of these "labels"? Second, view yourself from the inside, from *your own* perspective. What are some of the stereotypes that you can dispel? What are some that might be true? What are some things about you that others wouldn't know through a mere surface-level encounter? Flatter yourself, but be honest, too. Finally, think of yourself as a stir-fry dish. What would you be called, and what would be the primary ingredients? Explain.

The key to these exercises is very specific and focused writing prompts that lead students away from obvious "big picture" topics. Notice how I try to incorporate very short narrative images in the questions themselves.

If you're teaching a literacy narrative, you might want to direct these exercises: people that affected your literacy, places where you wrote, objects that were connected to your literacy, "literary events," how *you're* a writer and reader. But "literacy" can be a very broad term, and I think it's a good idea to present it to students broadly. Consider this: Literacy can be drawing or painting, being well versed in the rules or the mastery of a sport or activity, finding the right words to explain to parents why you got home so late past your curfew, repairing a car or building something, making a quilt, or talking trash about a friend. Almost any topic can relate to literacy, one way or another, so more general prompts can help your students who aren't able to think of a topic involving writing or reading alone.

Once students have brainstormed in these five areas, have them do a clustering exercise to see what items match up directly and tangentially from their lists. Good topics are often smaller events (with people, places, and objects) that can be made larger through linking elements and making connections, choosing appropriate details, and finding significance. Letting students know before they choose topics that you're looking for writing that includes connections, details, and significance helps them understand what topics might work or not work so well.

Drafting and Revising

Strong exercises to help students generate ideas and text can make drafting easier. We might see "drafting" as a very broad term; often, after students have arrived upon topics, revisited their first writing exercises on people, places, objects, and events, read and done more writing with a focus on the topic they've chosen, most of the preliminary work of drafting is out of the way. Have your students write about the ideas they've generated, and encourage them to add specific details. By doing these activities, they've generated the most commonly omitted details of any narrative, and they are ready to develop a draft.

Ask students to begin their rough draft with "I," to tell the story from their own perspective and to fill in their details where appropriate. Telling the story directly is often the easiest way for students to get it on paper or screen and gives them a text to work with.

When they've completed a draft, consider having students rewrite, starting their second drafts with an engaging line that you pull from the middle or end of their first drafts. You can do this by walking around the class, quickly skimming their drafts, or by looking them over once they've posted them online. You may be met with a little resistance, but explain that there are hundreds of ways they could approach this draft, so why go only with the first? Your strategy in choosing a line for them to begin with is twofold: to find a "hook," an engaging line that gets them right into the heart of the story, and to make them look at the chronological possibilities of narrative.

Organizing, Transitions, and Time Markers

Events happen in some order in life, but our memories can put them in any order we want. Narrative writing can bend time, too, and one of the hardest things to teach about narration is how to make good choices about order and clarity. Here are a few exercises that might help:

- Have students literally "cut and paste" a draft. Not on the computer—have them print it out and then cut and separate each and every paragraph. Have them trade draft pieces with a classmate (preferably one that hasn't seen this draft at all), and have that classmate piece it back together. If the classmate has trouble, it's a sign that the author might need to work on the sequence of events. But also invite students to consider the possibility that stories don't always have to be told in chronological order. Scenes can be reordered or "collaged" to reveal meaning or to make significance clearer.

- Play "Stand-Up Comic" as a transition exercise. Write out a number of silly, odd, or "confusing" sentences with no context. Lead an exercise where your students have to find ways to connect two non-related sentences by using the old standby that many comedians use: "And speaking of . . . "

- For time markers, explain that every *time a sentence or paragraph shifts in time, a reference should be made to something significant that has already happened in the narrative*: Before I went in the Navy. . . . After my sister gave birth. . . . At the same time as the bird flew into the window . . .

- Tell a story in class. Seated in a circle, have each student make up a story, adding one or two lines and building the story from the lines told by the previous speaker. Each new speaker has to start with a time marker: "Three years ago . . . " "Before Megan passed her driving test . . . " "Right after Kenny screamed for rebellion. . . . "

- When you read, look for good examples of time markers and save them to show your students, as they will benefit from seeing examples by experienced writers. Ask students to bring examples from their own reading.

Choosing and Maintaining a Stance

Fiction writers often speak of the writer's voice, but writers disagree on a definition of just what "voice" means: do writers have an "authentic" voice that reflects their true selves, or do they construct various voices to meet various rhetorical demands? You may find that talking about stance avoids this predicament by focusing on the ways writers may alter their stance to achieve their purposes. You can practice in the classroom by having your students rewrite short narrative passages, adopting different tones: angry, passionate, indifferent, cynical. You can also ask students to alter the narrator's point of view, retelling Bragg's story from his father's perspective or Nichol's from her English teacher's point of view. Or go outside the narrative and retell it from another perspective entirely—Bragg's from the point of view of a psychologist, or Nichol's from an official at the state Education Department.

If you're brave, you can demonstrate orally. Dust off that old John Wayne impersonation and then try telling the same tale with your bad go at Britney Spears or Jack Nicholson. Ask students to add their own versions.

Find and share examples of writing that has a strong stance and ask students to bring examples. You might also, by analyzing the language of some examples, show that stance and tone are often a matter of word choice and sentence length. For more on the relationship between voice and stance, see Chapter 21 in this book.

Adding Detail

Description has to be memorable. Think of a man (or woman) wearing only a coat, opening the coat quickly. What do you remember the most? That detail is probably the most appropriate for your writing. And it's not always the most common or expected detail; it could be the person's navel the size of a half-dollar, or it could be a tattoo of Batman's head on the flasher's left thigh.

Using comics and films. Comic books and graphic novels have some of the clearest narrative drives of any style of writing, and the authors of these works know which details to include and which to leave out. Since narrative writing is often about action and "visual" or sensory stimulus along with some reflection, why not use some comics as models? Students can rewrite scenes based on the dialogue bubbles and comic panels. What details do they need to add to match the comics' imagery and narrative drive without the help of the images and actions in the panels? Conversely, have students rewrite their narratives in comic book form and discuss what happens. They may draw details they can then add to their writing.

A similar activity can be done with film, something a friend and colleague of mine does with great success. For example, play a brief (3–5 minutes or less) scene without any sound. Play it again and have the class discuss details they notice as the scene unfolds. Then have students try to write dialogue that they think fits the details. Play the clip again with sound and discuss the different interpretations.

Showing, not telling. Stories are told, yes. But the creative writing mantra—Show, don't tell!—is actually valid, if we approach it knowing that we can't and shouldn't get rid of telling altogether. Think of "telling" as the glue that holds the showing together. And what is "showing"? You might demonstrate by give them a one-person show. I sometimes walk into class and play-act like I'm drunk or otherwise not with it: I'll take off my shoes, drop things, and say inappropriate things. When the show's over, I'll have students recreate the scene on paper.

Have your students try one or both of these strategies:

- Use *sensory detail* (taste, touch, sound, smell, sight) to go beyond adjectives and adverbs. For example, ask students to use *concrete nouns* and *vivid verbs* to portray words like "big" or "angrily."

- Mix *dialogue* or *action* with any necessary reflection. Ask students to add several lines of dialogue to a reflective paragraph or to replace a passage that tells something about a character with a passage in which the character does something that shows what had been told.

Consider, too, these familiar phrases: "action speaks louder than words" and "a picture paints a thousand words." That's what appropriate detail is all about: pictures and actions transferred through the written word. We can make language move (action), and we can make it vivid (a picture).

Showing students a model—a brief paragraph that tells, followed by a longer revision that shows—can help them see what "showing" is and understand how significance comes about through reflection. An example I wrote can be found in Chapter 27 of this book, "Teaching about Writing Processes." But you can also make up your own.

Articulating the Narrative's Significance

Though there are many narrative approaches to choose from, after helping students experiment with tone and details you should present theme or "significance" to the students. Every writing has a theme, which starts, simply, as an abstract noun such as love, fear, or determination. You might help students hypothesize about the theme of their narrative early, so they can choose appropriate details, but remember that their theme or significance may not reveal itself until they start writing or have even finished a complete draft and asked someone else what it means.

In a narrative, the writer is often both a participant (a character) and an observer (a distanced commentator and interpreter). This commentator or interpreter often reveals the significance. A narrative is not a fairy tale, so readers are not looking for "the moral of the story." Steer students away from such endings as, "And so I <u>learned</u> never to put glue in my little sister's milk." Also, try to help students avoid vague expressions such as "I learned to strive hard for my goals" or "I learned that nothing can stop me." We are looking for the significance, which is often revealed through the narrator's descriptions of events as he or she looks back at them, revealing a present perspective on a past event: The observer relays the significance while telling and showing the participant's story. Other students who are not as close to the topic are often better at finding significance as opposed to a moral. Don't force authors to identify a theme too early; perhaps let a classmate lead them in that direction in a workshop.

Evaluating Narratives

How do we grade narratives? Despite the subjective nature of reading and evaluating a narrative, it can be done. You might present your students with a rubric before you actually grade their work. List every single criterion you could possibly use to evaluate it (or show the class your list and see if they have anything to add—see Chapter 9 in this book on responding to writing for tips on establishing criteria collaboratively). Explain that, depending upon their narrative choices, some criteria might not apply, giving them stylistic options. Below is the rubric I use for narratives. Notice the N/A column? This section is essential because of all the possibilities that narratives present.

Writing and Creative Writing

Despite any tensions between so-called creative writing and other English composition and literature courses, in truth, there's usually little separation beyond preference and

Narrative	Very Strong	Strong	Average	Weak	N/A	Explanation
Beginning						
Stance						
Significance						
Details (characters, setting, action)						
Dialogue						
Organization						
Point of view						
Transitions, time markers						
Ending						
Grammar, mechanics (sentence structure, punctuation, etc.)						

politics. All writing is creative in the sense that it wasn't there before the author put it to paper. He or she created it. And each of the divides between modes of studying writing has some sort of bridge over it; for example, narrative writing in a composition course draws a lot from the storytelling features of creative writing or fiction writing. But you don't have to be a "creative writer" in the categorical sense to teach narrative or to write it yourself. Creative writing strategies *can* be employed in composition classes. One book on fiction writing is especially appropriate for classes that teach narratives, especially literacy narratives and memoirs: Stephen King's *On Writing*. This book is a hybrid: On one side it's a compelling memoir or series of narratives on King's development as a writer, and on the other side it's a simple "how to" on telling stories using detail, significance, and other things we've touched on here. As a bonus, many students already know and like King's stories.

Finally, you don't have to be "imaginative" or shuffle around in bunny slippers while mumbling philosophical ideas to yourself to be qualified to write narrative. Imagination evolves from memory, reflection, careful attention to detail, and good storytelling—and these skills, which we all have, are what's important in writing good narratives.

Other Useful Chapters in the *Field Guide*

1–5 RHETORICAL SITUATIONS
15 MEMOIRS
21 COLLABORATING
22 GENERATING IDEAS AND TEXT
28 BEGINNING AND ENDING
29 GUIDING YOUR READER
32 COMPARING AND CONTRASTING
35 DIALOGUE
37 NARRATING
23–27 DRAFTING, ASSESSING A DRAFT, REVISING, EDITING, PROOFREADING

Useful Readings

Bishop, Wendy. "Crossing the Lines: On Creative Composition and Composing Creative Writing." *Colors of a Different Horse: Rethinking Creative Writing Theory and Pedagogy.* Ed. Wendy Bishop and Hans Ostrom. Urbana, IL: National Council of Teachers of English, 1994. 181–197.

King, Stephen. *On Writing: A Memoir of the Craft.* New York: Pocket-Simon & Schuster, 2000.

Mirtz, Ruth. " 'You Want Us to Do WHAT?" How to Get the Most Out of Unexpected Writing Assignments." *Elements of Alternate Style: Essays on Writing and Revision.* Ed. Wendy Bishop. Portsmouth, NH: Boynton/Cook, 1997. 105–115.

23 Analyzing Texts

A student reading her history textbook notices that it presents a different explanation for an event than her high school textbook did and wonders which one is correct. She sets the book aside and picks up a magazine where ads for various creams each say one is perfect for her skin. Flipping to an article in the magazine, she reads about a politician's campaign to save the environment, though she thinks she remembers hearing on the news that the same politician had voted against a bill protecting water quality. This student, like everyone else, is bombarded with information that must be carefully analyzed, not just for its truth or falsity, but also for the ways in which it is designed to influence us, both overtly and covertly. Chapter 7, ANALYZING A TEXT, teaches students to read a text critically and examine it carefully.

Analyzing a Text

Many students arrive in college with limited experience reading nonfiction texts critically. Their high school English curricula probably focused on the reading and interpretation of literature, often characterized as articulating a response to literary texts. In their other courses, they were expected to read their textbooks not as rhetorical documents but as unbiased factual material. As a result, a close, critical reading of a nonfiction text presents a new challenge; they must learn to read in different ways and apply techniques they may have learned in literature study to informative or argumentative texts. Their goal, however, is not response or interpretation but analysis and, possibly, evaluation of the text to determine how the language and structure of the text and its use of aspects of the rhetorical situation attempt to guide readers' thinking. In this assignment, students should not try to create a coherent interpretation of the text as they would in a literature class; rather they should aim to take the text apart in order to understand its purpose and the ways its author uses textual elements to achieve that purpose. The resulting essay uses evidence students create through analyses of the text to support their assertions about the way the text works—and, often, how well. Here's what first-year graduate teaching assistant Andrea Nay has to say about teaching students to analyze a text:

> First, I must remember that this type of writing is brand-new to many of my students. As Sheena, one of my students, writes, "I think the reason why it's coming so hard is that I never had to do any serious English work." The most important common point

I found is that most of my students are quite happy to write their own opinion, but academic analysis comes far more difficult to them. Jana, another student, notes, "I am not good at this kind of analysis because I am an opinionated person and there are not too many places for opinion in this paper." I feel I may have confused some students by starting off the unit having them write me a "Dear Andrea" letter responding to the focus article with their own opinion. That started them, right off the bat, lacing their analysis with their own biased comments. This carried through into their papers, and my workshops and conferences were mainly spent helping them extract their own "rants" from portions of their drafts.

As Nay correctly notes, students are more accustomed to stating their own opinion or reacting to ideas than to analyzing nonfiction texts. Therefore, students often find the task of analyzing a text challenging, so you need to offer considerable help. Modeling, walking the class through analytical techniques, and encouraging even modest progress are all likely to be needed at various points along the way as students try out unfamiliar ways of thinking and writing.

Using the Readings and Teaching the Key Features

You can use readings not only to help students understand how a textual analysis might work but also to help them see what they already know about analyzing texts. You might introduce David Rubin's "It's the Same Old Song" by playing the Eagles' song "Hotel California" and asking students to discuss the meaning of the lyrics. You might give students copies of the Gettysburg Address to analyze before reading what William Safire makes of it. And you might ask students to discuss the implications of some contemporary print ads or television commercials to introduce them to Doug Lantry's analysis of three soap ads from the past. Asking students to identify the Key Features of each text—where the writer provides a summary of the text, pays attention to its context, presents a clear interpretation or judgment, and offers reasonable support for his or her conclusions—will help them understand each writer's techniques and the demands of their assignment. After students have read these three analyses, they'll have background to help them see the techniques each writer uses, and they'll begin to exercise their own critical reading skills.

Getting Started and Choosing a Text to Analyze

Choosing an appropriate text for your students to analyze is your first challenge. A good way to understand some of the difficulties the text will present for your students—and whether or not it's a good one to assign—is to analyze it yourself, using some of the techniques you'll ask your students to use. Guidelines for choosing an appropriate text include the following:

- Look for relatively brief texts. Newspaper editorials are often good choices, as they typically focus on a single, narrowly defined topic and deal with it in a few hundred words at most. Op-ed essays can be useful, though they sometimes are less focused than editorials. Even letters to the editor of newspapers can be fruitful choices. Other possibilities include sections from college or high school textbooks, parts of longer news or magazine articles, texts of Web sites, and civic or government documents of various sorts.

- Choose a text with a single, clear thesis statement. Many op-ed pieces contain more than one statement that may serve as a thesis for a section of the essay. Some begin with a fairly lengthy introduction, followed by a thesis placed roughly one-third through the essay. Single-thesis texts may represent only part of the pantheon of possible essay styles, but they function like frogs in biology classes: simple, but still complex enough to be challenging to dissect.

- Look for a text with a structure that can be outlined without undue difficulty and that won't require students to spend too much time figuring out the meaning. Most instructors find that almost any text, even one that seems simple, grows in complexity and depth as students analyze it, and the point of the assignment is the analysis—not mastery of a complex concept.

- Know how much contextual research you'll ask of your students. If you choose a text on a subject of contemporary interest, students will know or be able to find out easily about the context of the information or argument. A document from the past, however, may require students to research the context within which the text was written.

- Consider the emotional response students may have to the text. If you choose a text on a controversial topic, you'll need to deal with students' responses to the text and its stance, allowing them to articulate their response before and during their analysis and drafting. As teaching assistant Sharon Tjaden noted while teaching an analysis, "My students are struggling with separating their responses and their opinions from analyzing this article." The more controversial the topic, the more difficult it is for students to respond objectively.

Once you've chosen an appropriate text, you might introduce the textual analysis assignment by modeling some brief analyses of visual texts or advertisements, letters to the editor, or other texts, including texts similar to the one students will analyze. Asking students to participate in these analyses will show them how much they already know about texts and how sensitive they are to nuances of language, arguments, and the ways in which texts attempt to manipulate their responses.

Doing the Analysis

A Guide to Analyzing a Text provides detailed advice to help students understand what they need to do and how to go about doing it. Once they have developed a tentative thesis, you should direct them to chapter 38, READING STRATEGIES, where they can find detailed advice on reading carefully along with several methods for analyzing texts. Once they've done several analyses from that chapter, they'll be ready to analyze their text's rhetorical situation, rethink their thesis, and rough out a conclusion.

Consider asking students to write answers to the questions in the "Previewing a Text" and "Annotating" sections of Chapter 38 in the *Field Guide*. You might ask them to annotate the text they're to analyze and compare their annotations with other students'. You might explain that who we are—our thoughts, experiences, and values—are a kind of filter through which we read or absorb information and that we have to recognize this filter and account for it as we begin to analyze. A good approach is to write a first response where we can get all of our reactions out in the open; only at that point can we read the article more objectively. Asking students to play the Believing and Doubting game (described in Chapter 38), either on paper or orally in groups, can help them see the text from at least two perspectives—and get past their own response to the text's ideas, so they can start to develop an analysis. Thus, you can avoid the problem Andrea Nay describes.

You can structure an analysis of the text in several ways. Here are some options:

- Choose the methods of analyzing that the class should complete, or work together with the class to decide which methods are most suitable for the text and the assignment as you've created it.
- Treat each method of analyzing as a separate assignment; for example, each student might be asked to create a top-

ical outline, a functional outline, a summary, or a list of patterns. Students might then compare their analyses in groups or as part of a class discussion.

- Have students work in groups, each group having as its assignment an analysis of the text based on a specific method or on a subset of that method: one group creates a functional outline while other groups look for patterns: of sentence types, of imagery, of repeated words or phrases, and so on. Then the groups could present their findings to the class for all to share.
- Have students analyze the argument as a group activity (see "Analyzing the Argument" in Chapter 38 in the *Field Guide*).
- Give students a quiz on argument fallacies. Many students enjoy ferreting out fallacies as well as deciding whether they are used as fallacies in the rhetorical context of a text, and a quiz really does provide incentive to read and study them. Students may later complain that they're seeing fallacies everywhere, an opportunity for you to smile and nod in response.

Writing an Analysis

The hardest part of writing a critical analysis is moving from analysis to a conclusion. At this point students must shift from collecting information through various analytical activities to creating a coherent essay based on a unifying theme: its response to its rhetorical situation. They have examined the text in three ways: in terms of what the text says, how it works, and what it means. Their analysis essay should include a brief summary that outlines what the text says, but it may then move in one of several directions.

How the text works. In this type of analysis, students focus on the means by which the text gets its meaning across. They may identify a particular strategy of appealing to the text's audience, characteristic use of language, or ways of presenting material (such as metaphors, examples, anecdotes, and explanations). They may draw on their functional outlines to show how the text's organization moves the reader from point to point to a particular conclusion or overall effect.

What the text means. Students focusing on the meaning of the text may focus on their topical outlines to show how the text moves from beginning to ending, building and elaborating on a single overall meaning—or to show that it begins on one topic but diverges from it. They may focus on the logic of individual statements and how that logic either does or does not hold from statement to statement. They may trace patterns of imagery or the writer's use of "loaded" language to show how the writer is writing from a particular stance or slanting the meaning to a particular purpose.

How well the text works. In either case, the analysis may also lead to an evaluation of the text's effectiveness, based on criteria drawn from the elements of the rhetorical situation:

- How effective is this text in meeting its purpose?

- How effective is it in meeting the needs and expectations of its audience or affecting its audience as its author intended?

- How well does it use the conventions of its genre?

- How well does its author convey his or her stance?

- And how well does it employ design in its chosen medium to achieve its aims?

Having students answer these questions about the text's rhetorical situation can help them revise their tentative thesis based on the results of their analysis.

Providing Evidence

Once students clarify their thesis, you may need to help them draw evidence from their analyses to support their assertions. To do this, have students look through their materials for patterns: What shows up more than once, either within a single analysis or across two or more? What relationships can be seen in the information? What do these patterns tell students about the text? How can they fit what they learn together? You may need to help them look for clusters of related information that they can use to create an outline to guide them as they draft their essays. "Ways of Organizing a Textual Analysis" can help them think about how to structure their essays, and "Writing Out a Draft" offers several options for drafting, which may have to be done in several stages. Be aware that the novelty of the textual analysis assignment will make it difficult for many students, so schedule ample time for conferences, workshops, Getting Response and Revising activities both from Chapter 7 and from Chapter 25, and opportunities for students to assess their own writing, using Chapter 24; many students will need several attempts before they fully understand the demands of the assignment.

Evaluating Textual Analyses

Focus on how well students apply the Key Features in their own writing. In addition, you should consider your goal for assigning this task: some instructors ask students for well-organized, polished final drafts; others, however, use the assignment to improve students' critical reading and reasoning abilities and are forgiving of structural problems or even surface errors that may increase in frequency when students are thinking hard about their writing's content. For more tips on evaluating text analyses and other student writing, see Chapters 9 and 12 of this book.

Other Useful Chapters in the *Field Guide*

1–5 RHETORICAL SITUATIONS
38 READING STRATEGIES
12 EVALUATIONS, if analysis leads to an evaluation of a text's effectiveness
17 TOPIC PROPOSALS
21 COLLABORATING
22 GENERATING IDEAS AND TEXT
28 BEGINNING AND ENDING
29 GUIDING YOUR READER
32 COMPARING AND CONTRASTING
42 QUOTING, PARAPHRASING, SUMMARIZING
23–27 DRAFTING, ASSESSING A DRAFT, REVISING, EDITING, PROOFREADING

Useful Readings

Booth, Wayne C. "The Rhetorical Stance." *College Composition and Communication* 14.3 (October 1963): 139–145.

Corbett, Edward P.J. and Robert J. Connors. *Style and Statement.* NY: Oxford, 1999.

Hickey, Dona J. *Developing a Written Voice.* Mountain View, CA: Mayfield, 1993.

24 Reporting Information

Students are accustomed to reading texts that report information because their primary form of reading throughout most of their education has been textbooks. They may also read newspapers, magazines, Web sites, and books focusing on their various interests. And many of them have written one or more research papers in high school that demanded that they combine several sources of information to create an informative essay. Nevertheless, they may find the assignment sequence in chapter 8, REPORTING INFORMATION, challenging. They may have difficulty maintaining a neutral stance toward their subject. They are likely to be encountering scholarly research and using the resources of a university library for the first time, and they may find that synthesizing the information they glean from their sources can be daunting. Writing an essay reporting information, though, will give students the experience of in-depth, college-level research and practice in conveying information to an interested audience that will stand them in good stead in other research-based writing assignments in first-year writing courses and beyond.

Using Readings and Teaching the Key Features

You might begin by asking students to write a two-part response to each reading in Chapter 8 of the *Field Guide*, first summarizing its content to show that they understand it and then writing a reaction. "The Hijacking of United 175" offers a detailed, even clinical description of one of the September 11 hijackings that will likely elicit strong reactions from students, who may find such a lengthy piece difficult to summarize. By contrast, "The Science of Screams" offers a relatively easy, brief explanation that may be easier to summarize than the hijacking piece. You may want to discuss the differences between writing about specific events and abstract concepts after reading these two essays. The third essay, "The Greatest Generation," presents a characterization of the people of a specific time and place, relying on interviews and historical facts to describe a group; you can use this essay and the others to show the range of possibilities in essays reporting information. You can then begin a class discussion by asking students to read from their responses. Next, review the Key Features of reports and ask students to discuss how those key features are presented in each of the essays. The 9/11 Report excerpt offers a tightly focused topic and accurate, well researched information; "Science" presents clear definitions of various terms and laws of physics and uses various writing strategies to explain them; and both "Hijacking" and "Greatest Generation" use maps and photos that can lead to a discussion of appropriate design. These activities will lay a good ground for students to begin thinking about their own report topics and strategies.

Getting Started and Choosing a Topic

Choosing a good topic can be a challenge for students. They may choose a topic that's far too broad to report in a relatively brief essay or that leads to an avalanche of available information that would be hard to sort through. A student interested in a topic relating to domestic abuse or violence within families, for example, found that typing "family violence" into a Web search engine resulted in almost two million hits, and "domestic abuse" gave her almost a million. Students may also choose topics that are phrased as arguments or that would be hard to write without becoming argumentative. A student who wants to write an essay exploring how the news media is biased, for example, is making a claim that must be argued. And students who want to write on topics like abortion or athletes' steroid use will have difficulty not only narrowing their topic but also finding information that is indeed impartial.

For these reasons (and more that your students will reveal as they present their topics to you), it's good practice to spend time with individual students and your class, helping them find and hone good topics. You might ask students to email you their proposed topics or to post them on a discussion board. You can then read over them and either discuss them in class or post your responses online. Students bene-fit from hearing or reading your suggestions for other students' topics, as many will change or adjust their own topics after hearing your critique of other, similar topics. Getting the topics in advance also allows you to do quick searches on your own to see if topics will lead to enough—or too many—sources of information or if using a synonym or rephrasing the topic will result in better source information. This research can be as simple as using a Web search engine or a library database, such as Academic Search Premier, and it can help you give students good advice on how to proceed.

You can then help students move from a preliminary topic to a working thesis by having them review the rhetorical situation in which they are working and narrow their topic by finding and reading some general sources. Often, students can do this efficiently by interviewing an expert on their topic—for example, a faculty member in the academic field or a local politician, journalist, business leader, mechanic, or farmer. Discussing their topic with an expert can help students limit their topics and point them toward good information, often information more current than is available through the library—and the interaction with a person can engage them with their topic. Then they're in a position to create a thesis and start doing serious research.

Helping Students Research Their Topics

If this assignment serves as your students' introduction to academic research, you may find that their concept of serious research differs from yours. Many students have no clear idea of what constitutes a scholarly source as opposed to a popular source, and careful definitions are sometimes insufficient to help them see the difference. Bringing in or downloading samples of scholarly sources to show students their distinguishing features can be helpful. For example, scholarly sources, unlike many news articles or encyclopedia entries, always list their authors and often their academic affiliations; scholarly sources cite their sources both in the text and in a list of sources at the end, while popular sources do not; and depending on the discipline, scholarly sources include an abstract, while popular sources do not. Students need help finding good sources in the library and online, so provide any help you can. The *Field Guide* offers detailed advice in Chapters 39–41. Here are some suggestions:

- Devote class time to searching for sources. If your school's library will allow you to hold class there, you can work with students as they search for sources in the library's catalog and databases. Often, reference librarians will make themselves available to assist both the students and you as you search. If you're teaching in a computer classroom, you can do this searching there.

- Hold research conferences. Instead of or in addition to working with all your students in class, consider holding research conferences, again where students have access to your library's holdings. I've had success by scheduling three students at a time for thirty-minute periods, helping those three find useful sources.

- Use the services of librarians. The resources available in university libraries grow and change rapidly, and only reference librarians can be counted on to keep up. So enlisting their aid as much as you can will not only help your students find information, it'll help you, too. Invite librarians to visit your class and point out how to access the library's resources. And model good research behavior by asking their help when you're stumped—as you will be.

- Help students rethink their topics if their original topic proves too difficult to find good information on. Sometimes students hit dead ends: there's simply nothing available on their topic, or—as is more often the case—there's too much, leading the student either to become overwhelmed or to think too generally about their topic. In either case, you can help by working with the student to adjust the topic, either making it more specific or more general, or exploring a related issue for which good information is available. For example, a student who wants to report on hypnosis will have trouble finding sources that lead to interesting information; the use of hypnosis by medical professionals, on the other hand, has a wealth of potential sources and the opportunity for further narrowing of the topic to a particular use of hypnosis in medicine.

- Require students to find more sources than they'll use. Like all of us, students practice economy: If you ask for at least three sources in an essay, some students will find and consult three sources. If you ask for eight to ten sources, though, students will find eight to ten, become much better informed about their topics, write better essays (we hope), and be able to choose the best sources, rather than rely on the first ones they find.

Help students organize their research, too. Consider asking them to create an annotated bibliography as part of the assignment, providing full bibliographic information that they can then simply copy and paste into a Works Cited or Reference page when they draft. Require them to photocopy each source they use—at least the pages containing bibliographic information and those containing information they cite—to label each one, and to include these copies when they submit their annotated bibliographies and drafts. This activity forces them to organize their sources and saves you time when you read their work, as you can quickly consult the sources to see how well they've quoted, paraphrased, summarized, and cited them. Requiring copies of sources also cuts down on intentional plagiarism while showing you instances of unintentional plagiarism—and presents a teaching opportunity.

Organizing, Drafting, and Revising

Reporting information well relies on clear organization, so it's a good idea to ask students to create an outline of their report before they draft it. The *Field Guide* offers three ways to organize a report that students should consider as they plan and offers advice on the various strategies— narrating, defining, comparing, and others—that writing a report may require. Still, you may need to warn students about common pitfalls of writing a report and have students look for them when they're ready to revise:

- Beginning too generally: A standard diagram showing how to introduce a report shows a funnel at the top, enjoining the writer to begin with a general statement and gradually zero in on a thesis statement. Students who have learned this technique sometimes take it to an extreme; for example, a student writing on the effect of negative emotions on our physical health began her essay, "Everyone has emotions." See *Field Guide* Chapter 28, BEGINNING AND ENDING, for some other ways of beginning.

- Turning the report into a how-to manual or argument: Sometimes students start out explaining a process, but at some point, they begin giving instructions, changing their focus from describing the information being conveyed to what "you" need to do to make something happen. Similarly, students sometimes become engaged in their topic and find maintaining a balanced stance difficult.

- Scaffolding: I use this analogy: when someone erects a building, they need scaffolding on the outside to stand on while they do the brickwork, put in the windows, and the like. Once the building is done, however, the scaffolding is removed so we see the structure itself. Statements like, "In the following paragraph I will explain . . . " or "In the article, 'Legislature Outlaws Visible Underwear,' it states that . . . ." are scaffolding that draw attention away from the information being reported to the paper and its writer.

- Problems with sources: Some of the most common include: not providing citations or signal phrases in the text to show where information came from; citing sources in the text that don't appear in the list at the end; and failing to provide photocopies of cited sources. A problem you may also encounter is the unacceptable paraphrase: A student may follow a source's language, structure, or both too closely. Most of the time, this problem involves a single paragraph or less, but once in a while a desperate student will borrow the structure of an entire source. Examples of unacceptable paraphrase may be found in *Field Guide* Chapter 43, but it's often useful to provide examples from your students' own writing, perhaps by showing the original and the paraphrase side by side, highlighting the similar passages.

- Ignoring conflicting evidence: When students research topics, they often find sources that offer differing views. They may react in one of three ways: They present both sources' views equally and uncritically, as if no conflict existed; they present both sources' views and end their essay by throwing up their hands and saying something like, "It's up to the reader to decide"; or they simply ignore one side's view, presenting the other as if there were no controversy. Instead, they should investigate the sources of the evidence to see if one has greater credibility than the other, and, if that proves inconclusive, present the controversy as a controversy: for example, "Experts disagree over whether or not we can reduce the risk of a shark attack when we swim in the ocean. Source A asserts _____, while Source B says _____." See *Field Guide* Chapter 38, READING STRATEGIES, and Chapter 41, EVALUATING SOURCES.

Of course, these are the same pitfalls you'll be looking for when you evaluate their finished work, along with their handling of the Key Features of a report. For more tips on evaluating reports and other student writing, see Chapters 9 and 12 of this book.

Other Useful Chapters in the *Field Guide*

A Useful Reading

Connors, Robert J. "The Rhetoric of Explanation: Explanatory Rhetoric from Aristotle to 1850" and "The Rhetoric of Explanation: Explanatory Rhetoric from 1850 to the Present." *Selected Essays of Robert J. Connors*. Ed. Lisa Ede and Andrea A. Lunsford. Boston: Bedford/St. Martin's, 2003.

25 Arguing a Position

In many first-year writing courses, essays arguing a position are central to the curriculum, and for good reason: As students write in courses across the curriculum, they will be asked to present arguments of one kind or another. Even reports that don't make an overt argument nonetheless represent the writer's version of the information and suggest to readers that that version is reasonable or correct. At the same time, students will be required to read arguments critically and therefore need to know how arguments are constructed. Chapter 9, ARGUING A POSITION, guides students through the process of developing an argumentative essay. Since writing a successful argument is a complex undertaking, you may find that, more than with other assignments, you'll need to assign various sections of the *Field Guide*, either for the whole class to use or for individual students as they generate ideas and text, do research, and draft their essays.

Getting Started

You might introduce the concept of arguing a position with texts in various genres and media, including magazine or television ads and hip hop or rock, to demonstrate that arguments—attempts to influence our thoughts or behavior—are all around us. Indeed, you might ask students to consider the role of corporate logos on their clothes to explore how these symbols may function as arguments. You then need to distinguish between arguments of the sort found in advertisements, arguments around the kitchen table (or on *Crossfire*-style TV programs), and academic arguments.

Using the Readings and Teaching the Key Features

Having students read the model essays in this chapter is a good way to introduce the Key Features of writing that argues a position, either by teasing out what makes each essay effective or by examining how each writer uses the Key Features. Lawrence Lessig's essay on electronic piracy states its clear and arguable position in the first sentence. Andy McDonie provides necessary background information before stating his thesis in the fourth paragraph. Anna Quindlan appeals to readers' values before stating, "Time to use the F word again." She provides good reasons, arguing that women's status "hasn't changed as much as we like to tell ourselves" and offers considerable support; McDonie offers examples from history and security practices by El Al to support his reasons. Each establishes a trustworthy tone in different ways that you may wish to discuss, and each offers careful consideration of other positions, again in very different ways. In any case, students need to be aware of the basic features of writing that argues a position.

To write a good argument, students must choose and refine a topic that is clear and arguable; provide a context for the topic; come up with good reasons and support for each one; appeal to readers' values (which entails understanding what those values are); write with a trustworthy tone; and show that they have considered other positions carefully and are presenting them fairly. The advice that follows covers each of these Key Features, grouped as you might teach them. ,

Choosing a clear and arguable topic. Students often think that they should choose "big" topics for argument essays, for example, abortion, gun control, or evolution. Such topics are seldom successful. Opinion on them is so polarized that finding reasoned debate and reasonable sources amid the avalanche of dogmatic and partisan source material available is difficult at best—and students who choose such topics usually begin with strong opinions one way or another, reducing their ability to explore ideas with an open mind. It's better for students to choose issues that they have some personal connection with, as source material on these topics often is more limited and less polarized than with the "big" issues. Even if they choose a major issue, their personal connection to it often

helps them narrow it, their knowledge of it aids them in contextualizing it for their readers, and their interest in the topic often leads to a better essay.

The section on Generating Ideas and Text in Chapter 9 asks students to examine their topic from several perspectives and in potentially unfamiliar ways to determine whether it's arguable and worth working on. This process leads them to the drafting of a thesis statement, which they then must qualify. Some students will need to search general sources in order to explore their topics adequately, so you may direct those students to Chapter 40, FINDING SOURCES, for help. You will likely find it useful to check their thesis statements at this point to make sure their topics are appropriate—arguable, narrow or broad enough, doable in the time available—before they do more research.

Crafting a Good Argument

A good argument is complicated, and taking into account the various aspects that can make an argument succeed or fail can be difficult for students. One way to help them is to deal with these aspects one at a time. Here are some tips for doing so.

Appealing to readers' values. Many students have done most of their writing either for an audience of one—a teacher—or, having been taught formal characteristics of writing, for no audience at all. Their need to define their audience is therefore new to them and deserves your attention as you teach. Insist that they seriously consider—in writing—the questions posed in "Considering the Rhetorical Situation," especially those about audience. You may want them to consider one additional question: What kinds of arguments is this audience likely to consider, accept, or reject out of hand? For example, an audience of political progressives is likely to consider an argument suggesting that Social Security creates a safety net that helps all of society but reject an argument suggesting that the pension program reduces workers' freedom to invest their money as they like; a conservative audience will likely do the opposite. In other words, the readers whom students choose to address strongly influence the kind of research they'll do (some audiences will prefer eyewitness testimony over scholarly research, for example) and the nature of the sources they use (conservatives will likely accept conservative columnist George Will's word over the more liberal commentator Paul Krugman's, and vice versa). Then, as students draft, they can appeal to their readers' values because they know who they're writing to and what evidence may move those readers. Here are some tips for helping students define and analyze their audiences:

- Have students select two or three different audiences, for example, "classmates," "parents," and "readers of the campus newspaper." Discuss how the rhetorical situation differs for each audience.

- Have students write a brief text, perhaps an email or instant message to a friend, and then rewrite it for various audiences. Discuss the changes each new audience required.

- Have students explore how readers' purposes can influence their reading. For example, an instructor's purpose in reading a student essay may be to see how well the student demonstrates knowledge and ability to compose; a parent's purpose in reading a student's email may be both to get information about the student's life and to be reassured that the student is doing well physically and emotionally.

Providing background information. Students who already know something about their topic might well use the techniques for GENERATING IDEAS AND TEXT in both Chapter 9 and Chapter 22 to be able to give an overview of the topic. Others may first need to gather background information from general sources as they explore their topics. If your assignment sequence includes a research component, students are likely to come up with sufficient background information as they read their sources; nonetheless, it's a good idea to remind students to look for and take notes on such information as they read.

Coming up with good reasons and support for those reasons. Reasoning clearly is primary to students' success. You should therefore spend some time on the developing of good arguments and the avoidance of logical fallacies. You might have students model essays or evaluate the reasons given in an advertisement. Have students collaborate (see Chapter 21 in the *Field Guide*) on brainstorming and then evaluate potential arguments for one another's drafts. You could write an argument with the class, listing potential reasons for a topic on the board and discussing which ones are suitable for the rhetorical situation you've outlined. Because many good reasons come to us through our reading and research, you should let students know that their reasons may well change as they learn more about their topics.

Doing research to find support. Most of the time, organized, in-depth research to find support is crucial to success in arguing a position. To help students, you should fold into your assignment sequence the activities in Chapter 39 for DEVELOPING A RESEARCH PLAN, Chapter 40 for FINDING SOURCES, Chapter 41 for EVALUATING SOURCES, Chapter 42 for QUOTING, PARAPHRASING, AND SUMMARIZING, and Chapter 43 for ACKNOWLEDGING SOURCES, AVOIDING PLAGIARISM. Even if you have assigned these chapters for a previous assignment, it wouldn't hurt to do a quick review. Students' challenge in finding sources to support an argument differs from that of finding information or supporting a textual analysis, so you may need to help them locate balanced sources or a balance among various sources. You may also need to help them evaluate sources to see if the reasons and evidence offered by the sources are themselves questionable. Students may also need to investigate the backgrounds and affiliations of their sources to assess whether the sources are

espousing an unstated point of view or philosophy. Some students may choose topics that require interviews or observations for adequate support; they can find help in doing those kinds of research in Chapter 40. Detailed advice on teaching these chapters can be found in Chapter 29 in this book.

Refuting or acknowledging other positions. As students do their research, they need to take into account the positions held by those with whom they disagree. In practice, they need to find sources that don't simply echo their own positions, evaluate those sources fairly, and summarize those positions clearly and without bias to show that they understand competing positions. Then they have to deal with those other viewpoints, either by refuting them completely or in part or by acknowledging that they exist, thus presenting themselves as reasonable people who have taken other views into consideration before deciding where they stand. Ways of helping students do this include the following:

- Have students write two drafts of their argument: one favoring their own position, the other favoring another position. Their goal is to be equally fair and equally passionate in arguing both positions. Refer to Believing and Doubting in *Field Guide* Chapter 38 for guidance.

- Have students look for the beliefs and values underlying opponents' views. Too often, people on one side of an issue can't comprehend how others could disagree, when their view seems so eminently sensible and correct.

Moving past the particular issue to the premises underlying people's positions can help students understand differing views.

- Look for common ground: see if students can find something on which they and their opponents agree, so they can build on that commonality, perhaps by softening their stand or by finding an alternative to polarized positions that both sides can live with.

Adopting a trustworthy tone. As students draft their arguments, they may well need to temporarily ignore the needs of their audience in order to organize and articulate their own views as well as they can. In assessing their drafts and revising, however, they should examine their stance and see whether their tone matches their intent. If they have presented good reasons and done adequate research, their content will be trustworthy. They need to listen carefully as they read their drafts to make sure their tone is confident and reasonable, not strident, angry, or overbearing. Occasionally, students believe that an effective argument bludgeons the opposition into submission, a serious problem with tone. Here are some ways to help students find an appropriate tone:

- Let students play with their voice, rewriting a paragraph from their drafts in an angry voice, a snide or satirical voice, a stiffly official voice, or a slangy voice. Then ask them to decide which of those voices—or combination of

them—might best capture their stance and influence their audience.

- Have students read their drafts aloud or read aloud selected passages from classmates' drafts that may be problematic to the writer. They will quickly hear problems with tone.
- Help students recognize that their voice should be consistently present throughout their draft, including paraphrases and summaries of their source material. If their paraphrases are too close to the original text, the result is a patchwork of voices that diminish the force of the argument— and might be seen as plagiarism. Make sure students can write paraphrases without looking at the original, and use direct quotations when they need specific phrasing from the original.

Evaluating Essays Arguing a Position

Evaluating arguments should focus on how well students apply the Key Features in their own writing. Since these features are complex, though, and may be achieved in many ways within a single essay, you may want to break down some into categories. For example, students may include necessary background information but fail to elaborate sufficiently its relevance to their argument; or they may provide convincing support but rely too heavily on a single source. For more tips on evaluating essays arguing a position and other student writing, see Chapters 9 and 12 in this book.

Other Useful Chapters in the *Field Guide*

1–5 RHETORICAL SITUATIONS

12 EVALUATIONS, for arguments about whether something is good or bad

14 LITERARY ANALYSES, for arguments that interpret a literary work

17 PROPOSALS, for arguments that propose some kind of solution

22 GENERATING IDEAS AND TEXT

28 BEGINNING AND ENDING

39–45 RESEARCH, for arguments that call on other sources and need documentation

29 GUIDING YOUR READER

23–27 DRAFTING, ASSESSING A DRAFT, REVISING, EDITING, PROOFREADING

Useful Readings

Fahnestock, Jeanne and Marie Secor. "The Stages in Scientific and Literary Argument." *Written Communication* 5.4 (1988): 427–433.

Fulkerson, Richard. "Technical Logic, Comp-Logic, and the Teaching of Writing." *College Composition and Communication* 39.4 (1988): 52–64.

Lynch, Dennis A., Diana George, and Marilyn M. Cooper, "Moments of Argument: Agonistic Inquiry and Confrontational Cooperation." *College Composition and Communication* 48:1 (February 1997): 61–85.

26 Teaching Other Genres

Richard Bullock, Michael Boblitt, and Paige Huskey

Texts are seldom "pure" representatives of a single genre. Instead, most texts combine genres to meet the needs of a rhetorical situation: A report on holistic medicine begins with an abstract and includes an annotated bibliography of articles and books on the subject; an argument against using animals to test cosmetics evaluates several alternatives and ends with a proposal to use computer modeling whenever possible. The Genre chapters in *The Norton Field Guide to Writing* all focus on a particular genre but can be combined according to your instructional needs. Each Genre chapter offers a definition of the genre, a good model, a list of its Key Features, and advice on generating ideas and text and then on organizing that kind of writing. This chapter offers tips on teaching the various genres.

If you're weaving one genre assignment into a larger sequence, you can lead students through the activities in the Genre chapter, folding them into your larger assignment. For example, after choosing a topic in Arguing a Position, students might do extensive research on it, creating an Annotated Bibliography of potentially useful sources. If you'd like students to focus on a single genre, such as an evaluation or proposal, simply assign the appropriate Genre chapter. These chapters all include links to other places in the book should students need more detail—help drafting, for instance, or describing, or incorporating source materials. If you know your students need a certain kind of help, you can assign the appropriate chapters; consult the sections at the end of each Genre chapter in this book for suggestions about other chapters in the *Field Guide* that might be useful. Chapters 3 and 20 in this book offer suggestions for designing writing assignments and developing course plans and assignment sequences using *The Norton Field Guide*.

Chapter 10, ABSTRACTS

Writing an abstract is an exercise in accuracy and economy. Students need to paraphrase and summarize a report or reading without distorting the information, while condensing it into less than 100–200 words. Creating prose with this precision can challenge students.

Using the Reading and the Key Features. Three examples illustrate the three types of abstracts students may one day be asked to write, either in their academic or professional field. Discussing how each example accomplishes the Key Features of abstracts will help students understand the different purpose of each type of abstract. For example, students may consider the types of information that are included in the summary of the "Boredom Proneness" study, the language that the authors use in order to remain objective and to convey information concisely, or the sentence structures which aid in brevity. You may also wish to compare the verb tenses in the informative and proposal abstracts to show the differences between an abstract that reports on a completed project and one that has yet to be done and discuss the authors' decisions about what to define (such as the Hopkins Symptom Checklist) and what to assume their readers already know.

Though every abstract should contain these Key Features, certain fields may require a specific format. For example, Phil Koopman, an Associate Professor at Carnegie Mellon University, suggests that all computer architecture abstracts "for both conference and journal papers . . . should follow a checklist consisting of: motivation, problem statement, approach, results, and conclusions" ("How to Write an Abstract." Electrical and Computer Engineering. 20 Oct. 1997. 17 July 2005 <http://www.ece.cmu.edu/~koopman/essays/abstract.html>.) It may be a good idea for those students who know their intended field of study, rather than drawing exclusively from the "Boredom Proneness" examples, to do some quick research on the Internet to determine any specific guidelines suggested for their discipline.

Some Tips for Teaching Abstracts. Here are some ways you can help them shape an abstract once they've drafted it:

- Revise for completeness. Does an informative abstract include a description of the text's subject, the method used, and the results or findings? A summary of the discussion of the results or findings? The conclusion or implications of the study? Does a descriptive abstract announce the subject of the study and provide an overview of the full paper? Does a proposal abstract announce the subject and summarize the method to be used?

- Revise for objectivity. When students have drafted an abstract, ask them or their peers to look for opinions or interpretations. The abstract must represent the larger text without distortion or bias.

- Revise for conciseness. Draft a wordy abstract and pare it down as a class, looking for unneeded adjectives and passive verbs. Have students work together to decide whether each word in their abstracts is needed. Have them write the abstract as a telegram that costs them $1 for each word. Ask students to reduce the number of words in the abstract by half, and see how close they get.

- Revise for coherence and readability. Having cut the abstract down to its barest bones, what can be done to make it read clearly and smoothly? Have students add transitions where necessary, repeat key words, and make sure each sentence is complete and grammatical.

Other Useful Chapters in the *Field Guide*

Chapter 11, ANNOTATED BIBLIOGRAPHIES

Annotated bibliographies are useful because the process of writing annotations for several potential sources demands that students understand the sources thoroughly and invites comparing and contrasting of the various sources, which, in turn, makes students more discerning readers and researchers. At the same time, annotated bibliographies present students with several challenges: finding sources to include, creating accurate citations of those sources, and writing accurate annotations. For advice on helping students find and cite sources, see Chapter 29 in this book.

Using the Reading and Teaching the Key Features. After reading the *Teen Film$* example, students may consider how each entry from the annotated bibliography may or may not be helpful to a person interested in writing a report on the teen film genre. You might adapt the questions from "Decide what sources to include" on p. 117 to *Teen Film$* to guide students in analyzing the appropriateness, credibility, balance, and timeliness of the entries—and even have students find the listed articles in order to assess the accuracy of the entries. After considering the language used and the information included in the examples, students may try rewriting the entries. Where can they add or condense information? How can they alter the wording to change the descriptive annotations into evaluative annotations? Because annotated bibliographies must serve a highly specified purpose in a limited space, it's important for students to hone in on the Key Features, which include a statement of scope, bibliographical information, a concise description of the work, relevant commentary, and consistent presentation. Helping students identify those features in the reading and discussing how the sample annotated bibliography entries communicate them can clarify the assignment's requirements and their writing goals.

Some Tips for Teaching Annotated Bibliographies. To write useful and accurate annotations, students must read potential sources carefully. Consider modeling such a reading, perhaps by positing a topic for a bibliography and then giving students an article or essay on that topic. You can then work with them to find the main idea or thesis, identify the writer's purpose and audience, and examine the content carefully to answer the following questions:

- What aspects of the topic are emphasized? What are deemphasized or omitted?
- What does the author assume about the audience's knowledge of or attitudes toward the subject?
- Does the evidence support the main idea?
- Does the writer show bias?
- Would this source be useful for writing about the topic?

Then ask students, working alone or in groups, to write a descriptive annotation—and then an evaluative one.

Other Useful Chapters in the *Field Guide*

Chapter 12, EVALUATIONS

Introduce evaluations by pointing out that we evaluate people, places, and things all the time: My English teacher is cool, the guys in the room down the hall party too much, the latest CD from U2 is better than their last one, this classroom needs to be painted. Implicit in those informal evaluations are criteria or reasons. You might ask students to list the criteria governing each of those evaluations. Then you can point out that formal evaluations work the same way: The writer identifies criteria by which something should be evaluated and then sees how well it meets those criteria and presents those findings as an argument.

Using the Reading and Teaching the Key Features. Ben Leever's evaluation of *Dawson's Creek* is likely to strike a chord with students, many of whom are familiar and concerned about the issues Leever discusses. Moreover, they are probably familiar with TV dramas which do not accurately depict the lives of typical teenagers. As such, students will probably want a chance to react to Leever's message, perhaps applying it to some other, current TV shows. While discussing his essay in class, try to steer the students toward the Key Features of evaluations by asking questions such as, "What does Leever think makes for a good teen drama?" or "Does Leever think *Dawson's Creek* is the perfect teen drama?" Providing a balanced and fair assessment may be difficult for some students, especially when dealing with controversial issues. Make sure to point out to students how Leever not only included but remained respectful of sources who disagreed with his position, thus strengthening his own credibility.

Some Tips for Teaching Evaluations.

Introduce criteria. Although students can already identify many evaluation criteria, spending class time to identify and clarify the specific criteria for the genre of work they'll be evaluating will help them understand what they need to look for and will allow you to guide them to more rigorous examination. A good approach is to examine together a single example from various perspectives in order to develop a list of criteria. Before you start, ask students to list the criteria they'd use to evaluate it. Then ask them if the criteria need to be revised or expanded.

If you want students to evaluate a TV show or movie, for example, a good way to develop criteria is to show them a brief sample; a music video or even a TV commercial can work well because you can show the same tape several times in a single class period. For each viewing, ask students to focus their attention on a single aspect and write a brief reaction:

- *Purpose.* What is this video or commercial trying to achieve? Does it achieve its purpose? Do you like it? are you entertained by it? Convinced by it? Why or why not?

- *Plot.* What happens? Does it make sense? Are there jumps or gaps in the narrative? Is there an ending or resolution? Is it convincing?

- *Characters.* Who are the characters? What do we know about them? How do we know?

- *Costume.* What are the characters wearing? Why? How does their dress contribute to the meaning, atmosphere, or overall impression?

- *Setting and background.* Is the film in color? Natural color or manipulated color? Black and white? What do you see in the background? What details do you remember? What else is in there? How does the setting contribute to the purpose?

- *Lighting.* Is the setting brightly lit? Dark and shadowy? How well can you see what's going on in the foreground or background?

- *Sound.* What sounds do you hear? Is there dialogue? Music? Voiceovers? Background sounds? View it again, with the sound turned off: How does the sound—and its absence—affect your experience?

- *Cinematography.* If the screen is like a picture frame, where are important objects or people located within the frame? What are the effects of their placement in the frame and their movement through it? Where is the camera located—at eye level? looking down from above? up from below?

You can then ask students to work individually or in groups to put these observations together, first by creating a brief summary or description of the work and then by identifying a small number of criteria—four-to-six is typical—that a music video or commercial should meet. For example, a commercial should have the following traits:

- Grab viewers' attention immediately
- Focus our attention on the product being promoted

- Entertain
- Be memorable, so that we remember it and the product it represents

Follow with a whole-class or group discussion of the way this work meets or doesn't meet the criteria, asking for evidence from their viewings to support their assertions. If you have time, you might ask students to research how others have evaluated similar subjects and to see if their own criteria need to be expanded or changed.

Choose something to evaluate. A common object of evaluation in writing courses is a media work: a movie, a television show, a song or CD, a Web site. Artwork is also a possibility, as is a work of architecture. You can ask everyone in the class to evaluate the same work, allowing everyone to contribute to the evaluation and discuss it as a class, but you'll then face twenty-five essays on the same topic. You can allow every student to choose whatever he or she wants to evaluate, but then discussion is more difficult because you're faced with one of two scenarios: viewing or listening to twenty-five different movies, TV shows, songs, or Web sites or evaluating students' essays without having knowledge of the object of the evaluation. There's something to be said for the second position: students should be able to describe what they're evaluating clearly enough that readers have enough information to know whether or not their evaluation is fair, even if readers aren't familiar with the work. If, however, you'd like to control the range of topics, here are some strategies:

- Create a list of works from which students may choose. Some instructors restrict the items on the list to works they're familiar with or to works they have had success with in the past. Others create lists containing only works within a single genre, such as action movies, situation comedies, hip-hop songs, fashion Web sites. The works should be accessible: Films should be rentable or available at area libraries, TV shows should be available on DVD or currently playing, Web sites should be up and running (but advise students to print and date the pages they're evaluating, since Web pages are often revised and sites disappear).

- Ask students to choose from the works on your list. You can then assign students to groups according to the work itself or according to the genre, if your list has more than one. The groups can then collaborate on establishing criteria and examining the work or works.

- Alternately, place students in groups first. In a class of twenty-five, four groups of five-to-seven work well. Each group should choose one work from the list. By grouping students first, you guarantee that everyone will have others to work with, and you limit the class's evaluations to four works.

- As a variation, you might encourage students to compare two similar works: two situation comedies, two Ben Stiller movies, two department stores' Web sites, two CDs, or two buildings on campus.

Draft an evaluation. Once students have chosen something to evaluate, give them time to obtain the work and watch or examine it several times over several days, probably a weekend, taking notes on different aspects or looking through the lenses of different criteria each time. If they're working in groups, encourage them to view the work together so they can point out observations to one another as they watch and as they discuss it together afterwards. They'll also need class time and your guidance to bring their individual notes together, revise their criteria in light of their research, and evaluate their subject, possibly comparing it with other, similar works. Their goal is to state a judgment as a thesis statement.

At this point students are ready to start planning and writing. Review the Key Features of evaluations and ask them to consider the rhetorical situation again in relation to their own project. You might ask them to write answers to the questions posed in "Considering the Rhetorical Situation" and review "Ways of Organizing an Evaluation" in Chapter 12 and then have them draft, assess their draft, get response, revise, edit, and proofread, consulting Chapters 23–26 as need be. For help in identifying reasons and evidence, go to Chapter 9, ARGUING A POSITION.

Other Useful Chapters in the *Field Guide*

Chapter 13, LAB REPORTS

Although lab reports are seldom taught in first-year writing courses, students are often required to write them in various science and social science courses, so pointing out this chapter to your students to use as a reference may be helpful to them. If your school has a Writing Across the Curriculum program, however, you may be called upon to teach students how to compose lab reports. Disciplines differ in their exact requirements, demanding more or fewer parts or naming them differently, so if you're working with a specific course or instructor, be sure to find out what's required—and emphasize to students that they need to do the same whenever they're assigned a lab report. Also, if possible you should do the experiment yourself to familiarize yourself with the methods, equipment, and expected results.

Using the Reading and Teaching the Key Features. "The Effect of Biofeedback Training on Muscle Tension and Skin Temperature" by Sarah Thomas offers a good example of the Key Features of most lab reports. Her title is clear and avoids the temptation to begin, "A Study of." She describes her Purpose clearly and concisely and notes similar work done by another researcher. Her Methods section is divided into four sections, each presenting specific details of the experiment itself. She presents the study's Results and Discussion, including two detailed charts, and includes a single Reference. After students have identified the Key Features of Sarah Thomas's lab report, they may consider: What types of information were included in each section? Would they be able to reproduce her experiment if asked? Did her results seem logical and convincing? Thomas's lab report also offers an excellent opportunity for students to practice writing abstracts, one of the Key Features not addressed in Thomas's lab report. Students could try to condense her report into each type of Abstract outlined in Chapter 10.

Some Tips for Teaching Lab Reports. Here are some tips that will make it easier for students as they prepare to draft their reports:

Take notes. A lab report succeeds or fails first of all on the accuracy and comprehensiveness of its content. For that reason, students need to take careful notes as they conduct experiments. To help them, consider requiring a lab journal to record each of their actions as they do them and to note carefully their observations as well as their thoughts. They should record their raw data in the journal and use its pages to tease out the implications of their findings. When they are ready to write the report, they'll have collected much of the information they need for the Methods, Results, and Discussion sections.

Draw from the research proposal. If your students write research or topic proposals (discussed in Chapter 17 of the *Field Guide*), they can adapt much from the proposal for the report itself. Research proposals vary from discipline to discipline but typically include an introduction that reviews the relevant literature; a discussion of proposed procedures, needed equipment, and methods of analyzing the data collected; and a discussion of anticipated results—writing that can be used as the foundation for the lab report itself. Caution students against simply copying and pasting, because it's unlikely that the actual research will match what was proposed. Students will need to revisit their purpose, expand their methods and discussion sections, and change verb tenses to show that the research has been completed.

Use visuals. Students may need to present data in the form of charts, graphs, or tables, so refer them to the *Field Guide* Chapter 47, PRINT TEXT, for guidance.

Create an abstract. Once students have finished their lab report, they'll need to write an abstract of it; see the advice on helping students write a good abstract earlier in this chapter and Chapter 10 in the *Field Guide*.

Other Useful Chapters in the *Field Guide*

Chapter 14, LITERARY ANALYSES

Analysis of literature is the heart of many university English departments, and most universities require students to take one or more literature courses as part of their general education requirements. For those reasons, you may wish to ask students to analyze a literary work in your course. If you do, emphasize that a literary analysis is a form of argument; as in other arguments, students need to make an assertion in the form of a thesis and use evidence from the text to support it. Careful attention to the Key Features, showing examples from your own, other students', or literary critics' work, can help establish your expectations for this assignment.

Using the Reading and Teaching the Key Features. Allowing students an opportunity to discuss their interpretations of Shelley's sonnet before they read Stephanie Huff's analysis may be a good way of demonstrating the myriad reactions which a literary work may elicit. Huff's analysis may then be read as an example of how a reaction can be shaped into a well-supported analysis by using the Key Features of literary analyses. Also, some students, after years of English classes, have developed a negative attitude toward analyzing literature, believing that it is "much ado

about nothing," but for those students, Huff's analysis is a good example of how we can find meaning in the minutest details of a work when we respect authors enough to give them credit—and hold them accountable—for the language they use.

Some Tips for Teaching Literary Analyses.

Help Students Choose a Method of Analysis. This chapter of the *Field Guide* presents three different methods for analyzing literary texts. The first, focusing on the text itself, is likely the most familiar to students from their previous education. The ways of analyzing texts in Chapter 38 can be helpful in focusing students' attention on specific textual features.

The second, focusing on their response as readers, may be familiar to some students, as the method has become popular in some high school curriculums. To introduce students to it, you might choose the first paragraph in a story or the first stanza of a poem. Write the first word on the board and ask students, "What might come next?" They may be able to guess whether the sentence is likely to be a statement or question, but little else. Add the second word, and repeat the question, then the third, and so on. Students will see that at a certain point, they can guess the shape and likely content of several words to come. As you proceed, add phrases, then entire sentences, to show that as we read, our choices narrow and broaden as we experience the words in sequence. By slowing down the reading experience, we can analyze it and create an interpretation based on our predictions and how the text fulfills or frustrates them.

The third method, analyzing the text as part of a context, can turn the literary analysis into a full-blown research project as students discover the author's biography and other works, the era or culture of the time of the work's original publication, the genre, or some other larger context of which the work forms a part. Analyses based on the other methods will often benefit from some research of this sort; in her analysis of Shelley's poem, Huff might have researched the influence of Plato's allegory of the cave on Shelley's thinking. A context-focused analysis may attract students who are more interested in history, culture, or technology than in literature; at the same time, a danger in this analysis is that the literary work itself may disappear as the student gets caught up in the context. Making sure the student's thesis focuses on the work in its context—and checking early drafts to make sure they relate to the thesis—can keep students' attention where it should be.

Provide questions for revising. Here are some questions for you and peer reviewers to ask about drafts of a literary analysis (adapted from Lolly Ockerstrom, *Teaching with a Purpose* [Boston: Houghton, 1992. 221–22]):

- Did the writer's analysis of this work improve your understanding of it? If so, how?

- Identify the writer's thesis. Is the thesis sufficiently focused, clearly worded, and analytical?

- Describe the organization of this essay. Is there a definite organizing strategy?

- Does the writer support the analysis with enough evidence from the work? Where does the writer need more evidence? Where is there too much evidence, or evidence without an explanation? Is this the best evidence to support the writer's analysis?

- Has the writer avoided summarizing the plot?

- Are quotations and paraphrases from the work correctly integrated into the writer's own prose? Are they introduced by signal phrases?

If you are studying literature, you may find some students' apparent opaqueness about literature and inability to analyze it particularly difficult to understand. It's good to remember that when you're very close to a subject, much of it seems self-evident, while to a novice it's challenging and puzzling. For the same reason, you may want to avoid asking students to read and analyze your favorite poems, stories, or novels because you may be disappointed by their responses to your personal preferences.

Be aware of common problems: You're likely to run into the following problems students writing about literature can have:

- *Seeking "the right answer" or assuming that all literary analysis is arbitrary.* Much of students' education consists of learning information and being tested on it, and their goal is, of necessity, knowing the right answers. They may generalize that literature, too, has a correct interpretation that English teachers, for perverse reasons, refuse to tell. Because literature doesn't lend itself to "the right answer," some students may conclude that interpretation is a meaningless game. Explaining how literary analysis makes an argument from evidence to support an interpretation may help correct both misunderstandings. You might also bring up examples from other fields—criminology, biology, history—to show how different analysts can use the same evidence but derive very different interpretations as a way to make the point that literary analysis is not a special case, but an instance of a common human activity.

- *Summarizing instead of interpreting.* Some students retell the story or summarize the action of the poem and think they've interpreted it. Usually, they do so because they don't know what else to do. Walking through an analysis of a brief text in class, or asking students to create topical and functional outlines (from the *Field Guide*, Chapter 38, READING STRATEGIES) can help them distinguish what a text *says* from what it *does*.

- *Failing to support assertions with textual evidence.* Often, students have trouble identifying the parts of the text that can support their thesis—or identifying patterns in the text at all. They're used to reading for meaning, and the interplay between the meaning of a text and the words that convey that meaning (especially literary meaning as opposed to literal meaning) is invisible to them. They might find activities from Chapter 38 of the *Field Guide* helpful here, especially color-coding. Students who take in information best visually may see highlighted patterns in words and phrases that they don't see otherwise. Some students can find evidence but stumble in using it to support their assertions because they have trouble articulating patterns within the evidence. They may benefit from making lists of textual features that they highlight in the same color and writing a sentence describing each list or from annotating the text as they read and reread, perhaps using different colors of ink for each reading's annotations.

Other Useful Chapters in the *Field Guide*

Chapter 15, MEMOIRS

Asking students to write about their lives can be rewarding both for them and for you. It's a topic most students find of interest, and they can develop their skills in narrating and describing by writing memoirs. Memoirs are a large genre; literacy narratives are simply memoirs that focus on a particular aspect of students' lives. For that reason, the advice in Chapter 22 of this book, "Teaching Literacy (and Other) Narratives," will be useful when you ask students to write memoirs.

Using the Reading and Teaching the Key Features. The reading can help students understand the genre, present a model for their own writing, and provide an example of the Key Features of memoirs. Although few students are likely to have a wartime memory like Chanrithy Him's, they may remember times when they were frightened or experienced some strong emotion; when they experienced an event that they didn't understand; or when an experience proved to be the beginning of a significant event in their lives. Discussing "When Broken Glass Floats" in the context of their own lives can help them see potential topics for their memoirs. The Key Features of memoirs include a good story, vivid details, and clear significance. Helping students identify those features in the reading and discussing how Him communicates them can clarify the assignment's requirements and their writing goals. Students often find significance to be a difficult concept to grasp. Discussing the reasons Him believes her story is important and needs to be told—and how that importance, both in the short and long term, is conveyed—can help students see how to show the significance of their own memoirs.

Some Tips for Teaching Memoirs.

Finding a topic. The first, and probably most important, task in writing a memoir is choosing a suitable topic that has significance for the writer. Given the variety in students' lives, what they might choose to write about is legion; however, many students don't understand the implications of *significance*. They may gravitate toward big topics that so many others share—prom, graduation, the state wrestling tournament—that they're drained of uniqueness and are hard to write about well and originally. Alternately, students may want to write about recent events—prom and graduation, yes, but also serious car accidents or post-graduation breakups—that they don't have enough distance from. Your first task, then, is to encourage students to consider significant and unique events in their lives, ideally events that took place at least two years ago, and events that only they may know about. Here's a short list of such topics from my life; you might create such a list yourself to share with your students:

- The day I looked in my sixth-grade teacher's car and found out she smoked
- When one of my grad school professors, seeing me struggle writing an essay on a comic novel, gave me per-

mission to use humor, saying "You're writing about a funny book; write a funny paper!"

- Seeing my father cry for the first time

In other words, a significant event can be a realization, a new perspective, or a memory revisited—something important for the writer but perhaps unknown to anyone else. Occasionally you'll encounter a student who insists that nothing of any importance has ever happened to him or her. It's helpful to sit with such students and ask them as many questions as you can think of about their lives and interests, seeing why, for example, they like to hunt or what it was like to move to a new high school their senior year. Usually, those conversations lead to several significant moments, and your next task may be to convince these students that you'd like to know more about them—and so would others.

Drafting the memoir. Students sometimes think they need to give readers a great deal of background information or start their memoir far earlier in the day or week than they have to. When they write a first draft, they may need to work up to the event that they're focusing on. When it's time to revise, however, ask them to consider just how much or how little background readers need to understand the circumstances and shape their stories so they can draw readers in, keep them interested, and express the significance clearly.

Here is the next challenge you'll face: helping students understand that a mem-

oir need not be a completely factual record of an event in their lives. Like other narratives, it must be shaped—omitting some details, emphasizing others, possibly even altering events—to both tell a good story and express the significance of the event for them. You should also help them focus not only on telling the story but on exploring its significance; in a memoir, *introspection* is just as important as *retrospection*. You might ask students to rewrite the memoir from multiple perspectives to see which point of view seems to work best.

Other Useful Chapters in the *Field Guide*

Chapter 16, PROFILES

Profiles introduce students to first-hand research by asking them to observe people, places, or events; interview key people; and organize their findings into a report that readers will find interesting and engaging. Students typically visit their subject one or more times, taking careful notes on what they see, hear, and experience, and then shape those notes and their memories into a detailed, focused account.

Using the Reading and Teaching the Key Features.

The reading presented in the *Field Guide* is particularly useful for discussing the Key Features of the genre. Students will be amused by Merlis's use of word play throughout his profile. M.D. stands not for medical doctor but for Metropolitan Doctor, where Metropolitan is a classic car and Doctor is a "shade-tree mechanic of the highest order." Merlis dubs the people who own Metropolitans as "Met lovers" and "Metheads" a play on words associated with baseball lovers and drug addicts who use methamphetamines. These examples can help students understand how Merlis crafts his piece from an interesting angle and uses engaging details to draw his reader in, of which both are Key Features of profiles.

You will also want to discuss the background or context Merlis includes in his piece. Ask students what they remember of Shirley Barnes aside from her relationship with Metropolitans. They may remember that she was once a professional dancer or that she learned to drive in 1960. Point out to students that their lack of answers is a good sign—it shows that Merlis's piece is focused, which is also a key feature of profiles. When discussing the assignment, you may want to clarify to students the difference between firsthand and secondhand accounts. Be sure they understand that reading a newspaper article and then relaying those facts in a profile would be considered secondhand since they did not witness the event with their own eyes and ears or do the research themselves.

Some Tips for Teaching Profiles.

Finding a topic. Students may choose to profile people in the area who have interesting occupations or hobbies or who have distinguished themselves in one way or another. They may profile places, ranging from areas in parks or other public places to buildings or structures, from retail stores to factories. Or, they may profile events such as a concert, a poetry reading, a rodeo, a stock car race. Encourage students to choose topics with which they aren't familiar; they need to be able to see their topic through fresh eyes, without the preconceptions that previous experience or familiarity brings. Guide them, too, to subjects that are clearly focused: "the lake" or "the campus" or "the supermarket" are all too broad and won't yield the sharp detail that makes a profile interesting. Also, make sure students choose topics they can gain access to. Students who choose a hospital operating room or a lawyer's office, for example, are unlikely to be allowed in; certain people—the mayor, a convicted felon—may be unavailable for interviews; and if the subject is located away from the campus area, students without cars may have difficulty getting to it. Finally, discourage students from choosing illegal or dangerous topics, such as drug deals or a gang leader; you don't want them to risk harm, and as a college teacher you don't have any confidentiality privileges, like lawyers and doctors, and don't want to know things that you'd have to share with law enforcement authorities. The best advice? Approve each student's topic before allowing them to pursue their research.

Doing research. Profiles require field research, placing demands on students that academic or Internet-based research doesn't. Specifically, they have to schedule appointments and interviews and times when they will observe their subjects. It's especially important to have students create a research schedule as outlined in the *Field Guide* Chapter 39, DEVELOPING A RESEARCH PLAN, to help them structure their time so they can get their research done with ample time to draft and revise their profiles—and, if need be, do additional research. Research will consist primarily or entirely of first-hand observing and interviewing; those two sections in the *Field Guide* Chapter 40, FINDING SOURCES, can help.

If they've done good research, students will have a lot of notes and evidence to sift through. Help them find patterns: A good angle or point of view offers a new way of seeing the subject, rather than simply confirming what most people already know about it.

Organizing and drafting. Once students have examined their research material and settled on an angle, they need to decide how to organize their profile and whether they have enough information. They may consider creating an informal outline (from *Field Guide* Chapter 22, GENERATING IDEAS AND TEXT) and then seeing how much information they have for each topic they want to

cover. If some of their research is thin, they can do additional field work—visit the event or scene again, do a followup interview—or do some research for background and more information on the topic. For example, if they were writing on the Circleville, Ohio, Pumpkin Festival but the festival is over, they could interview one of the organizers, see what's been written about the Pumpkin Festival itself, or look for information on agricultural festivals and fairs to see how Circleville's festival is part of a long American tradition. Warn students to focus on their subject rather than on themselves as researchers or observers; some students draw unnecessary attention to themselves by statements like, "Then I asked her . . . ."

Other Useful Chapters in the *Field Guide*

40	see the sections on INTERVIEWS and OBSERVATIONS
1–5	RHETORICAL SITUATIONS
22	GENERATING IDEAS AND TEXT
28	BEGINNING AND ENDING
29	GUIDING YOUR READER
34	DESCRIBING
35	DIALOGUE
37	NARRATING
23–27	DRAFTING, ASSESSING A DRAFT, REVISING, EDITING, PROOFREADING

Chapter 17, PROPOSALS

A proposal is a kind of argument, but proposals present students with some unique challenges in terms of choosing a topic, justifying the need for the proposal, and shaping their proposal for their audience.

Using the Reading and Teaching the Key Features. The reading offered in the *Field Guide* is useful for pointing out to students the Key Features of proposals. In addition, you may want to mention areas where the writers could have chosen a different stance or solution in an effort to help students understand the choices they will need to make as they write their own proposals. For instance, one of the Key Features of a proposal is a well-defined problem. In their essay, King and Bannon define the problem as "unmanageable levels of debt" for student borrowers where "monthly payments are more than 8 percent of their monthly income," yet in the preceding paragraph they've pointed out that a college degree is worth "more than $1,000,000 over a lifetime in the workforce." Some opponents to their proposal, therefore, might argue that the benefits of pursuing a college degree outweigh the costs, even if graduates must live on peanut butter and jelly while paying off their loans. However, as King and Bannon also point out, and most would agree with them, low-income students are more likely to "forgo a college education altogether" rather than risk the burden of debt.

You will also want students to note the appropriateness of King and Bannon's tone, which is a key feature of proposals. Help students see that the authors state their concerns and solutions matter-of-factly, citing sources to give their argument the authority it needs. Ask students how they think King and Bannon's proposal would have been received if they had used a harsh, angry, or demanding tone. Another way to get students to understand the importance of using appropriate tones and words is to encourage or even require them to actually deliver their polished proposals to their intended audience.

Other Key Features of proposals include a recommended solution and a call to action. Point out to students that King and Bannon have first stated their solution in one terse statement: "Congress should increase grant-aid funding, reduce the cost of student loans, and provide flexibility within the student loan program to help make college more affordable for all Americans." They go on, however, to break this down into several concise calls to action, providing paragraph headings and even a bulleted list. This helps readers follow their logic, which makes their solution more convincing—another key feature of proposals.

Some Tips for Teaching Proposals.

Choosing a topic. The problems for which students can best propose solutions are often specific, local issues in their community or on campus. The broader or more abstract the problem, the harder it will be for students to write about because they'll have trouble identifying a specific audience and specific solutions. If they choose something local, for example, the lack of weekend tech support for computer equipment in the dorms, they not only can discuss the problem in specific terms, they also can find out who is responsible for technical support on campus, analyze the rhetorical situation as it applies to them as students writing to a university administrator, and direct their proposals to that person. They can also evaluate the problems to see whether they need a proposed solution: Will the problem go away by itself, be solved too easily, or be seen as trivial by readers?

Defining the problem. Make sure, through conferences or topic proposals (also discussed in this chapter) or both, that students' proposals are clear, focused, and significant and that they know to whom their proposal will be addressed. Approving their topics before they start can forestall many problems.

Doing research. Students may not initially have a solution (or they'll have one that may or may not be feasible) but will need to research the problem to find out its dimensions. If this research involves interviews or observations, it's important for students to recognize that field research places demands that academic or Internet-based research doesn't. Specifically, they have to schedule appointments and interviews and times when they will observe their subjects. It's especially important to have students create a research schedule as outlined in the *Field Guide* Chapter 39, DEVELOPING A RESEARCH PLAN to help them structure their time so they can finish their research with ample time to draft and revise their proposals—and, if need be, to do additional research.

Drafting. Proposals often consist of two arguments: one to frame the problem and a second to support the preferred solution. You may want students to explain why the issue is a problem, to help them understand that problems are not necessarily self-evident; after all, one person's problem may represent another's happy status quo. Then, have them write about a proposed solution or solutions. Although the finished draft may or may not present alternative solutions—that may be a function of the problem itself, or may reflect a particular audience—students should anticipate and think about alternatives to show that they've weighed their preferred solution against other possibilities.

Other Useful Chapters in the *Field Guide*

Chapter 18, REFLECTIONS

Reflections—essays in which the writer shares his or her thoughts on a subject—are challenging to teach because their subject matter, form, and style are nearly limitless. Reflections are places for writers to play with ideas, unlikely juxtapositions, unconventional organization, and innovative language—all in the service of exploring a line of thinking about a subject. That's also what makes them fun for students to write, read, and share, because they can compose with a freedom few have had permission to experience in their writing in school.

Using the Reading and Teaching the Key Features. The reading provided in the *Field Guide* is a wonderful example of just how playful and yet serious reflections can be. Cooper begins his essay by describing in great detail the act of sighing, something most people wouldn't give a second thought to. Specific details, such as "you can no more contain it than your hands can cup a lake," compel us to keep reading and are a key feature of reflections. However, it is not until Cooper relates memories of his mother and father sighing and his interpretations of their sighs that we begin to understand why he is so fascinated or intrigued by his topic—another key feature of reflections.

You may want to have your students, either as a class or in small groups, draw an outline or some type of visual map of Cooper's essay. In this way, students will better understand how Cooper's reflection is structured to help readers make connections and follow his logic. Ask students to try to rearrange Cooper's essay in a way that it still makes sense, but perhaps leads to a different conclusion. Explain to students that, although structure is a key feature of reflections, there are many options with which they will probably want to

experiment. Chapters 28 and 37 in the *Field Guide* can give students more ideas for organizing or structuring their essays.

Some Tips for Teaching Reflections.

Choosing a topic. Here, the topic is less important than what students do with it. Sighing and other bodily emanations, observations ("My mother, my grandmother, and my sister all share a way of standing with their arms folded"), interesting facts ("40,000 Americans are injured by toilets each year"), speculations ("What if dogs could talk?")—all are grist for reflections. Students may be able to write about their topics using their own knowledge of them. However, most reflections are enriched if the writers do some research, deepening their understanding of their topic and gaining additional insight and perspective on it. Asking students to do some research on the topic of their reflection is a good way to improve the quality of your students' drafts while lessening the chance that they'll rely on their (often not inconsiderable, but sometimes painfully sophomoric) wit.

Organizing. Since reflections are by their nature idiosyncratic, their organization can take many forms. The charts presented in the *Field Guide* may be helpful, but students may benefit from these tips, too:

- Provide several examples of reflections. "Sighing" offers one kind of reflection, but showing students several different models can help them see both common elements—some kind of organizational scheme, an overall focus and unity to the essay, even if it wanders—and the breadth of possibilities open to them. Consider giving them one example from a Dave Barry piece to show how discursive and tangentially relevant some pieces of a reflection can be, as long as the writer can tie up the loose ends by the end.

- Have students write a draft as a PowerPoint presentation. As odd as it sounds, asking students to turn their essay into a series of slides may help them achieve a better organization by showing them how the pieces—the individual slides—fit together (or don't). If the slides just stop, students can see that some sort of conclusion is needed. And they can easily move the slides around to play with different organizational patterns.

- Caution students not to turn their reflections into arguments. As students write, they may switch from reflecting and playing with ideas to arguing a point. In group work, ask readers to watch out for such a shift, which may reflect not a loss of control but a new understanding of the subject or a new commitment to a particular position. If so, the student may not need to revise the reflection but instead may need permission to switch genres to reflect his or her new learning.

Reflections are by nature playful (though they are often serious in intent and tone), so you and your students may find the Rewriting activities in the *Field Guide* Chapter 25, GETTING RESPONSE AND REVISING, helpful as students revise their drafts.

Other Useful Chapters in the *Field Guide*

Chapter 19, REVIEWS OF SCHOLARLY LITERATURE

A review of literature offers students the opportunity to come to grips with the most important scholarly work on a specific topic. It's a challenging assignment, because students have mostly done research either to report information or to support an argument; they haven't been asked to look through the scholarship on a topic, decide what's most important, and write a review that characterizes it fairly and clearly. As a result, they need to approach choosing a topic, doing research, organizing their findings, and drafting an essay in new ways.

Using the Reading and Teaching the Key Features. You will want to discuss the Key Features of reviews of scholarly literature using the example provided in the *Field Guide* so that students will have a better grasp of this somewhat difficult genre. Have students follow along as you identify how Johnson has effectively narrowed her topic in the first paragraph. She starts with a broad overview: "In the history of education, few topics have sparked such public debate as the teaching of reading," and ends with a very concise statement: "Two basic views of reading instruction grew out of this activity: the skills-based approach . . . and the meaning-based approach." In this way, Johnson has defined her focus and is able to transition quickly to her summaries of the research.

Johnson devotes a separate section to each reading approach, first discussing its history and origination and then giving a brief overview of its elements. You may want to point out to students that Johnson carefully avoids making value judgments about the two approaches or comparing them in a pro-versus-con method. Explain to students that accurate, objective summaries are a Key Feature of reviews of scholarly literature.

Johnson spends the last three paragraphs summarizing the issues that have arisen in relation to the two approaches. She writes that current research confirms that "balanced reading instruction in the classroom combines the best of phonics instruction and the whole-language approach." By critically evaluating her sources (another Key Feature), Johnson is able to present her findings in a logical and focused review and to draw important conclusions.

Some Tips for Teaching Reviews of Scholarly Literature.

Choosing a topic. To make their task manageable, students need to choose a limited topic. If they are writing a literature review

as part of an assignment sequence leading to a report or argument essay, their first step might be to create a tentative thesis statement that can govern their literature review as well. You can then help them further limit their research by asking them to define the following:

- *Range of the search.* You may ask students to limit their search to a particular type of scholarly literature, such as theoretical works, practical applications, statements of policy, quantitative research, or qualitative research.

- *Scope of the search.* You may restrict students to journal articles, books, Web sites, government documents, or other resources, or ask them to search only in the scholarly literature of a single discipline.

Doing research. As they would in compiling an annotated bibliography (*Field Guide* Chapter 11), students doing a literature survey need first to read widely to determine what sources are indeed the most relevant for their topic. Refer them to *Field Guide* Chapters 39–41 for guidance in devising a research plan, finding sources, and evaluating them. In addition to the advice on reading presented in Chapter 19, students need to be on the lookout for recurring themes, ideas, and arguments, as well as repeated references to certain works or authors. Work that is cited repeatedly should be consulted for possible inclusion in the review. Discerning patterns in the ideas and research presented in several books or articles can help students "place" the information in their own developing sense of the topic, which in turn will make organizing their reviews easier.

Organizing and drafting. It's useful to remind students that their review of literature should be an essay organized around concepts and ideas, not a summary of everything they find. If they identify major trends, schools of thought, or controversies within the literature, they can organize their reviews around those. Some students, of course, may need your help in seeing trends and in moving from the individual arguments to a sense of the common threads running through a group of sources. Try modeling the assignment by presenting three or four sources and highlighting common terms, concepts, or referenced authorities; discuss what they have in common; and work with the class to summarize that commonality in a single sentence. Do the same with differences, and discuss whether the sources should be grouped as one or divided into two or more groups, according to the degree to which they share premises or method, agree or disagree. You might also offer students specific frameworks within which to group the literature: three possibilities include historical (how can these works be grouped in time?), geographical (how can these works be grouped by country or location?), and descriptive (how are some of these works similar or different?). Students may benefit from the advice in *Field Guide* Chapter 31, CLASSIFYING AND DIVIDING.

You can also help students see how to draft their discussion of each group of works by examining the sample review in *Field Guide* Chapter 19. Each section in the literature review begins with a descriptive thesis like "The skills-based approach to reading was highly influenced by the work of Jeanne S. Chall." The rest of that section uses evidence from selected sources to support the thesis. The author uses a few direct quotes but primarily paraphrases and summarizes the literature she cites as she synthesizes it.

Students may be reluctant to do more than summarize the literature because, as students, they may feel that their opinions cannot hold any water in comparison to the weight of the experts they are consulting. Even graduate students may have those concerns; in fact, they're similar to the feelings most people have at several points in their lives of being frauds who only enjoy their positions because no one's found them out yet. So you may want to discuss these feelings in class, both to reassure students that it's okay to feel that way and to help them understand that part of entering a new community—school, work, or social—involves pretending you belong and know the language and moves, even when you don't.

Other Useful Chapters in the *Field Guide*

Chapter 20, RÉSUMÉS AND APPLICATION LETTERS

Although usually reserved for courses in business or technical writing, instruction in creating résumés and application letters is often greatly appreciated by students, many of whom are seeking part-time or summer work and may be clueless about presenting themselves effectively on paper. This chapter offers help in teaching these important documents.

Using the Reading and Teaching the Key Features. Although the examples in the *Field Guide* are useful for illustrating the Key Features of résumés and application letters, you may also want to have students spend some time reviewing numerous types and styles of both. Viewing samples written for various purposes and audiences will help students develop a large inventory of active verbs and better understand how to effectively relate their own qualifications in a succinct, organized fashion using a design that highlights their noteworthy information (all Key Features of résumés). Students may benefit from learning that employers, on average, spend no more than a minute reviewing each applicant's résumé to determine if the person is worthy of an interview or further consideration. An easy way to have students test out their résumés is to have

them exchange with a classmate and scan each other's drafts for one minute. When the time is up, have them hand back their résumés and share with each other everything they can remember reading. This activity will help students understand the importance of being concise and presenting information effectively.

When discussing application letters, point out to students that in addition to using a businesslike format and presenting qualifications succinctly, students will want to stay primarily focused on how they can best meet their potential employer's needs. For instance, Praeger writes, "Since your internship focuses on public relations, my experience in the field should allow me to make a contribution to your company." This is more effective than if he had said, "Since your internship focuses on public relations, I can expand my current knowledge and expertise." Mention to students that writing centers, job centers, and libraries are wonderful resources, too. Many offer advice, handouts, and even mini workshops—all free of charge! In addition, the following Web sites provide numerous samples and can be helpful for teaching résumés and application letters:

<http://www.jobweb.com>
<http://owl.english.purdue.edu>
<http://resume.monster.com>
<http://msn.careerbuilder.com>

Some Tips for Teaching Résumés and Application Letters.

Choosing content. When putting together a résumé, some students need to choose among their many activities to keep to a single page. Help them distinguish between personal information or hobbies that employers are unlikely to care about and activities that show their abilities to good advantage. Some students who didn't have jobs or pursue activities in high school may have trouble filling a page. These students may benefit from such activities as clustering and looping (in *Field Guide* Chapter 22, GENERATING IDEAS AND TEXT) or from doing research on potential employers or careers (Chapter 16 in the *Field Guide*, PROFILES, offers useful advice on this kind of research, as does "Doing Field Research" in Chapter 40). You may need to confer with such students to help them see that activities they may see as irrelevant, such as volunteering at their church or helping the local T-ball coach, can be presented as valuable activities that show their skills and character.

Drafting, revising, editing, and proofreading. Readers of résumés and application letters expect specific information in a specific order; résumés are highly stylized documents that don't invite much creativity (with the possible exception of job seekers in "creative" fields, such as advertising). Help students phrase their educational and work experience using action verbs to show what they *did*: Offering a list of such verbs, asking students to find action verbs in sample résumés, and revising some entries with the class can help them see what to do. It's useful to emphasize to students that application letters are arguments: The writer is presenting an argument that he or she should be considered for a job. As such, application letters need to present reasons and evidence, just as in any other argument. In both résumés and application letters, students should make their points in parallel form. Finally, plan on spending considerable class time on editing and proofreading. These documents should be flawless, without a single typo or misspelling, because busy employers look for ways to make the number of applicants they must evaluate manageable, and evidence of carelessness is a good reason for rejection.

Designing. To make their print résumé and letter each fit on a single page, students may also need help in manipulating design elements, including font size and use of white space. *Field Guide* Chapter 47 offers design advice. The documents should be printed on good-quality white paper with a laser printer—special "résumé papers" or folders aren't likely to impress potential employers, and in fact may annoy some. Consider going over how to address a business envelope and fold the documents to fit inside, skills that students used to email may not have mastered.

Other Useful Chapters in the *Field Guide*

Useful Readings

Bartholomae, David. "Inventing the University." *When a Writer Can't Write: Studies in Writer's Block and Other Composing Process Problems.* Ed. Mike Rose. NY: Guilford, 1985. 273–85.

Bazerman, Charles. "The Life of Genre, the Life in the Classroom." *Genre and Writing: Issues, Arguments, Alternatives.* Ed. Wendy Bishop and H. Ostrom. Portsmouth, NH: Boynton/Cook. 1997. 19–25.

Elbow, Peter. "The Cultures of Literature and Composition: What Could Each Learn from the Other?" *College English* 64.5 (May 2002): 533–46.

Freedman, Aviva. "The What, Where, When, Why, and How of Classroom Genres." *Reconceiving Writing, Rethinking Writing Instruction.* Ed. Joseph Petraglia. Mahwah, NJ: Lawrence Erlbaum, 1995. 121–144.

Ockerstrom, Lolly. *Teaching with a Purpose.* Boston: Houghton, 1992. 221–222.

Trupe, Alice L. "Academic Literacy in a Wired World: Redefining Genres for College Writing Courses." *Kairos* 7.2 (Summer 2002).<http://english.ttu.edu/ kairos/ 7.2/index.html>.

Young, Art and Toby Fulwiler, eds. *When Writing Teachers Teach Literature.* Portsmouth, NH: Boynton/Cook—Heinemann, 1995.

27 Teaching about Writing Processes

For many students, writing a text is an activity that has typically taken place the night before it's due. Some students believe that they write best "under pressure." Few have been required to think on paper about their topics, been given guidance in fleshing out their ideas with memories or research, or been asked to revise, except to "fix" errors pointed out to them on their drafts. If they have been asked to write using a full range of writing processes, they may have experienced them as rigid, even lockstep: First, you brainstorm; then you write an outline and then a draft; then you revise it, edit it, and turn it in. Many students may not understand how writers create good writing or how they can use the activities in this chapter flexibly to accomplish what they need to do. See Chapter 3, "Designing Writing Assignments" in this book for suggestions of ways to create sequences of assignments incorporating these processes along with various genres and strategies. Remember, though, that the best way to encourage students to use the processes of writing is flexibly, honoring their needs and acknowledging what works for them. Here are some suggestions for teaching using the processes of writing:

- Give students choices, but ask that they experience several strategies, so they can make informed choices about what works for them—and so they have alternatives if one method doesn't work.

- Ask students to describe how they write an academic essay. Invite them to describe it in a flow chart, diagram, list, or narrative, and then compare various students' processes to show how they can differ.

- Suggest that students write in brief sessions with breaks between to make writing part of their daily routine: freewriting on their topic one day, outlining the next, writing a beginning that evening, and so on. Or tell them to stop when they feel their creative juices drying up—in the middle of a paragraph or the middle of a sentence, if need be. They should quickly jot down a few notes about how and why they want to continue—and then do something else for awhile.

- Suggest that students set intermediate deadlines for themselves, for example, an outline by Wednesday, a rough draft by Friday. If their personal deadline is several days before the actual deadline, they then have time to improve their draft before submitting it. One way to enforce the deadline is to make an appointment for a conference with you or with a tutor at the campus writing center.

- Include time during class for students to write, share their writing, and talk about it. Teachers demonstrate what's important by their use of class time.
- Write with your students. Teachers also demonstrate what's important by what they do—and if you do assignments with your students, you can then talk with them as one writer to another about what you did, what worked for you, and what didn't.

This chapter offers advice and tips for teaching each chapter in the PROCESSES section of the *Field Guide*.

Chapter 21, COLLABORATING

Students may not enter into collaboration willingly. Some students have endured bad experiences with group work, others took seriously their teachers' admonitions to "Do your own work," and still others simply do not trust that the advice given by their peers is trustworthy and may think the teacher, as the bestower of the grade, is the only voice that matters. For those reasons, you need to lay some groundwork to make collaborating a successful part of your writing class.

First, you need to establish and maintain an atmosphere of trust and safety in your classroom so students will willingly share their ideas and work with one another. Early in the term, perhaps beginning on the first day of class, do some activities to help students get to know one another. You might pair students to interview one another and introduce their partner to the class, ask students to describe themselves in such a way that someone standing across the room could pick them out and then have students find each other, or do other ice-breaking activities to help students see one another as individuals. Ask students to share some writing with one another and with the class, with the simple rule that no one responds, except to clap at the end. Put students into groups and have them respond only positively to one another's writing, discussing three things they like about the draft.

How you assign students to groups is both a matter of pedagogy and a matter of taste. For informal activities, you might simply ask students to get into groups of four or five, letting them choose their partners. When you assign more serious group work, such as responding to drafts or doing collaborative projects, you're better off assigning students to groups. Instructors commonly divide students in various ways: they may want each group to include a mix of writing ability or to reflect the class's ethnic, racial, gender, or other diversity; sometimes you may need to create groups to separate students who do not work productively together.

The physical arrangement of groups can affect their functioning. If you're teaching in a room with moveable desks, insist that each group member's desk faces everyone else's equally; if the students are sitting in a row, the quality of their interaction will suffer because the students on the end can easily opt out of participating (and, indeed, may be unable to hear or see). If you're in a classroom with stationary furniture or teaching in a computer classroom, you may need to arrange the groups so that students are seated in two rows or working across a computer table—or allow students to sit on the floor or in the hall. If possible, move groups to the corners of the room, with one or two groups in the middle, to provide as much space between the groups as possible.

When you assign group work, establish clear rules about how students should behave: They should focus on the work and not on personalities, modulate their voices so the groups can work productively without disturbing one another or classes in other classrooms, and, in general, treat others as they want to be treated. When students read one another's work, give them advice on how to be good readers:

- Let the writer lead you by asking questions or requesting that you focus on certain parts of the draft.
- Be positive—look for what works well, rather than for mistakes—but be honest. Try to balance criticism and praise.
- Focus on the writing, not the writer. Describe what the *writing* says and does, rather than saying, "*You* do this or that."

- Be specific and constructive. Offer suggestions if you can; for example, "I'd like to know more here—maybe a couple of examples," or "What if you rearranged this sentence to say . . . ."

You can also help groups function by assigning roles. For example, one student might be the timekeeper, in charge of making sure that each student's work is given equal time; another might be the moderator, charged with seeing that every group member has opportunities to contribute and that one person does not dominate the group. Another student might be the recorder who takes notes on the group's work and reports the group's results to the class. Give the class a specific time period in which to work and call out the time periodically to remind students how much time remains. Consider giving students *less* time than you anticipate their task taking; for example, if you think the group work should take thirty minutes, give them twenty or even fifteen. You can always give them more time if they need it; and if they don't, you can move on.

Reporting results is itself a powerful way to keep groups working. If you assign a specific set of tasks that must result in an oral report to the class or a completed worksheet or text, students will be more likely to approach the work responsibly. It's also useful to have a backup activity—also leading to a product—for the groups that finish their first task far sooner than you had planned!

To keep groups working, walk around the room, monitoring their conversations, or sit at a desk in the middle of the room, where you can look at one group or a book while listening to another. Some groups will get to work and do exactly what you want, even if you never go near them; other groups will work when you're in the vicinity and lapse into conversation once you're on the other side of the room; and some groups will require you to sit with them to direct their activities. If you are needed for five minutes to clarify the task or your expectations for it, that's okay; however, if the group won't work unless you're sitting with them (fortunately, a rare occurrence), the group isn't functioning and should probably be disbanded, its members assigned to other groups.

Chapter 22,
GENERATING IDEAS AND TEXT

Often the biggest challenge for generating ideas and text is convincing students to loosen up, to give the activity a chance. Some students may see such activities as inefficient, preferring to jump directly to drafting prematurely; others may have tried such activities in the past and felt that they weren't helpful. Here are some ways to help convince students to try the activities:

- Stress that freewriting, brainstorming, and other generating activities won't be graded—or that you'll grade on length or amount of elaboration, perhaps with a three-point system: 3 = lots of writing, playful and thoughtful; 2 = goes beyond the minimum; 1 = meets the minimum requirement.

- Offer choices, so students may select a method that matches their abilities and ways of thinking. People who tend to think in words may prefer freewriting or listing, for example, while visual thinkers may prefer clustering or even sketching a picture. Some students may feel at home writing on a computer, while others need to use pen and paper.

- Encourage students to create outlines or numbered lists, or to move from these activities to the Organizing sections of the Genre chapters in the *Field Guide*. Rosemary Deen, in "Notes to Stella," says that "Structure pulls material out of the mind. You pluck something out of the mind's plenty that you would otherwise not pay attention to because you need it to complete your structure" (62).

- Make it clear that if the activity doesn't work, you won't force students to do it. At the same time, if their subsequent writing lacks content or is poorly organized, you should reserve the right to ask students to return to these activities to help as they revise.

Chapter 23, DRAFTING

Although "Drafting" stresses that drafting is exploratory and tentative, some students find the task daunting. They don't know where to start, they reach a certain point and grind to a halt, or they fear loss of control over their ideas as their prose leads them in directions they hadn't anticipated.

These students need encouragement and comfort: If they can't think of a way to begin, suggest that they start somewhere in the middle. If they hit a wall, suggest that they revisit activities in Chapter 22, GENERATING IDEAS AND TEXT, that worked for them before, or that they stop trying to write that section and begin another section or paragraph. If they find that their writing is leading them to a topic or a perspective on their topic that they hadn't planned, they can decide to see where the new topic leads, planning to rewrite the beginning to fit their new ideas; or they can try to figure out where in the draft their thinking abandoned their plan and try again to write what they'd planned. Before they do, however, they should consider carefully whether their new ideas are indeed a distraction or represent better ideas than they came up with earlier.

If writers are blocked and cannot write a draft, you can suggest some ways to get them going:

- *Revise your standards.* Some writers feel a need to perfect each sentence before moving on to the next. Many student writers feel such pressure to avoid error that they can't write anything. These writers need to be reassured that there'll be plenty of time to clean up their prose later, that their first priority must be getting text on the page or screen so they'll have something on which to work.

- *Write a letter.* Suggest that blocked students write a letter explaining what they want to say in their draft. By the time they've finished, they'll have a draft that they can rewrite to meet the demands of the genre in which they need to write.

- *Say it out loud.* Ask blocked students to explain orally what they want to say in their draft, to you, to another student, or into a tape recorder. Once they're done, they'll have rehearsed it and can usually put it into writing.

Chapter 24, ASSESSING YOUR OWN WRITING

Donald M. Murray observes that "the writer's first reader is the writer" (58). The advice in this chapter of the *Field Guide* begins with that premise: Before students have others read their writing, they should read and assess it themselves. Students are more likely to take these activities seriously if you assign them.

- Ask students to color-code their formal and informal writing. This activity can lead to good class discussions about what students characteristically do when asked to respond to readings or speculate about concepts—and what college faculty expect of them.

- Have students answer the questions in the sections on Considering the Rhetorical Situation in this chapter and also those questions in the Genre chapter they're working from to prepare them for revising and rewriting.

- Ask students to answer the questions in Examining the Text Itself as another way to help them see how their writing measures up.

- Have students analyze their own writing using the analysis techniques in Chapter 38, READING STRATEGIES: writing outlines of what their draft says and does, identifying patterns in their writing, and analyzing the argument.

Chapter 25, GETTING RESPONSE AND REVISING

You can use the advice in this chapter to encourage students to move from "fixing" their drafts—usually meaning that they change only what you have marked in your responses—to more global revision of their texts. This process isn't easy for some students, who struggle to get one draft written and honestly can't see how they might have written it differently. So encouragement and modeling with your own writing—perhaps by revising or rewriting a paragraph in class, thinking aloud as you make changes—can be helpful, as can your responses to students' writing. See Chapter 9 in this book for tips on responding to students' writing.

Here's an example of how you might model the thoughtful revising behavior you want from your students. Students' initial drafts may briefly sketch anecdotes or descriptions that need to be fleshed out so readers can understand what they're saying and why they're including it. In the following paragraphs, writing teacher Brady Allen revises a childhood memory from an initial anecdote to a memoir that also makes an argument. Allen introduces the memory in general terms:

My teacher said I'd done the assignment wrong, that I'd crossed the line, that my drawing was dirty. I had an argument with her about not being fair with me, and I was scared to death because she was so intimidating. She was big and mean looking, But I stood my ground, and I made her rethink things.

The underlined parts are all labels or vague descriptions that offer little information. Look now at his revision that adds details to bring the memory to life:

I stood in front of Mrs. Jones, and I clutched my artwork in my hand. It was a drawing of an apple—only my apple was upside down and had a head and face, arms and legs, and a stem where a penis might be. I had scribbled a title along the bottom: "You Are What You Eat." My classmates had thought it was funny.

Mrs. Jones was perched atop her thick-heeled shoes, staring down through her glasses across the bridge of her nose. Her forehead was wrinkled and she was grinding her teeth. She frowned at me; it was a staredown.

I felt a fat bead of sweat slip from my underarm, slide down my side, and disappear into the band of my Fruit of the Looms. But I stood my ground and looked into her unblinking eyes.

"That was not the assignment," she said, finally.

Here the specific details—the showing—give credibility by creating a scene and characters readers can see, hear, and sense. Allen doesn't stop there, however; he adds another layer, of reflection, which takes the narrative beyond a simple anecdote to an argument for students' rights to protect their creativity. At important points, he adds reflections, which are underlined here:

Mrs. Jones was perched atop her thick-heeled shoes, staring down through her glasses across the bridge of her nose. Her forehead was wrinkled and she was grinding her teeth.

Looking back, I see that it was something of a façade. She was a fifth-grade teacher built to terrorize, sure, but I think she was only *trying* to be scary. I would get to know her better throughout the rest of the year, and I remember her as a woman afraid of losing control. We all know how a soft-spoken teacher can be usurped by class clowns, especially rowdy fifth-grade boys. She wanted to avoid that, and frowning over her nose from atop her tall shoes was her means.

So she frowned at me; it was a staredown.

I felt a fat bead of sweat slip from my underarm, slide down my side, and disappear into the band of my Fruit of the Looms. But I stood my ground and looked into her unblinking eyes.

I'm not sure why I really felt the need to stand up to her. I knew the drawing was "obscene." That's part of why I drew it that way after all. I know I didn't really have any concept of censorship at that age, but I think even then there was something inside me that knew my artistic freedom was in jeopardy. Somewhere in the back of my mind I knew I had to defend my art. Something told me that my creativity, my urge to expand the boundaries of the assignment, was more important than the petty "perversity charge" of my teacher. My creativity hadn't hurt anyone, had it? No. It was a simple apple with human anatomy. I mean, come on.

"That was not the assignment," she said, finally . . . . ."*Your* apple has body parts. *Appendages*," she said. I recall that she made the word appendages sound like it was a pile of maggot-infested crap. *Ah-peeen-daaageees.* Like merely having an appendage went against some strict religious doctrine.

"I know, but. . . . Look at my apple." I held the paper up, and turned it upside down so that the apple itself was right side up. I recall my hand shaking slightly, the paper rustling softly. "My apple has the same bad spots—it looks the same as the one on the table. I just added to it."

"Did I tell you to add to it?" Her nostrils flared, and I could see her jaw working where she was still grinding her teeth.

I said nothing. Just locked with her eyes.

"Did I?" she asked again.

"No."

"You'll stay after school and wash my boards for the rest of the week. Okay? You'll take the second bus home. Do you understand?"

"Yeah, I guess."

" 'Yes,' not 'Yeah, I guess.' "

"Yes."

"So, what have you learned from this?"

I thought about this for only the briefest of moments, and then I said, "That you've got no imagination."

I thought she was going to wear her teeth down to the gums, the grinding got so bad. I thought I was going to catch some hell. She poked me in the chest with one meaty finger. But what Mrs. Jones did after that surprised me: she smiled slightly and said simply, "Maybe you're right."

With these additions, Allen moves beyond the perspective of the classroom anecdote itself to his current, adult interpretation of this childhood drama. He shapes the narrative by telling, showing, and reflecting on it and so shapes readers' interpretation as well. You can create similar, multiple revisions to illustrate how to revise to improve a text's focus, argument, organization, clarity—or anything else.

Rewriting is useful for at least two reasons: When students rewrite a draft in a completely new way, they are forced to see their writing with new eyes, making various changes to fit a new rhetorical situation; such revision can be challenging in a way few students have experienced previously. And that makes it fun to do: since students already have a "serious" draft, asking them to play with it lets them explore various alternatives without risk. In the process, they often discover ways of integrating some of their rewrites into their original and sometimes decide to focus their attention on the rewrite, abandoning the original. You can assign rewriting in various ways: you can have students do quick rewrites in class; you can have them work collaboratively on one another's drafts; you can have them rewrite a single paragraph of their choice (or yours); or, you can require that they produce a completely new draft that's at least as long and as carefully thought through as the original.

Chapter 26,
EDITING AND PROOFREADING

For many students, what they were taught to call "revising" is really editing and proofreading. And some of them have been taught that editing and proofreading are the only parts of the writing process that really matter. You should try to convince students that they can put off serious editing and proofreading work until the final stages of writing a text—that there's no point in fixing a sentence or phrase that might be revised out of the text. Also, as students revise, they'll see problems or straighten out sentences or spellings, so many editing and proofreading issues will disappear as they go over their work. But once their texts are in the overall shape they think is best, they need to go over the texts carefully, making them as clear and correct as they can for the simple reason that readers are often intolerant: They judge a writer's ideas and personality by the correctness of their prose.

The *Field Guide* does not include a handbook, but Chapter 26, EDITING AND PROOFREADING, offers advice for students on major questions they need to ask about their paragraphs, sentences, and words. In addition, you may ask students to look for patterns of errors in their writing, as they might in analyzing the writing of others (see *Field Guide* Chapter 38, READING STRATEGIES). From this exercise, students can compile a record of their error patterns, allowing you to provide focused, detailed instruction in the correct forms. You may also assign worksheets on such problems; several are available on the Web, and more may be available in your campus writing center. These records can also help students edit, using them as checksheets to make sure those errors don't appear in their work.

When you see a student's early drafts filled with mistakes, don't panic. Often, students who are struggling with new concepts and unfamiliar genres can't successfully manage the rules of language at the same time. Some students who speak dialects of English compose in their home dialect first. In both these cases, as students gain control over content and organization, many of the errors and nonstandard usages will likely disappear—and what's left is where you should focus your teaching.

Chapter 27,
COMPILING A PORTFOLIO

Chapter 10 of this book, "Teaching with Writing Portfolios," offers detailed advice on assigning, maintaining, and evaluating writing portfolios and is a good place to start. When you ask students to create portfolios, you can use the questions in "Considering the Rhetorical Situation" either as a way to help students choose the sort of portfolio they'd like to create or as a framework for defining the kind of portfolio you'd like them to create. In other words, you may wish to offer students considerable freedom or carefully define for them the portfolio's purpose, audience, included genres, desirable writer's stance, and range of media and design options.

Students usually find a list of required and optional pieces useful, and you will, too, since the first requirement for any required piece in a portfolio is simply, "Is it in there?" As Chapter 10 notes, asking for all drafts and source material for essays helps students assess their progress while helping you read their material efficiently.

Similarly, asking students to organize their portfolios carefully helps them see what the portfolio contains while aiding your reading and evaluating.

For many instructors, students' reflections on their portfolio contents is very important in assessing their growth as writers and potential for independent work once they leave the writing course. Ask students to read the Sample Self-Assessment and discuss it, identifying the various elements of a good self-assessment and the evidence Nathaniel Cooney uses to support his statements; note how the assessment itself demonstrates Cooney's writing ability as much as any other piece in his portfolio.

A Literacy Portfolio. This is a special portfolio that nicely accompanies the literacy narrative assignment in Chapter 6. You can assign it as a way to create a bridge between the literacies students bring with them to your classroom or the literacy instruction they've had before reaching you and the expectations of college writing. The assignment itself is deceptively simple: "to put together a portfolio that chronicles your development as a reader and writer." As students collect materials from their past and organize them for presentation, they often make striking discoveries, find books or papers they'd long forgotten, and connect various significant literacy events. And as they share their portfolios with other students, they learn that others have had similar experiences and enjoyed some of the same books, and they see possibilities for adding to and reorganizing their own portfolios—and they get to know other students in the class. Most students find this a very rewarding experience. Here are some tips for making the assignment work:

- *Create one yourself.* As is generally true, doing what you're asking students to do will help you explain it to them while providing you with a model for them to see. You can use your portfolio to show them what they might include in theirs and various ways of compiling the material: plastic sleeves for essays, photo album pages for individual sheets, two-pocket folders for bulky items, even boxes or baskets for oddly-shaped items.

- *Assign the portfolio early* and give students several weeks to work on it. Some students need to travel home to get material; some need to get their parents to dig papers and picture books out of closets, attics, and basements. They'll also need time to organize what they find and annotate each item.

- *Offer options.* Some students have little to collect, because of frequent moves around the country, house fires, or simply a disinclination to keep old schoolwork. Such students may compile portfolios of current writing, writing done for work, or even remembered writing—brief descriptions of pieces of writing or reading they remember as significant but that they don't have. (One schoolteacher who had lost everything in a fire created a moving portfolio composed entirely of the memories he had of important papers in his life, from his daughter's birth certificate to his divorce papers.) Some students who have few artifacts of their reading or writing have many of other kinds of literacy, including artwork, sports, auto mechanics, and music—allowing alternate forms of literacy to dominate some portfolios may draw otherwise disengaged students to participate in this project (and enrich the portfolios of other students, too).

- *Share the portfolios.* You should share your portfolio with them as an introduction to the assignment. Most instructors spend class time flipping through the pages and explaining each item orally; you might ask students to do the same, perhaps assigning two or three students to share theirs at the beginning and end of each class period. Alternately, you can ask students to bring their portfolios on the due day and place them on their desks; they can then circulate around the room, reading one another's portfolios and discussing the contents with one another. If students scan materials and create an online literacy portfolio, you can ask that students visit one another's sites during or outside class. It's useful to close the sharing activity with a brief writing activity, asking students to reflect on what they learned about one another's literacy—and their own.

Useful Readings

Boynton, Linda. "See Me: Conference Strategies for Developmental Writers." *Teaching English in the Two-Year College* (May 2003): 391–402.

Dawkins, John. "Teaching Punctuation as a Rhetorical Tool." *College Composition and Communication* 46:4. Rpt. Josephine Koster Travers, *Teaching in Progress.* 2nd ed. NY: Longman, 1998. 438–455.

Hartwell, Patrick. "Grammar, Grammars, and the Teaching of Grammar." *College English* 47.2 (1985): 105–127.

Micciche, Laura R. "Making a Case for Rhetorical Grammar." *College Composition and Communication* 55:4 (June 2004): 716–737.

Murray, Donald. *A Writer Teaches Writing.* 2nd ed. NY: Houghton, 1985.

Perl, Sondra. "Understanding Composing." *College Composition and Communication* 31.4 (December 1990): 363–369.

Sommers, Nancy. "Revision Strategies of Student Writers and Experienced Adult Writers." *College Composition and Communication* 31 (December 1980): 378–388.

Tobin, Lad. "Introduction: How the Writing Process Was Born—and Other Conversion Narratives." *Taking Stock: The Writing Process Movement in the '90's.* Ed. Lad Tobin and Thomas Newkirk. Portsmouth, NH: Boynton/Cook—Heinemann. 1–14.

Teaching Writing Strategies **28**

Defining. Analyzing causes and effects. Comparing and contrasting. Writers constantly employ these and other strategies as they write, whether they focus primarily on a single strategy or combine several strategies in order to achieve their purposes. Other strategies—for creating effective beginnings and endings, guiding readers, using dialogue, and reading critically—are useful in many writing situations. The chapters in this section of the *Field Guide* are designed to help students as they write and read, so encourage them to refer to the Strategies chapters as they plan and draft their work. They may find that one strategy, such as analyzing causes and effects or classifying, becomes the major strategy they use when writing some essays; for others, they will combine several strategies—narrating an anecdote, defining a key term, comparing several things, and so on.

Each of these chapters offers guidance in deciding how to use the strategy and a brief example, followed by ways of organizing a text using the strategy and an outline of the rhetorical situations in which using each strategy is a good idea. If students are writing a text that primarily uses one strategy, they can follow the suggestions in that chapter as they plan and draft. If they're combining strategies, they may choose among the options to suit their needs as writers. See Chapter 3 in this book for suggestions on integrating STRATEGIES chapters into sequences of assignments leading to a finished text. You may find yourself discussing these strategies with students more often during one-on-one conferences, as their varying topics and approaches to those topics will dictate their need for specific strategies. Here are some additional pointers for helping students use these strategies effectively.

Chapter 28,
BEGINNING AND ENDING

Chapter 28 explains several ways for students to begin and end their essays. You might ask students to draft several opening and closing passages and then compare them to see which most effectively achieves their purposes. Some students may need to play with several opening paragraphs in order to find a direction for their papers and to develop momentum for further writing. Some may need to wait until they've finished a draft to write a beginning, so they can write knowing what they're introducing. Others might benefit from drafting the ending first, to help them work toward a goal. Students might also share their drafts in groups to see how each affects an audience. Some additional tips for helping students with beginnings and endings include the following:

- *Use "Considering the Rhetorical Situation" to help students choose an appropriate beginning and ending.* Ask them to consider the general questions in this chapter in light of their understanding of the genre in which they're writing—and refer to the questions on the Rhetorical Situation in the Genre chapter for more specific ways to think about them.

- *Encourage them to think in terms of content, not paragraphs.* Many students believe they need an opening paragraph and a concluding paragraph. That's often not enough space to provide a useful introduction or a satisfying conclusion. One teacher I know suggests devoting the first page to the beginning, with the thesis at the bottom of the page, and the last full page to a conclusion. Showing models of multi-paragraph beginnings and endings can help, too.

- *Consider an essay a journey to a new place—not a round trip.* Students taught rigid formats may write essays in which the first and last paragraphs are virtually interchangeable. Note that beginnings and endings serve different purposes—and so should contain different information, even when the conclusion restates the main point, so that readers feel satisfied.

Chapter 29, GUIDING YOUR READER

The advice in Chapter 29 helps students in the creation of titles, thesis statements, and topic sentences and presents advice on using transitions effectively. It's a good idea to refer students to this chapter repeatedly as they plan and draft their texts. Here are some ideas for helping students write good titles and thesis statements:

Titles. Have students write five, or ten, or twenty possible titles and choose the one that they like best. Have other students choose from their list or compose a thesis based on the titles. Have students come up with a title as they work on generating ideas and text to help them focus their thinking. See if key phrases in their thesis statements can be combined or modified to act as a title. Explore the differences between titles in newspapers, popular magazines, and scholarly works by sharing examples from all three media and having students analyze them for structure, content, and intent: do they try to entice the audience to read the piece? Provide a concise summary of the content? Entertain? Something else? Have students find several titles that they like or that make them want to read further and then discuss what qualities of the titles make them effective.

Thesis statements. Chapter 29 outlines a process for generating good thesis statements, so you may assign your students to follow the three steps outlined in the chapter. In addition, students may benefit from the following advice:

- Thesis statements are tentative. As students write, their drafts may head in a direction different from their original thesis, and it's okay to change the thesis statement accordingly. They do need to be sure that every other part of the draft relates to the new thesis, though.

- A good thesis statement is meaningful for its intended audience and suggests that the writer will have something interesting to say about the topic. Have students ask of their thesis statements, "So what?" For example, while an audience of undergraduates may be uninterested in a thesis like, "It snows too much in the midwest"—it's hard to see what there is to say about such a topic—they're likely to find a thesis like this more meaningful: "Financial aid to college students, including Pell grants, should be eliminated to reduce the influence of the Federal government."

- The thesis of an essay that makes an argument should state a position that others could oppose or challenge. If it doesn't, there's no argument. For example, the statement that "Beef tastes best when grilled" can't be argued because it's a matter of taste.

- Sometimes a template can help students compose a thesis. Here are three models from the Web site of the Writing Center at the University of Wisconsin-Madison:

A. Although most readers of _____ have argued that _____, closer examination shows that _____.

B. _____ uses _____ and _____ to prove that _____.

C. Phenomenon X is a result of the combination of _____, _____, and _____.

Topic sentences. Topic sentences in paragraphs—sentences that state the main idea of the paragraph—function not only to signal to readers what a paragraph is about but also to help readers move from paragraph to paragraph, idea to idea. Help students by beginning the first sentence of a paragraph with a summary of the previous paragraph, by repeating key terms or restating the previous paragraph's content in a word or phrase, combined with "This," as the example by Deborah Tannen ("This episode . . . ") does. You can ask students to find such signal phrases in their reading and analyze how they function in the text. Students can trade papers and underline the topic sentences in each other's paragraphs. You can also help students write effective paragraphs by pointing out that the various approaches for organizing in the "Strategies" section of the *Field Guide* can be applied to single paragraphs as well.

Transitions. To clarify for students the need for transitions in their writing, remove all the transitions from a brief text and show it to students, asking them how the various ideas and sentences relate to one another and then inserting transitions where they think best. Now show the original with transitions, and compare the results. If you use PowerPoint, you can create a series of slides—the first showing the first sentence of the passage, the second showing the first two sentences, the third showing the first three, and so on—to dramatize the reader's journey through the text and show how transitions help guide the reader's understanding. Have students exchange papers and circle the transitions in each other's drafts.

Chapter 30, ANALYZING CAUSES AND EFFECTS

Analyzing causes and effects is challenging, because there are seldom definitive, clear chains of causes and effects and because in many cases the task requires writers to reason backward from an effect to the probable causes of it or speculate that a certain cause will probably lead to certain effects. Both are abstract and tricky, and speculating about possible or probable effects is particularly difficult for many students, as their arguments may quickly devolve into conjecture, fallacious reasoning, or "common sense," which is often anything but. They're better off using this strategy to analyze the causes of a specific event for which evidence exists. If they need to analyze the plausible effects of something, they need to be aware that their analysis must be grounded in evidence: analogous situations, similar events, testimony by experts.

If you're asking students to Argue a Position (Chapter 9) but focusing their argument on analyzing causes and effects, you might ask the class to work together to identify promising topics. Then discuss each one to see if it has these characteristics: it will be interesting for the audience to whom the students are writing; it's researchable—information on possible causes is available; and its causes are arguable.

A danger of the cause-and-effect strategy is oversimplification: arguing that B follows from A, when in reality B might also result from the influence of C, D, and E. Emphasizing the classification of causes and effects as plausible, probable, or likely—not statements of fact—can help students see the need for selecting and interpreting as well as making an argument. To emphasize the interpretive nature of cause-and-effect analyses, students should take extra care to include signal phrases that introduce their sources, as the credibility of their sources will help them make their case. A signal phrase like, "Jonathan Pope, former director of the Institute on Applied Behavioral Sciences and author of seven books on the subject, states that . . . ." makes it clear that the source is authoritative—important in any argument, but especially so in one of this nature.

Chapter 31, CLASSIFYING AND DIVIDING

To help students understand this strategy, you might present several items—names of cars or popular singers, fast food menu items—and ask students to classify them into groups, identifying the characteristics of each group and why each item fits into it. Alternately, you might present large categories—automobiles; music; fast food—and ask groups of students to divide each one into subcategories. In both cases, ask students to articulate the criteria they use to classify or divide. Your goal here is to help students see that classifying and dividing can be done in various ways; for example, automobiles might be classified by make, function, color, performance, or "coolness," to name a few categories. When possible, students should devise categories that are clear and distinct—or be able to justify a scheme that permits something to be part of more than one category. In their writing, the categories should relate directly to their purpose; if I'm writing about emissions controls on trucks, for example, whether pickup trucks seat two, three, or five is likely irrelevant, unlike their gas mileage and tailpipe emissions.

If you're asking students to Argue a Position (Chapter 9) but focusing their argument on proving that something is a member of a class, you might begin by giving them some sample assertions (W. Mark Felt, Deep Throat, was a hero; a nearby deserted factory should be declared a hazardous waste site) and then asking the class or groups of students to identify the characteristics of the class (What are the characteristics of a hero? Of a hazardous waste site?). They could then see that the task of arguing is to demonstrate that their topic has or doesn't have each of those characteristics.

A common pitfall of the classifying and dividing strategy is to confuse it with

the goal of the essay, to assume that classification or division of something is inherently interesting and worth writing about, rather than a way of understanding a topic. Describing the characteristics of Red State and Blue State voters, for example, might be useful for analyzing two main political currents in the United States, but the essay needs a clear purpose to go beyond mere listing. Students may also need help in making sure that each category they identify is described consistently, using similar criteria to place items in each category and devoting similar amounts of text to each category.

Chapter 32,
COMPARING AND CONTRASTING

When comparing and contrasting two items with the purpose of showing the superiority of one over the other, students will sometimes be unfair in their characterizations of one item, noting only the strengths of one and the weaknesses of the other; you should urge them to acknowledge the strong points of both items because maintaining a judicious, fair stance will increase their credibility for readers.

If you're asking students to Argue a Position (Chapter 9) but focusing their argument on comparing and contrasting two or more things, you might give them terms that they may see as very different. Ask them to identify the differences—and then ask them to identify similarities, too. For example, "Conservative" and "Liberal" are often viewed as opposites. Yet both stand for philosophies of government; both imply ethical stances; both advocate policies on a wide range of issues. This sort of discussion can help students see that their comparisons need to be even-handed.

You might extend discussions of comparing and contrasting by asking students to create analogies, perhaps by starting with clichéd analogies—"My love is like a red, red, rose," "He dropped like a sack of potatoes," "Her face turned as red as a beet"—and seeing how students might revise them to make them fresh and new. Students might practice block and point-by-point organizations by drafting information both ways and discussing each method. Some students will benefit from creating charts or illustrations that help them see the points of their comparison.

Chapter 33, DEFINING

How you define something determines how you—and, potentially, your audience—see it. Helping students see that definitions aren't static or universally agreed upon, that how we define the words we use strongly influences our thinking, is important. To illustrate, you might give students a short list of contested terms—stem cells, character, inheritance tax—and ask them to find out how various people and institutions define them. Then you can discuss how the definitions lead to certain arguments and perspectives. You might also discuss what linguist George Lakoff calls "frames" that define social issues. For

example, one way of framing the issue of taxation is to talk about the need for "tax relief," which implies that taxation is something from which we need to be relieved; a different way of framing the issue is to talk about taxation as "paying our dues as Americans," which implies that paying taxes is a patriotic act. The frames we use, Lakoff says, define our thinking (Powell).

It's also useful to point out that for most purposes in writing, a bare-bones dictionary definition isn't sufficient; ask students to examine the examples of definitions in the chapter to demonstrate how far beyond Webster's they go. This is also a good time to note that regular dictionaries are only one source of definitions; to get useful definitions, students may have to look in specialized dictionaries, etymological dictionaries, textbooks, encyclopedias, and scholarly books and articles. To underscore this fact, you might ask groups of students to find definitions of a single term in several different reference works and compare their findings. You might also ask students to choose a term to define in each of the ways described in the *Field Guide* and explore how each might serve a different purpose.

Chapter 34, DESCRIBING

Describing plays an essential part in many genres and media. Students, however, often need to be nudged to provide descriptive details rather than labeling or classifying. For example, an acquaintance may be described as a geek, or a music CD as cool—but those labels tell us little, other than the writer's overall evaluation. Ask questions: How do you know this person is a geek? What does this person wear, say, and do that makes him or her geeky? Why is this CD cool? What about the music and lyrics makes this CD cool? Or have students write out a description of someone sitting near them (providing guidelines, of course, to avoid negative or hurtful descriptions). Collect them and hand them out randomly; then ask students to silently find the person being described.

In addition to the suggestions presented in this chapter, you might also show students various ways of using description by adapting a technique first presented by Young, Becker, and Pike (1970):

Think of your subject as a *particle* (as if it were a static object sitting still, by itself):

- *Describe it as something standing alone.* What features make it different from others? (Young, Becker, and Pike use as their example a particular, old oak tree: " 'Old Faithful' contrasts in size and age with the surrounding trees.")

- *Describe it as a specific variation of its concept or idea.* How much can it differ from others like it before becoming something else? (The oak "is shedding its leaves more slowly than the other trees. Although still stately, it has passed its lifetime peak of mature, vigorous health.")

- *Describe it as part of a larger context.* How should it be classified? What is its typical position in a time sequence, as a person may be a baby, an adult, or a senior citizen? What is its position in space—as a tree may be part of a forest, or grow by itself in a yard? (The oak "is composed of roots, trunk, and branches, leaves, and reproductive system [not readily discernible, thus an unknown for this inquirer]; each part is composed of subsystems [again, not discernible & thus unknowns]. Since all trees have roots, trunks, branches, and so on, this oak probably differs from other kinds of trees most clearly in the particularities of its subsystems. . . . ")

Think of it as a *wave* (as if it were moving, growing, changing, dynamic):

- *View it as something that changes over time.* What physical features distinguish it from similar objects or events? What is its core or center? (The oak "is now old, nearly leafless, with one broken limb and numerous scars where others have fallen off. Ten or twenty years ago it was the same tree, but not at its inception as a seed. Then it was only potentially a tree. When it falls and rots or is cut up into lumber, it will lose its identity.")

- *View it as a dynamic process.* How is it changing? ("It is clearly rotting; some of the branches are already dead and other show signs of decay.")

- *View it as part of a larger, dynamic context.* How does it interact with its environment? Does it have clear borders, or does it blend into its context? (The oak's "subsystems support, feed, and repair each other by means of a physiological network. The state of the system differs from hour to hour [e.g., in the regulation of moisture loss] and from day to night [in the handling of carbon dioxide]. Some parts of the system can be lost, either temporarily [leaves] or permanently [some branches] without destroying the system.")

Think of it as a *field* (as if it were a network of relationships or a part of a larger network):

- *View it as an element of larger classification systems.* How are the parts organized: in time, in space, in relation to one another? (The oak "is a member of a class of trees called hardwoods, . . . part of a larger class system that includes all trees. . . . It dwarfs the second-generation trees around it.")
- *View it as an element of larger physical systems.* How do particular parts of the system vary in how they interact with the larger systems of which it's a part? ("As part of a scene, its branches stand out sharply against the sky . . . , but from a distance its dark trunk merges almost indistinguishably with the trunks of surrounding trees. . . . It shelters wildlife; it draws raw materials for growth from the earth in which it is rooted and in turn enriches the earth with its fallen leaves.")
- *View it as an abstract system within a larger system.* How does it fit into the larger system? What features and components make it a part of the larger system? ("A system in itself, it fills a place in a larger system, a niche in the ecology of the area. . . . ")

Chapter 35, DIALOGUE

To show students how dialogue can tell readers much about speakers and help writers achieve their purpose, ask students to analyze some dialogue, considering questions like these, adapted from *The English Teacher* Web site: What dialogue gives clues to the speaker's occupation? Nationality or ethnicity? Social class or position? Personality? Character? Intelligence or education? Where does the dialogue refer to or advance the text's narrative or argument? (Danielson)

Your students may attempt to write dialogue containing dialects of English. Writing dialect is tricky: done well, it can clearly convey the speaker's heritage and social class; done poorly, it can seem condescending or inappropriate. If some of your students wish to try to capture a speaker's dialect, offer these suggestions:

- Write out the dialogue in Edited American English first, so that the meaning is clear.
- Select a few key characteristics of the dialect to use, and revise the dialogue to include them consistently. Actual dialect can be difficult to transcribe, partly because many dialectal differences involve differences in pronunciation that are hard to capture without a special alphabet (for example, the

regional differences between *pin* and *pen*), and partly because actual speakers aren't consistent in their use of dialectal features. In addition, some dialects contain features that students may not know without linguistic study that may well be inappropriate for your class (such as verb tenses in African American Vernacular English).

- Ask students to do their best to use the dialect they actually heard the speakers speak, rather than falling back on stereotypical dialect.

Chapter 36, EXPLAINING PROCESSES

If students explain a process that is familiar to them, a potential pitfall is inattention to the needs of their audience, because their familiarity with the process leads them to take for granted steps and explanations that someone unfamiliar with the process needs in order to complete it. One way to demonstrate this problem in class (and have some fun, too) is to ask students to write out instructions for making a peanut butter and jelly sandwich. Take to class bread, peanut butter, jelly, a knife, and a disposable tablecloth (this gets messy) and, following their instructions literally, make some sandwiches. They'll quickly see how unstated steps can lead to unintended consequences—and they can eat the evidence. Also, you'll be able to demonstrate that to explain a process well also requires describing, narrating, defining, and even classifying.

In addition, the more complex the process, the more readers need some orientation in the form of an introduction that identifies the process and its purpose and briefly summarizes the primary stages of the process. Readers will keep this overview in mind as they go through the details of the process. The ending of a process explanation may vary: it may simply end with the end of the process, with a brief summary of the process or its main stages, or with some commentary on the process.

Students' purpose also affects how they explain processes. The chapter focuses on explaining how something is done to inform readers, and explaining how to do something by writing a set of instructions. If the process is complex, you might suggest that students break the process into stages, with steps within each stage, to make the overall task easier. Doing this also lends itself to a series of illustrations, one or more for each stage, or a flow chart.

Chapter 37, NARRATING

Narrating is a strategy used by writers in virtually all genres. You can demonstrate this fact by showing students how narrating is used, not only in Chapter 6, WRITING A LITERACY NARRATIVE, but in the readings in many other chapters as well. Here's a partial list:

- ANALYZING A TEXT: William Safire includes several brief narratives in his analysis of The Gettysburg Address, using several time markers: "Then," Finally," "Lincoln, thirteen years later."

- REPORTING INFORMATION: "The Hijacking of United 175" is a detailed narrative structured around precise noting of the time, from 7:58 a.m. to 9:03:11 a.m., when the plane struck the World Trade Center.

- ARGUING A POSITION: Lawrence Lessig's "Some Like It Hot" presents narratives of the emergence of piracy in various mass media. Andy McDonie includes a history of the government's efforts to suspend the rights of certain groups in his essay.

- LAB REPORTS: The "Procedures" section of lab reports, including this one by Sarah Thomas, consists of a narrative outlining how the experiment was conducted.

- MEMOIRS: Chanrithy Him's "When Broken Glass Floats" narrates a frightening incident of her youth in Cambodia.

Additional teaching issues and suggestions related to this strategy are covered in detail in Chapter 22 of this book, "Literacy (and Other) Narratives."

Chapter 38, READING STRATEGIES

Many of the students you'll encounter in first-year writing courses have extensive experience in reading for meaning. They have read textbooks to learn facts and concepts and have read literature, often for plot and theme. However, they have far less experience or training in reading non-fiction texts critically, examining the words and sentences of the text and exploring the contexts within which it was produced and reading to determine whether information is correct, dated, incomplete, or biased—in other words, whether it's a good source or not. The activities in this chapter are designed to help students read more critically as they analyze texts (in Chapter 7 of the *Field Guide*) or find and evaluate sources (in Chapters 40 and 41). Here are some suggestions for using these activities to good advantage:

- When you introduce the rhetorical situation, have students read a brief text and analyze it as the activity on Previewing a Text in Chapter 38, READING STRATEGIES asks, killing two birds with one stone.

- Ask students to submit responses to texts they read to make sure they're reading accurately and responding appropriately and not, for example, reacting to something they've misread or misunderstood. You might ask students to submit two-part informal writings for assigned readings: one paragraph of summary, to show that they understand the piece, and another paragraph of response, to show that they've thought carefully about it.

- Ask students to annotate a text collaboratively, perhaps writing on an overhead transparency or using the Comment feature of their word processor. Then each group explains to the class why they annotated as they did, and the groups compare notes to see what everyone agrees are the most noteworthy passages of the text.

- If your class is analyzing a single text, divide the class into groups and ask each group to analyze it using one of the methods described in Chapter 38: one group creates a topical outline ("What it says"); another creates a functional outline ("What it does"); a third color-codes repeated words and phrases and a fourth counts parts ("Identifying Patterns"); and a fifth creates a flow chart of the text's structure. Then the groups share their work with everyone, creating a pool of information from which individuals can draw as they develop their own analyses. You can do the same with the questions in "Analyzing an Argument."

- Ask students to study the logical fallacies listed in the chapter, noting that they represent only a sample of the fallacies that philosophers and rhetoricians have identified. Then present some excerpts from texts and some print or TV ads and ask students whether they contain fallacies and, if so, which ones. You're likely to have a lively debate, not only over identifying the fallacy but over whether it's indeed a fallacy—or simply an effective sales or argument technique (or both!).

Useful Readings

Connors, Robert J. "The Rise and Fall of the Modes of Discourse." *Selected Essays of Robert J. Connors*. Ed. Lisa Ede and Andrea A. Lunsford. Boston: Bedford, 2003. 1–12.

"Developing a Thesis Statement." <u>The Writing Center: University of Wisconsin: Madison</u>. 2004. 14 January 2005. <http://www.wisc.edu/writing/Handbook/thesis_composedraft.html>.

Danielson, Leif. *Teaching Dialogue Analysis*. 1999–2004. 14 January 2005. <http://teacher2b.com/ literature/dialogue.htm>.

Qualley, Donna. "Using Reading in the Writing Classroom." *Nuts and Bolts: A Practical Guide for Teaching College Composition*. Ed. Thomas Newkirk. Portsmouth: Heinemann, 1993. 101–126.

Powell, Bonnie Azab. "Framing the Issues: UC Berkeley Professor George Lakoff Tells How Conservatives Use Language to Dominate Politics." *UC Berkeley News*. 27 October 2003. 14 January 2005. <http://www.berkeley.edu/news/ media/releases/2003/10/27_lakoff.shtml#father>.

Salvatori, Mariolina. "Conversations with Texts: Reading in the Teaching of Composition." *The Writing Teacher's Sourcebook*. 4th ed. Ed. Edward P. J. Corbett, Nancy Myers, and Gary Tate. New York: Oxford UP, 2000. 163–174.

Young, Richard, Alton Becker, and Kenneth Pike. *Rhetoric: Discovery and Change*. NY: Harcourt, 1970.

29 Teaching Research and Documentation

Why do we ask students to do research? Research helps students become better thinkers, investigators, critics, and writers. Asking them to find, evaluate, and synthesize the ideas and words of others helps them form and express their own ideas. Ultimately, such activities will help them become better students, able to examine concepts and arguments from a thoughtful, informed perspective, and better citizens as well, less vulnerable to emotional appeals and attempts to mislead them.

Students who have experience with researched essays often conceive the assignment minimally: Pick a topic for which there's lots of information (such as abortion or gun control); do as little research as possible, often looking only for sources that agree with the position they already hold or finding one source that presents "the" opposing view so they can have a "con" to balance their "pro"; string quotes and paraphrases from the sources together to create a draft that meets length requirements; write an introduction and conclusion that could be interchangeable; and make sure the finished paper looks neat. Your task in teaching researched writing is to help students understand that

doing research involves much more. Good research engages the researcher, and that engagement carries over into the writing. Academic research requires examining sources that may hold various points of view and seeing why they agree or disagree, and then creating a text that carefully articulates those various perspectives, drawing from them thoughtful conclusions.

Research assignments can appear daunting at first: Find, read, and use several sources of information to write an essay of five-to-ten pages. Breaking the assignment into a series of smaller tasks, though, makes it manageable for students and for you. Here's a sample sequence using the *Field Guide*:

- Make a list of possible sources (Chapter 39, DEVELOPING A RESEARCH PLAN, and Chapter 40, FINDING SOURCES)
- Compose an annotated bibliography (Chapter 41, EVALUATING SOURCES, and Chapter 11, ANNOTATED BIBLIOGRAPHIES)
- Summarize the positions taken by several sources (Chapter 42, QUOTING, PARAPHRASING, AND SUMMARIZING)
- Draft a tentative thesis (Chapter 29, GUIDING YOUR READER)

- Make an outline (Chapter 22, GENERAT-ING IDEAS AND TEXT)

- Write a draft (Chapter 23, DRAFTING, Chapter 42, QUOTING, PARAPHRASING, AND SUMMARIZING, and Chapter 43, ACKNOWL-EDGING SOURCES, AVOIDING PLAGIARISM)

- Assess and get response to the draft (Chapter 24, ASSESSING YOUR OWN WRITING, and Chapter 25, GETTING RESPONSE AND REVISING)

- Document sources (Chapter 44, DOCU-MENTATION, and Chapters 45, MLA STYLE, and 46, APA STYLE)

- Revise (Chapter 25, GETTING RESPONSE AND REVISING, and Chapter 26, EDITING AND PROOFREADING)

Research assignments usually form part of a genre-based or inquiry-based assignment, such as essays reporting infor-mation or taking a position. For that reason, much of the advice in this chapter is generic, to be adapted as needed for the particular kind of task your students face. The sections below offer advice on using the chapters on Research and Documentation.

Chapter 39,
DEVELOPING A RESEARCH PLAN

Helping students choose a topic. Students typically start with big topics, often a sin-gle word or phrase: stem cell research, gay marriage, legalizing marijuana. The *Field Guide* offers advice on narrowing a topic to make it manageable, but you can add to the advice in various ways.

Help each student with his or her topic. A research project typically stretches over several weeks, so it's worth your while to make sure students are working on top-ics that are unlikely to cause them trouble down the road. Three ways you can do this: (1) *Ask for a* TOPIC PROPOSAL. Have students write out a formal or informal description of what they'd like to research and why. You can collect these on paper or via email and respond to them individually, or have students post them to an online discussion board, where they can read one another's proposals and your responses. (2) *Hold a workshop in class.* Students, especially those who are having trouble coming up with a topic, benefit from hearing other students' topics and from hearing how you respond to them. Ask students in your class to briefly describe their topics (or read their topic proposals aloud) to you and their classmates and then respond, perhaps ask-ing other students to chime in as well. After responding to seven or eight, you'll find students revising their topics before their turn comes. (3) *Hold topic conferences.* You can also ask students to come to individ-ual conferences to discuss their topics. Again, asking them to write a topic pro-posal and either bring it with them or sub-mit it to you ahead of time will help them clarify what they want to do and help you respond appropriately.

Encourage students to choose topics in which they have an interest and a personal connection. Their own interest in a topic will lead them to invest time and energy in the research and writing and will likely produce a better text in the end than a topic they've chosen because they think it's expected or it's easy or it's one they wrote on in high school.

Guide students away from topics on issues like abortion, legalizing marijuana, gun control, and others that are subjects of ongoing, hot debate in society. Although these are important issues, two problems can make these topics very difficult for students: There's so much information available, so many arguments from so many passionate people, that students may be overwhelmed and unable to sift through the mass of data to core arguments; also, students who choose such topics often have a definite position and have difficulty seeing other points of view, let alone treating them fairly.

Also, steer students away from topics on which they're likely to have trouble finding information. Topics on legal or medical cases or sensitive corporate or government information, for example, require access to sources that they're unlikely to have. If you can hold topic conferences or workshops where you have access to your library's online catalogue and databases, you can quickly determine if a topic is likely to be a dry well or to require access to sources that can't be obtained within the time constraints of the course. Also, don't let students choose topics that might lead to harm; a colleague once had a student who wanted to do field research by going underground at a crack house—not a good choice.

Don't let students write on topics they wrote on in high school or wrote on for another course. Aside from issues of recycling—if they simply rework a paper done previously, they aren't doing the work of your course—most schools forbid submitting papers to more than one class unless both instructors agree to it.

Helping students see their biases. Ask students to explore not only what they already know about their topics, but what their opinions and beliefs on it are as well so they understand their potential biases. This process is important so students approach their research task knowing that they need to balance sources that bolster their position with sources that offer other viewpoints. You might also help students see multiple perspectives on their topic by asking them to consider what other positions—more than one—people might hold on their issue: ask questions like, can you be in favor of X in some circumstances but against it in others? Is there a middle ground between two extreme positions?

Emphasizing the need for organization. Students sometimes collect, photocopy, and download source material willy-nilly, forcing them to sort through piles of material to find sources they need. Ask them to follow the advice in Keep Track of Your Sources and bring their source material to show you. Emphasizing that the advice in the *Field Guide* on organizing their material is important is a start, but you may want to ask students to try some of the following methods for keeping on top of their research material.

Filing. Simply having one place—a notebook, a folder, even a paper bag—devoted solely to research material on one assignment will help your most organizationally challenged students. Be flexible, since people need to organize in different ways to suit their personalities and ways of working. Asking students to bring all their research to class or conference in some sort of container can be helpful to them. In class, they can then organize the material if they haven't already done so: Bring markers, sticky notes, a stapler, scissors, a three-hole punch, and transparent tape so students can help one another categorize, annotate, and organize their notes and research.

Double-entry notebooks. Show students the double-entry system for taking notes: In a spiral notebook, they write on the left-hand page direct quotations, paraphrases, and summaries of source material as well as observations or interview notes. On the right-hand page they write reactions, insights, questions, connections—the thinking they need to do about their sources that will help them integrate the material into their own work.

Annotations. Students are generally unused to annotating source material—and if it's from a library, of course, they shouldn't write on it! But when they photocopy material or print it from the Web, they should underline or highlight important passages and write notes in the margins to help their understanding and to identify useful material. Refer students to the sample annotation in Reading Sources with a Critical Eye (*Field Guide* Chapter 41) for advice.

Research portfolios. If students are keeping notebooks or folders with their research material and notes, and if you ask them to submit their source material when they submit their finished essays, they have most of the raw material to create a research portfolio. In a research portfolio, students present a record of the processes of thinking, researching, and writing that led from the initial assignment or topic idea to the finished product. The students then can reflect in writing on those processes, how well they worked and what they might change in the future. Reviewing their research portfolios needn't consume much time: Have them place their materials on their desks and, while they're doing an activity in class, quickly flip through each student's material. Place on each portfolio and in your gradebook a quick evaluative mark (check plus, check, check minus) plus give a brief oral description of what the mark means (very well organized, acceptable, needs work) and you're done.

Chapter 40, FINDING SOURCES

By and large, first-year students rely for their research efforts on the World Wide Web and their local public library. These are useful places to find general sources for their preliminary research, but they need to learn to focus their search efforts on more scholarly sources for their college work.

Consulting reference librarians. Because electronic research tools evolve so quickly, librarians have more up-to-date knowledge of where to look and how to search than anyone else. In many students' minds, librarians are the people who shushed them when they whispered and wouldn't let them borrow the really interesting books, so they need to understand that librarians in academic libraries are not only helpful, they're indispensable to thorough research. Here are suggestions for introducing your students to the services of your school's research librarians:

- *Invite a librarian to your class.* Many librarians have prepared workshops during which they describe what the library offers and how to access it.

- *Meet in a computer classroom or lab.* If you can arrange meeting in a classroom with access to the library's catalogue and databases, the librarian can demonstrate how to use them, and then your students can start searching while you and the librarian circulate, offering advice and troubleshooting.

- *Investigate your library's services.* Some libraries offer guided tours, workshops, searching scavenger hunts, and other services that bring students to the library, where they learn how to use its services.

Encouraging students to interview experts. Specialists in the subject on which they're writing can help students focus their topics, offer ideas they hadn't considered, provide the most current information available, and point them toward valuable sources they might have missed in their own searching.

Permitting students' research to influence their topic choice. While it's good to set a deadline after which students cannot change their topics—desperate students sometimes use a last-minute topic change to substitute a plagiarized paper for the one they're having difficulty writing—giving them the opportunity to allow their research to influence their treatment of the topic reinforces the concept that research is a learning process.

Chapter 41, EVALUATING SOURCES

Evaluating sources is really a twofold activity: Students first evaluate sources as they find them, quickly discarding obviously unsuitable ones and moving on; but next they need to evaluate the remaining sources carefully for their suitability and relevance for their needs. Students often use whatever they find, whether or not it's appropriate. To keep that tendency in check, consider asking them to complete a worksheet on which they answer questions about each source: You might select a few questions from *Field Guide* Chapter 41 and staple the worksheets to photocopies of the sources they plan to use.

Some students may misread their sources. While the ways of misreading are many, a common concern, especially with historical topics, is reading sources not as informational texts but as stories. Students may read for plot and character, as they were taught in their literature courses, not as arguments written for specific purposes. They may try to structure their own essays the same way, writing a narrative of their examination of their sources rather than a report or argument.

Students also tend to believe that what their sources say is the truth—after all, if it's in print, it must be the truth, right? After years of reading textbooks, which are not usually open to questioning, this attitude is understandable. Consequently, students may have difficulty when they encounter two or more sources that contradict one another. They often cannot reconcile the differences and therefore assume that one or the other is wrong, when each may represent a different argument, written at different times for different audiences, rather than statements of fact. As Margaret Kantz writes in "Helping Students Use Textual Sources Persuasively," "facts and opinions are essentially the same kind of statement: they are claims . . . . [T]he only essential difference between a fact and an opinion is how they are received by an audience" (195).

You might give students a list of statements that either are true but disbelieved by many people or that are false but believed by many (Snopes.com, a Web site that debunks urban legends, is a good source of both). Ask them to label each as fact or claim; and then, after you reveal which is which, use their reaction as a springboard to discussion. You might also present students with some sample sources and have them play Peter Elbow's

Believing and Doubting game (described in *Field Guide* Chapter 38), either individually or in groups. Or present headlines from news articles that carry bias from various perspectives and have students rewrite a current headline to change its bias by substituting new words for the originals.

You may find it worth your while to spend part or most of a class period on evaluating Web sites. Students find searching the Web very attractive and comfortable, so they often rely on unrefereed Web sites rather than scholarly sources. Show them some Web sites and have them evaluate their credibility, using either the questions in the *Field Guide* or on one of the many Web sites that offer guidelines on evaluating Websites. Discuss what features make some Web sites seem to be credible— or not.

Chapter 42, QUOTING, PARAPHRASING, AND SUMMARIZING

Quoting. Many students need help integrating quotations smoothly into their own prose. A useful minilesson on doing so might include not only the uses of signal phrases but also the use of a colon at the end of one's own sentence (For example: *My father's first reaction to seeing my grades was swift and surprisingly gentle: "Go to your room; we'll discuss this later."*)and incorporating brief quotations grammatically and gracefully into a sentence, including omitting words and using brackets and ellipses. As an in-class exercise, give students a brief text along with three or four excerpts from sources that support the text's assertions; have students incorporate the source material into the text. You might combine this activity with advice on acknowledging sources: what needs to be acknowledged and what doesn't.

Paraphrasing. Paraphrasing correctly can be challenging for students and accomplished writers alike, so spending some time working with your students on creating good paraphrases is often useful. Consider having students paraphrase a brief text and compare their versions, demonstrating that the ideas in a text may be expressed in various ways. Have students read a text and then create a paraphrase without looking at the text itself until it's time to see whether everything in the text is included accurately in the paraphrase.

Deborah Healy has her students tease out the ideas in a passage, then points out phrases they should avoid when they paraphrase it, and then shows a good example that demonstrates how the grammar, wording, and order of ideas should change.

The original text
Named for James Brady, the White House press secretary who was shot and wounded by John Hinckley Jr. during the attempted assassination of President Ronald Reagan in March 1981, the Brady Bill establishes a national waiting period and background check for the purchase of a handgun. (Bender, 1995: 137)

Main Ideas
Brady bill = named for White House press secretary James Brady

Brady was shot during an assassination attempt on President Reagan
Brady bill provisions = people who want to buy handguns have a waiting period and check on their backgrounds

Phrases to avoid from the original
Named for James Brady, the White House press secretary who was shot and wounded by John Hinckley Jr. **during the attempted assassination** of President Ronald Reagan in March 1981, **the Brady Bill establishes** a national waiting period and background check for the **purchase of a handgun**. (Bender, 1995: 137)

A good paraphrase
Bender (1995) explains that people who want to buy handguns in the US now have a waiting period and a background check as a result of the Brady Bill. The bill was named after White House press secretary James Brady, who was wounded during an assassination attempt on President Reagan. (137).

Also, giving students access to online plagiarism-detection tools such as Turnitin.com can help students see where they are using the language of the original text. I use this tool at the rough draft stage to help teach students to paraphrase—not at the final draft stage, where using it is a policing tool.

Summarizing. Students may find summarizing correctly a difficult task. Some will produce paraphrases; others will distort the original beyond recognition. Some tips for helping students produce effective summaries include the following:

- Have students identify the thesis of the passage and restate it in their own words. That sentence becomes the first sentence of their summary.

- Have students highlight or underline the main ideas in a text (you might model this activity using the highlighting function in your word processing program or on an overhead slide); then ask them to turn over their highlighted text or start a new document and draft a summary of it without looking. Then have them compare their summaries, working together to create a "best" summary.

- Have students write a summary for one audience and then rewrite it for a different audience. Discuss the changes they made and the reasons for the changes.

- Have students write a paraphrase; then a paragraph-long summary; then a three-sentence summary; then a one-sentence summary of the same material. Impose word limits to see how concisely they can summarize a passage.

Chapter 43,
ACKNOWLEDGING SOURCES,
AVOIDING PLAGIARISM

Most plagiarism in first-year writing courses grows out of ignorance or desperation, not dishonesty. Many students have a limited or mistaken concept of what constitutes plagiarism, for example, that it means only using someone else's exact words, and sometimes a certain minimal number of them. Quite a few students honestly believe that anything they find on the Web is fine to use without attribution. Some cultures have concepts of what constitutes intellectual property that differ from ours, and though nonnative students who have studied in the United States for several years may know our rules, some students who have recently arrived in the U.S. don't. (See Chapter 19 in this book for more advice on teaching second-language writers.) Some students have no intention of plagiarizing but, faced with an assignment they don't think they can do, download an essay from the Web or from their roommate's computer and hope for the best. Only a few students deliberately set out to mislead instructors by turning in plagiarized work, and some of them do so because they see so much unattributed or copied writing or "sampled" music all around them. Still, all students need to know what is considered plagiarism in academic writing, as academic audiences define it—and how to avoid it. Here are some tips for preventing plagiarism, which is much better than dealing with suspected plagiarism in submitted essays:

- Emphasize that using the words *or ideas* of others without attribution constitutes plagiarism. Show examples, including unattributed paraphrases. Send students to Web sites that discuss plagiarism. Make sure they read and understand your school's academic dishonesty policies.

- Create writing assignments that make plagiarizing difficult. Slightly alter your requirements each time you teach a course, so that students' work will differ from previous courses' essays. Ask students to choose topics—or shape assigned topics—to some personal interest in the subject, both to increase interest and to individualize their research and writing. Require some recent sources; some student papers have been circulating for several years, so their sources are suspiciously dated, but even papers whose Internet sources predate your introduction of the assignment should raise a red flag.

- Monitor students' generating, researching, and drafting activities by collecting drafts and holding conferences. Establish deadlines for changing topics, so desperate students can't find and submit a plagiarized essay at the last minute.

- Remind students that you know about and have visited online term paper mills, such as Evil House of Cheat and Schoolsucks.com.

- Consider using online plagiarism-detection programs such as Turnitin.com or EVE2. Some instructors use these programs only when they suspect plagiarism; some insist that all students submit their final drafts for checking. I prefer to use Turnitin.com as a teaching tool, asking students to run their rough drafts through the program in order to see where they might need to revise to avoid plagiarism. (Note too that some instructors and students question the ethics of Turnitin's policy of maintaining a library of student work without the students' permission.)

If you suspect a student of plagiarizing, be as certain as you can that the work is indeed plagiarized before making accusations, by checking the paper's sources, submitting the work to a detection program, or simply searching in Google for unusual or key phrases. In my school's writing program, simply showing the suspect essay to other instructors who have taught the course recently gets surprisingly good results; students often recycle writing done just the previous semester, apparently assuming that writing teachers never talk amongst themselves. If you find that a student did indeed submit plagiarized work—or if you strongly suspect it but can't prove it yourself—check with your writing program administrator for your school's policies for dealing with plagiarism and, if necessary, for help before confronting the student.

You may also want to acquaint yourself with the ongoing debate over plagiarism, academic dishonesty, and intellectual property. Good Web sites that offer information on plagiarism and on this debate—and several good links—include Penn State's "Cyberplagiarism: Detection and Prevention" (http://tlt.its.psu.edu/suggestions/ cyberplag/) and a bibliography of articles on plagiarism by Syracuse University professor Rebecca Moore Howard (http://wrthoward.syr.edu/articles. html).

Chapter 44, DOCUMENTATION; Chapter 45, MLA STYLE; Chapter 46, APA STYLE

Very few students in first-year composition classes will be majoring in English or the other humanities disciplines that use MLA style. Most will major in a social science that requires APA or a business, scientific, or engineering field that uses some other citation method. For that reason, students should learn that citation systems are indeed *systems* with shared features. Whatever system they use to cite sources, it will demand that they include similar information to show where they got their information and to permit others to find the information if they want. The systems differ in how that information is presented, the order in which it is presented, and the punctuation used to separate items within each citation. The *Field Guide*'s advice on documentation is color-coded to make those systematic similarities clear to students.

That's not to say that you shouldn't try to teach MLA and APA or some other system. Teach the system that you're comfortable with or that your program prefers. If you teach the basic concepts well, students will be able to adapt the principles to other systems as they need to.

Some tips on teaching documentation:

- Give students sample texts to document. Students will likely be familiar with single-author texts and popular magazines and can find the appropriate documentation information fairly easily. Many students have never seen an academic journal, however, and may need help understanding how they differ from other periodicals.

- Focus attention on documenting Web sites. Show students how to cite various Web sites and how to find the necessary information—and how to cite the page if the information (such as the posting date for the page or site) can't be found.

- Tracking down the source of some Web documents can require sleuthing: Show students how to backtrack to a home page by deleting sections of the URL. For example, a Web page discussing the health effects of drinking water containing perchlorate, chemical used in rocket fuel, has the following URL:

http://www.councilonwaterquality.org/science/health_effects.html

Deleting everything behind the final slash yields:

http://www.councilonwaterquality.org/science/

This page offers several links to scientific data on perchlorate, while removing *science/* leads to the home page of the Council on Water Quality, an industry-funded public interest group. Backward searches can be important since search engines often find online source materials that turn out to be—but aren't labeled as—student essays (and sometimes high school student essays rather than credible sources).

- Give students a brief text that includes source material that needs to be cited, and have them add in-text citations and create a Works Cited page for it.

- Give students a "cheat sheet" containing examples such as excerpts from a paper you've written showing various citations. Sometimes students get lost in a long text.

Useful Readings

Bishop, Wendy and Pavel Zemliansky, eds. *The Subject is Research*. Portsmouth, NH: Boynton/Cook, 1981.

Healey, Deborah. *Paraphrasing Steps and Samples*. 9 Sept. 1999. 7 May 2005. <http://oregonstate.edu/~healeyd/162/162paraphrase.html>.

Howard, Rebecca Moore. "Plagiarisms, Authorships, and the Academic Death Penalty." *College English* 57.7 (November 1995): 788–806.

Kantz, Margaret. "Helping Students Use Textual Sources Persuasively." *College English* 52:1 (January 1990): 74–87.

Price, Margaret. "Beyond 'Gotcha!': Situating Plagiarism in Policy and Pedagogy." *College Composition and Communication* 54 (2002): 88–115.

Mellon, Constance A. "Library Anxiety: A Grounded Theory and Its Development." *College and Research Libraries* 47:2 (March 1986): 160–165.

Teaching Media / Design **30**

Overt attention to matters of design is relatively new in the teaching of composition. Of course, formatting according to MLA or APA style has been taught for many decades, but with the advent of computers with sophisticated word processing programs, the development of presentation tools like PowerPoint, and the rise of the World Wide Web, design options—and media choices—are available in just about everything we write. Email programs allow us to print in boldface or italics and choose our messages' backgrounds. Since our students face design and media choices every day, it makes sense to help them make informed choices. These three chapters offer brief introductions to design features of print, spoken, and electronic texts and advice on how to guide students to employ those design features effectively.

Chapter 47, PRINT TEXT

When we write something on paper, we're obviously creating a print text. When we create a set of PowerPoint slides or a Web page, though, we're also working with print text along with a variety of graphics and media options. This chapter presents advice for designing text using letters and words, no matter what medium they're delivered in.

The best general advice to give students about designing print text is to exercise restraint. Computers give us the ability to create print texts in an abundance of typefaces and colors, to warp and distort the fonts, and to add illustrations and backgrounds. However, under most circumstances, those effects are more irritating to readers than helpful. Add to that the unfortunate fact that the current rules for MLA and APA formatting preclude not only such typographic pyrotechnics but also simple but useful options for using boldface type and white space to aid readers. Therefore, students' print text design options are likely to be limited by disciplinary standards.

Although their typographic options may be somewhat limited in print texts, they have more options for including visuals. The computer also allows writers to insert visuals—photographs, charts, graphs, tables, drawings—into print texts easily and gracefully. Students may be reluctant to include visuals in their papers because they're unsure whether visuals violate academic standards for formal papers. Talk to them about the importance of asking their professors how much design freedom they allow in their assignments: Some college teachers and some assignments welcome innovative, visually interesting submissions, while others require a conservative approach.

Still, you can help students design documents by demonstrating how a well-designed document can improve readers' understanding of the content. Technical writer Beth Conney Lisberg likens good document design to the principles informing well-designed public parks. Each, she says, should pay attention to these five principles:

1. *Navigation.* Make it easy to find the table of contents, glossaries, indices, appendices, and other manual components. Within a chapter, use page anchors such as headers/footers. Use headings that show hierarchy.
2. *Circulation.* Use components that unify each chapter: overviews and summaries, new features, information boxes. Break tasks into visible chunks.
3. *Space.* Allow space for users to take notes and locate headings and notes. Create real white space with margins, virtual space by setting off special information.
4. *Equipment.* Include the correct tools, such as charts, tables, infographics, good illustrations. Create tables of contents that describe tasks. Create superb indices. Provide exercises to practice new skills.
5. *Safety.* Provide no unpleasant surprises. Give documents visual consistency.

Lisberg's analogy provides both a rhetorical justification for working with text design and easy-to-grasp ways of thinking about the roles visuals, white space, headings, and consistency play for readers.

Design Options for Writing Assignments. One way to introduce students to design is by adding design elements to other writing assignments. For example, you can expand the Analyzing Texts assignment (*Field Guide* Chapter 7) by asking students to analyze the effectiveness of the design on the text's overall message. How does the design appeal to the intended audience? Does it reflect the writer's stance? Will it help achieve the desired purpose? You might also consider offering students the opportunity to redesign one of their essays, choosing a different font, adding images, setting off key information as a list, turning a narrative or report into a photo essay. Many students will find it an exciting challenge.

You can also invite students to revise something they've written in a different medium—to turn an analysis or argument into a PowerPoint presentation, or to adapt an essay into a Web page. Such assignments offer you the opportunity to then ask how the message changes as the medium changes. Which version meets the demands of the rhetorical situation better, and why?

Chapter 48, SPOKEN TEXT

Spoken texts in most classes consist of speeches or oral presentations, often accompanied by visual aids in the form of PowerPoint slides, overhead projector transparencies, or writing on a chalkboard. As you may know or remember, moving from the student's desk to the instructor's place in a classroom—let alone behind a lectern or in front of a microphone—can be daunting. For that reason, it's useful to offer coached practice sessions, perhaps in small groups in your office, before asking students to present to the class or a larger group. Some of the problems students encounter when asked to present orally include the following:

- *Stage fright.* Many students are terrified of speaking in front of a group. Opinions vary on how instructors should deal with such students, ranging from insisting that they do the assignment just like everyone else to offering alternatives, such as videotaping their presentation and showing the tape or writing out their presentation, with copies for everyone in the class. You might offer students different degrees of exposure: sitting at their desks, using a lectern, or sitting at a table rather than standing in front of the class. If the course includes a significant oral component, consider creating a series of assigned presentations, each one more formal, to allow frightened students to acclimate slowly. Give students opportunities to speak to small groups before they speak to the entire class. In fact, most speakers get more comfortable, the more they speak in front of a group, so offering more, rather than fewer opportunities to speak can be helpful.

- *Reading the script.* Even though students should be discouraged from reading a

script when they present, they should prepare for a talk by writing a script and an outline. The student who stands, clutching a sheaf of papers, reading every word, is painful to watch and listen to. Encourage students to speak from outlines or notes, but if they need to read—as some speakers (including me) do—help them write the speech for oral delivery: mark pauses, shape sentences to resemble speech, and include stage directions, such as when to change slides or even (in extreme cases) when to smile. Encourage them to rehearse before a friend or a mirror.

- *Talking to one's shoes.* Inexperienced or shy students often avoid eye contact with the audience, mumbling with head down. Others stand woodenly, sometimes hiding behind (and often clutching, white-knuckled) a lectern. Coach such students to look out at the audience, speak to the back row, and use gestures; and encourage them to write stage directions to that effect on their scripts or notes. Many students habitually speak very quickly, and with the added nervousness and desire to be finished that come with speaking publicly, they may be impossible to understand. Again, coaching can help, along with notes to themselves on their outlines: Slow Down.

- *Restraint and pacing.* If students follow the advice in the *Field Guide* and keep their PowerPoint slides or transparencies simple, to act as enhancements or outlines of their spoken texts, they'll have cleared a major hurdle for presenters: copying the entire text of their speech onto slides and reading them. Even so, students need to monitor the pace at which they change slides to make sure they're visible long enough for their audience to read them.

Making your expectations clear. Your students' presentations will be better if you clearly identify what you expect them to do. Your assignments should answer these questions:

- What is the purpose of the presentation? What is its goal?
- Who is the audience? If it includes people in addition to the class and teacher, who are they?
- What topics should students present? Will they be given a list from which they can choose, or will they choose a topic on their own?
- What is the occasion, and what tone is appropriate? Are humor, parody, or satire permitted, or should this be a serious event?
- How long should the talk be?
- How should presenters dress? Formally, informally, in a costume?
- What criteria will be used to evaluate the presentation?
- Are visuals, props, or handouts required? How will they be evaluated?
- If groups collaborate on a presentation, must every group member be an active participant in the presentation, or can some students be writers and others performers?

Scheduling enough time. Requiring students to present to the class can take a lot of time. If you have twenty-five students, each one responsible for a ten-minute presentation, you need to allot 250 minutes of class time, not including the minutes between each presentation for setting up props, loading PowerPoint shows into the computer, and passing around handouts. In most schools, that's close to two weeks of class. Also, consider the effect on you and your students of watching five presentations each day for five days straight; it would be difficult to be the presenters on that last day. For those reasons, consider spreading oral presentations or teaching demonstrations or speeches through the term, perhaps one or two each class day.

Chapter 49, ELECTRONIC TEXT

When students create Web sites for a course, they usually post their sites on a server at their school. If you plan to ask your students to create a Web site, contact your school's Web administrators to determine the policies and procedures and online resources for the Web server your students will use. Many students also have access to Web server space through their own Internet Service Provider or free Web sites like geocities.com. If possible, get or make a simple graphic that shows students where files are physically located along with the filenaming hierarchy and clear, descriptive file and folder names. Showing students what they should do first will help them get started and keep them from giving up because "their page doesn't work." As writing instructor Jane Blakelock, the Wright State English Department Webmaster, observes, "That's the area that sinks the design ship, no matter how pretty." Some other tips for helping students create effective Web sites:

Using models. Show students Web pages that do what you want students to do. In general, good sites are uncluttered, use a consistent design throughout, have strong contrast between text and background, and use a navigation system that's obvious and simple to use. Many students' tastes run to fancy sites containing ornate fonts, busy backgrounds, flashing elements, and levels of complexity that not only are rhetorically devastating, but are probably beyond their capabilities or even the resources available to them. So showing them sites that are clean, readable, and easy to navigate can help students see that such sites enhance communication of the contents, rather than competing with it.

You can also use models to show students various ways of distributing their content among a number of pages, to take advantage of the layout and graphic design possibilities afforded by the Web's navigation and presentation capabilities. Have students compare various ways of organizing sites, discussing the rhetorical effects of each. Have them diagram potential ways of organizing their sites, pointing out that

organizational charts are the Web version of outlines—or have them begin with an outline and then turn it into a chart.

Finally, have students analyze Web pages as they would other texts, using the techniques described in *Field Guide* Chapter 38, READING STRATEGIES. You may also wish to add an additional criterion that is important to Web pages and may be a requirement at your school: accessibility.

Teaching students about style sheets. Consider teaching students to use style sheets to control margins and layout, color, font and other non-content design features. Style sheets set up rules for the way text looks on a page, so every heading (for example) appears onscreen in the same font and with the same margin. If you want to change the appearance of your site, you can do so by changing the rules on the style sheet instead of changing each element separately. You can find several good tutorials for using style sheets by entering "style sheets tutorial" in a Web search engine.

Teaching students about table and cell size. Tables create rows and columns of boxes, or cells, into which information is put to control Web page layout. Students may want to follow the convention of defining table and cell size by percentages instead of pixels so that the table will adjust proportionally to the size of the monitor display. Have students test their pages on a range of monitor display sizes. A good source of information and step-by-step modeling for tables is the Web site of the

Adaptive Technology Resource Centre at the University Toronto: http://www.utoronto.ca/atrc/tutorials/actable/.

Teaching students about designing for accessiblity. As the Internet becomes available to more and more people, making sure Web sites are accessible to everyone is increasingly important and may be a requirement of your school. Computer devices and programs can magnify Web site text and read Web sites aloud or convert them into Braille. Adaptive devices allow people with various physical disabilities access to the full range of the Web's capabilities. Here is some advice you can give students to help them take such special needs into consideration:

- _Follow basic design principles_. A clear organization, consistent design and layout, concise, precise language, and freedom from errors will benefit all visitors to your site.

- _Use clear, simple language._ Be as clear and precise as possible. Use simple words (for example, "use" instead of "utilize") to enable speech synthesizers and Braille devices to recognize the words more easily.

- _Provide introductions to special features and acronyms._ Introduce lists in your text ("The following list provides six ways to make your site accessible."). Spell out acronyms, abbreviations, and initials the first time you use them: "YSHS (Yellow Springs High School) is the home of the Bulldog Marching Band."

- _Integrate links into your text._ "This site includes <u>photos of the Thurber House</u>" is better than "To see photos of the Thurber House, <u>click here</u>" because screen readers pull out links and create a list of them. A list of "<u>click here</u>" links isn't helpful.

- _Use "Alternative Text" tags for all images and image maps._ "Alt" tags contain text descriptions of images or image map contents. Some browsers display this informative label when you move the cursor over the image, allowing page visitors to decide whether or not to wait if the image is too large to appear quickly. More importantly, adaptive software will read these descriptions to visually impaired page visitors, thus making page contents more comprehensible.

- _Use a template for organizing headings and subheadings._ If you create your Web site using an HTML editor, you can specify various heading levels, like these:

Heading 1	**MOST IMPORTANT**
Heading 2	**Very Important**
Heading 3	_Important_
Heading 4	not so important

(If you are using a style sheet, you only need to establish these heading font choices a single time.) When headings are identified in the software commands, adaptive software that translates written text into speech supplies varied speech tones that allow visually impaired site visitors to understand how the site's content is organized and flows.

- *Pay attention to color.* Many people have problems perceiving colors (especially, but not limited to, red and green), so relying on colors for any aspect of your site's message may not work. The safest combination is black text on a white background. Fairly safe is any primary color (except yellow) on a white background, or any two colors that contrast highly with each other. Several good resources on general color use and color blindness concerns are listed in the Graphics and Colors section of Wright State University's web design course resource page: http://www.wright.edu/cola/LA399/res _graph.htm.

- *Avoid flashing, scrolling text, and other animation tricks.* For the most part, blinking or moving text or graphics should be reserved for personal fun pages, like embellishments in a journal that you might share with close friends but would not offer to the world at large. Pages designed for general access should exclude most animated or psychedelic features. They not only tax eyesight and make content less effective, they can cause real problems for visitors with seizure disorders.

- *Test your Web site for accessibility.* Two sites can help you do this: (1) *Bobby* is a Web page accessibility testing program. To test your page or download a copy of Bobby, go to *http://bobby.watchfire.com.* (2)

Lynx allows you to view your pages with a text-only web browser. To view your page or download a copy of Lynx, go to *http://delorie.com/web/lynxview.html.*

Useful Readings

EDUCAUSE Learning Initiative. *7 Things You Should Know about WIKIs.* 2005. EDUCAUSE. 27 July 2005. <http://www.educause.edu/ir/library/ pdf/ELI7004.pdf.>

Gurak, Laura, et.al., eds. *Into the Blogosphere: Rhetoric, Community, and Culture of Weblogs.* 2005. 27 July 2005. <http://blog.lib. umn.edu/blogosphere/>.

Hill, Charles A. "Reading the Visual in College Writing Classes." *Intertexts: Reading Pedagogy in College Writing Classrooms.* Ed. Marguerite Helmers. Mahwah, NJ: Lawrence Erlbaum Associates, 2003. 123–50. Rpt. *Visual Rhetoric in a Digital World.* Ed. Carolyn Handa. NY: Bedford, 2004. 107–130.

Kramer, Robert and Stephen A. Bernhardt. "Teaching Text Design." *The Technical Communication Quarterly* 5:1 (1996): 35–60.

Lisberg, Beth Conney. "The Architecture of Designing Documents." *1999 Proceedings.* Society for Technical Communication. 17 February 2005. <http://www.stc.org/conf-proceed/1999/PDFs/stc-34.pdf>.

Williams, Robin. *The Non-Designer's Design Book: Design and Typographic Principles for the Visual Novice.* 2nd ed. Berkeley: Peachpit, 2004.

Contributors

Brady Allen teaches composition, fiction writing, honors courses, and literature at Wright State University. He has published short stories in many horror, crime and mystery, sci-fi and fantasy, and literary journals and anthologies in the United States, England, and Ireland, including *Strangewood Tales*, *Crimewave*, and *The Black Mountain Review*. He recently received an Individual Artist Fellowship from the Ohio Arts Council, and some of his stories have received honorable mention in *The Year's Best Fantasy and Horror*. He is also co-editor, with Scott Geisel, of *MudRock: Stories & Tales*, a fiction magazine that publishes authors from all over North America and focuses on publishing both popular or "genre" tales alongside more literary stories. And he co-organizes the annual MudRock Short Fiction Contest for Wright State undergraduate students and the MudRock/Dayton Metro Library Teen Short Story Contest for grades 6–12 in Dayton, Ohio.

Mike Boblitt is a Teaching Assistant at Wright State University in Dayton, OH, where he is working toward an M.A. in Composition and Rhetoric. He enjoys writing fiction.

Adrienne Cassel is an Assistant Professor of English at Sinclair Community College in Dayton, Ohio. She has designed and taught over a dozen online classes. She is co-founder and director of the Five Rivers Poetry Project, writer-in-residence for the Dayton Art Institute, and an instructional designer for Wright State University. Her poetry has appeared in the *Northwest Review*, the *Bennington Review*, 5 A.M., *Nexus*, and *Flights*. Her research interests include the life and work of June Jordan and Pearl Cleage, women writing prose poetry, and diversity and online learning. She lives in the historic Wright-Dunbar (as in the Wright Brothers and Paul Laurence Dunbar) neighborhood of Dayton with her husband and their two dogs. Her passions are poetry and traveling—especially traveling to Atlanta, Georgia, where her daughter and two granddaughters live.

Jimmy Chesire is a writer, teacher, counselor, and coach. He teaches first-year composition, creative writing, and business writing at Wright State University. He's published short stories, a memoir, a novel, *Home Boy*, and, with photographer Irwin Inman, *A Thousand Strikes: T-Ball Yellow Springs Style*. *A Thousand Strikes* chronicles Jimmy's nineteen years as coordinator of the Yellow Springs, Ohio, T-ball program where there are no fees, no sign-ups, no registration, and no requirement to play every week; where there are no runs, no outs and no strike outs: "You get a thousand strikes in T-ball." Jimmy has finished and is trying to sell his second, as-yet-unnamed, novel, has a completed first draft of a third one, and is currently at work on a fourth.

Carol Cornett is a Lecturer in English and Director of the LEAP Intensive English Program at Wright State University. She teaches ESL courses in composition, grammar, reading, speaking and listening, and classroom communication for international teaching assistants. Her research interests include authentic assessment and self-assessment, which have led to presentations at regional and international conferences and an article in the *International Journal for Teachers of English Writing Skills*.

Deborah Crusan is Associate Professor of TESOL/Applied Linguistics and Director of ESL Programs at Wright State University. She has published articles about writing assessment in *Assessing Writing*, *TESL Reporter*, and other journals. She teaches courses in assessment, grammar, and linguistics as well as a course in classroom communication for International Teaching Assistants. Her research interests include writing assessment, particularly for placement of ESL students, directed/guided self-placement and its consequences for second language writers, oral proficiency testing of

International Teaching Assistants, and the politics of assessment.

Melissa Faulkner is a teaching associate and Ph.D. student in composition and rhetoric at Miami University in Oxford, Ohio. She received her M.A. from Wright State University. Her second field of study is working class studies.

Scott Geisel teaches composition, fiction writing, business writing, and literature at Wright State University. He has also worked with the Writing Center and Writing Across the Curriculum programs at Wright State. He is a fiction writer and founding co-editor of the tri-annual all-fiction journal *MudRock: Stories & Tales* (www.mudrockpress.com). His short stories have appeared in a variety of journals, and *MudRock* is distributed across the North American continent.

Maureen Daly Goggin is the Associate Chair of the English Department and Associate Professor of Rhetoric at Arizona State University, where she teaches rhetorical theories, history of rhetoric, and writing. Author of *Authoring a Discipline: Scholarly Journals and the Post-WW II Emergence of Rhetoric and Composition* and of *Inventing a Discipline*, she has published numerous scholarly articles and chapters on the history of rhetoric, visual rhetoric, visual literacy, gender and race, and the history of needlework sampler making. She is currently co-editing a book on race, gender and sexuality in personal ads, and another book on material culture.

Paige Huskey is a Teaching Assistant at Wright State University, where she is working toward an M.A. in Literature. She enjoys reading and writing fiction, coaching youth basketball, and spending time with her husband and three children.

Melissa Toomey is a teaching associate and Ph.D. student in composition and rhetoric at Miami University in Oxford, Ohio. She received her M.A. from Wright State University. Her second field of study is social linguistics, with a special interest in literacy studies.